9.24   6—

THE SUMMIT
OF HER
AMBITION

THE SUMMIT OF HER AMBITION

The spirited life of Marie Byles
1900–1979

Anne McLeod

Marie in Norway on her around-the-world mountaineering adventure, 1928.

After scaling the peak she captioned this photograph "The summit of my ambition".

My enduring gratitude to Dr Erika Yeates.

By illuminating Marie's psychology, you helped me understand her through understanding myself.

Published by Anne McLeod

Copyright © 2016 Anne McLeod

Printed 2016
Reprinted 2016
Reprinted 2019

Anne McLeod asserts her moral rights as author.

National Library of Australia Cataloguing-in-Publication entry:

McLeod, Anne, author. Cohn, Laurel, editor.

  The summit of her ambition: the spirited life of Marie Byles

  ISBN 9780646941417 (paperback)

  1. Byles, Marie Beuzeville. 2. Women lawyers—Australia—Biography.
  3. Women conservationists—Australia—Biography. 4. Women
  explorers—Australia—Biography. 5. Women mountaineers—
  Australia—Biography. 6. Feminists—Australia—Biography. 8.
  Spiritual life—Buddhism.

920.720994

Designed & typeset by Lauren Statham, Alice Graphics
Printed and bound by IngramSpark

Cover photo: Marie Byles and Marjorie Jones, "Enjoying the summit of Crystal Peak" (New Zealand 1935) Marie Byles photographic collection, State Library of NSW

Foreword

The Hon. Elizabeth Evatt AC

I FIRST met Marie Byles in 1974 when a group of women lawyers visited her at home on the 50th anniversary of her admission to practice, to pay homage to her achievements. At 74 she was then rather frail, but strong in mind. Many years before, my mother had held Marie in awe when she was the brilliant head girl at the school they both attended. Marie later became the first woman to be admitted to legal practice in New South Wales, and my mother held her out to me as a role model when I was a law student. But even then, I did not know the full extent of her achievements.

Anne McLeod's biography reveals the many sides of Marie Byles' enigmatic personality. She takes us on Marie's journey through a life of great activity, in which she fought for many causes, for the equality of women, for social justice, for conservation of our native environment against the encroachment of development and consumerism. Besides running a busy legal practice, she was devoted to bushwalking and mountaineering, activities cut short too early by injury.

Marie wanted more from life than these pursuits. Her restless spirit sought inner peace, and led her on a quest to India, Burma and Japan, to learn the wisdom and teachings of Buddha and Gandhi. Her contradictory nature made these lessons hard for her to absorb personally. Nevertheless, she was deeply committed and persevered with her studies. This enabled her to write books that brought to many in the West the wisdom she had sought from teachers of Buddhism.

As described here, Marie was an enigmatic and elusive woman. She was ahead of her time with her commitment to equality, peace, justice and humanity. She lived a life of simplicity, against the consumerist trends of society. She sought to stay in harmony with nature, in her home and lifestyle. Her strong will enabled her to overcome her personal frailty, including disabling illnesses and a brutal personal attack. But her strength of mind also led to contradictions in her nature, which seemed to inhibit her from enjoying close relationships and from attaining the tranquillity she sought; only late in her life was she able to reach a state of harmony with herself.

Contents

Preface

I FIRST came across Marie Byles in 1993 while in northern India visiting sites significant to the Buddha, among them the Bodhi tree at Bodh Gaya under which he gained Enlightenment. My understanding of his life and teachings was enhanced through reading *Footprints of Gautama Buddha*, told from the perspective of a young disciple. This book enabled me to relate to Buddha as a real historical figure while absorbing the atmosphere of spiritual strength and tranquillity that still existed in those locations 2500 years later.

I had no idea that the author was Australian. Two years later, I was surprised to read in the *Sydney Morning Herald* about an open day at Marie Byles' home that she had gifted to the National Trust before her death in 1979.

On my visit to "Ahimsa" – named for Gandhi's principle of non-violence – I learnt that Marie (pr. Mah-ree) had been the first female solicitor of New South Wales who fought for women's equal rights in law. A devoted bush-walker, she became an influential environmentalist whose Buddhist regard for nature's primacy informed her advocacy. The breadth of her activism and scale of her achievements were remarkable. Why, I wondered, wasn't she more widely known?

Searching through her papers in the State Library of New South Wales, I discovered letters, diaries and her newspaper and magazine articles. As legal correspondent for women's magazines in the 1920s and '30s, she outlined discriminatory laws that ensured women's inferior social position and advised her readers on how to subvert them. In the journal of the Sydney Bush Walkers club she wrote of exhilarating expeditions into wilderness areas and the embryonic conservation movement. Her first published book, *By Cargo Boat and Mountain – the unconventional experiences of a woman on tramp around the world*, enthralled with daring mountaineering adventures throughout Europe and Canada, culminating in the ascent of Mt Cook in the Southern Alps of New Zealand in 1929.

Many who knew Marie through the legal profession, bushwalking, conservation and Buddhism were available to share their impressions. Because she was known for her forthright views and elevated consciousness, I was challenged with, 'If you haven't met Marie, how can you possibly write about her?' When I proved not to have a thorough knowledge of all her literary and philosophical influences, I was dismissed. Bushwalkers wanted to know if I was a bushwalker – if not, then obviously I was unable to appreciate the essence of her life and spirit.

A pattern emerged from many of these discussions: Marie was a force of nature, but no saint. In fact, conflict was present in many aspects of her life. This was difficult to reconcile with the committed Buddhist and disciple of Gandhi. Having put her on a pedestal, I became judgmental. Once I read her private diaries, however, I empathised with her depression and self-doubt as she attempted to put her values and beliefs into practice – her divine discontent. I knew then I could do her story justice.

CHAPTER 1

Dare to Have a Purpose Firm

1900–1917

Dare to be a Daniel,
Dare to stand alone!
Dare to have a purpose firm!
Dare to make it known.

"Dare to Be a Daniel" by Philip Bliss
(1873)
Congregational Church hymn

THIS HYMN was the creed by which Marie Byles' parents taught their daughter to seize her destiny and make her place in the world. She was born in England at the end of the nineteenth century, a time of social change as the Victorian mindset was dying with the monarch. Her mother marched with the suffragettes in the struggle for equal rights for women that disrupted civil society in their campaign for the vote. Her father was the son of a minister who had been forced to leave the Congregational Church because of his unorthodox views. As Marie reflected:

> My grandfather must have been embarrassingly broad-minded for he erected a notice at the door of his new church: "Jews, infidels and heretics – all are welcome." The term heretic was one of pride in our family, not of shame.

Marie Byles enjoyed being 'an heretic among the orthodox' and undermined the establishment while working from within to change it. In 1924 she triumphed over the patriarchal legal profession, who were adamantly opposed to allowing in women, to become the first female solicitor to practise in New

South Wales. Despite being told that she would be only a solicitor's clerk, she established a successful legal practice and became a powerful role model for other women in law. Acting as honorary solicitor she worked on behalf of feminist activist Jessie Street's organisation, the United Association of Women, to change laws that discriminated against women's rights in marriage – most cruelly, in the guardianship of their own children.

Through her study of arts, law, economics and geology, Marie had the intellectual conviction to raise society's consciousness regarding equal rights in law and the value of our natural inheritance. Instead of the fame and fortune she could have achieved in the legal profession, she devoted herself to the preservation of the environment.

A dedicated bushwalker since childhood, Marie joined the embryonic conservation movement in 1929 and became a zealous advocate for wilderness regions. At the forefront of the national parks movement, she employed her legal skills to ensure valuable tracts of land were reserved for the benefit of future generations. As honorary solicitor for the peak conservation organisation in NSW, the Federation of Bushwalking Clubs, Marie was, in effect, Australia's first environmental lawyer. An original deep ecologist, her Buddhist beliefs informed her appreciation of the intrinsic value of nature – regardless of its usefulness to human needs. Marie Byles deserves greater recognition for her sustained commitment to nature preservation and the part she played in the history of the environmental movement in NSW.

Her most outstanding quality was her ability to overcome each crisis and summon the inner resources needed to continue her trailblazing journey. Drawn to conquer mountains, the devastating failure of an expedition she led to south China in 1938 was the catalyst for a journey of self-discovery. It took Marie into realms she could never have found on a map and forced her to re-evaluate her life. Her strong will, her most powerful ally, sabotaged many of her attempts to find true peace of mind. This ultimate challenge, to fundamentally change and evolve, created deep conflict – and almost caused her self-destruction.

MARIE BEUZEVILLE Byles was born 8 April 1900 in Ashton upon Mersey, northwest England, to a mother with artistic, liberal – and most importantly, feminist – inclinations, and a father who epitomised the Victorian-era Empire-building drive. Her later conviction to stand up and speak out on a range of social issues was a characteristic that could be traced first to her parents, both strong and assertive individuals, down both sides of the family tree that reached back to the 1500s with intermarriage in 1796. Their Huguenot ancestors, the Beuzevilles, provided a model of outstanding courage and resourcefulness.

Forced to leave France in 1666 and flee to England because of religious persecution, they left in detachments in order to escape detection. According to family legend Marie, the twenty-four-year-old daughter, disguised herself as a peasant and led a donkey with two pannier baskets in which her two younger brothers were hidden. The little boys were implored not to move or make a sound, 'or the cruel soldiers would surely kill them'. They were almost safely to the port of Calais when a party of Huguenot-hunting soldiers rode towards them. The captain questioned the pretty young woman who bravely concealed her terror, declaring that only vegetables were in the baskets, as he could see for himself. 'We'll soon prove that!' the captain said as he unsheathed his sword and plunged it into a pannier, then rode off laughing. When the soldiers were out of sight Marie took shelter in the woods and threw off the vegetables. Her brother Francis was bleeding profusely from a wound on the arm. 'I didn't cry,' said the brave little boy. If he had, there might well have been a different family history.

Marie Byles was in no doubt about the critical influence her parents played in her development. In her unpublished autobiography "Many Lives In One" written near the end of life, she wrote that she was brought up 'in an atmosphere of indifference to prevailing standards'. When her parents met, her mother, Ida Margaret Unwin, was a talented young artist studying at the Slade School of Fine Art in London, the first to offer female students the chance to study from the life model. Ida marched in suffragette processions and fought for dress reform as she considered corsets to be 'instruments of torture' that restricted women's use and enjoyment of their own bodies. Refusing to wear skirts that trailed on the ground, she risked being called a prostitute by youths who threw stones at her as she walked down the street.

Marie's father, Cyril Beuzeville Byles, was employed as a signal engineer on the Lancashire and Yorkshire Railway, one of the largest railway companies in Britain and the first to introduce electrification of its signals. British class divisions meant that Ida's parents did not approve of their marriage. Despite their objections, Ida married Cyril in January 1899 and settled in his hometown of Manchester. She was thirty years old, two years older than her husband. Marie was a puny infant who wailed incessantly but her proud parents bestowed on her the family name Marie Beuzeville after her resourceful Huguenot forebear. She was three when her brother David was born. Baldur, named after a Norse mythological god, arrived a year and a half later. While Ida and Cyril's marriage was a happy one, with each being devoted to the other, it became a model of affection without sustained intimacy. After their third child was conceived, they no longer shared the same bed.

Ida was a freethinker whose progressive attitudes to childrearing meant the children enjoyed a close relationship with their parents. Marie reflected, 'There was no scolding or nagging and of course no slapping, and very few commands were issued; if they were, they were naturally obeyed.' Ida's rule of 'Don't say don't, say do,' exemplified her parents' attitude and allowed Marie to develop a strong self-concept. She was four years old when one teacher called her a little girl. 'I am not a little girl,' she piped up indignantly. 'What are you then, dear?' 'I'm a big girl,' she insisted.

> Had I known it, this was to be the architectural design for the life that was to follow – always a little higher, always a little further than was normal. It also probably showed an unpleasantly inflated ego, even at that early age.

As an adult, Ida's philosophies: "Dare to be a Daniel, dare to stand alone", and "We cannot be true to ourselves unless we are indifferent to what others say about us", inspired Marie to question the status quo and venture into male-only domains.

Her father's influence was just as great in forming her values. The children's introduction to conservation principles came when Cyril protested the enclosure of public lands. Begun in Tudor times, the fencing and sale of common land previously used by landless labourers and smallholders to live off was largely complete by the end of the 1800's. This economic measure, enforced by the Enclosures Act, was taken to make agriculture more efficient but it meant that villagers could no longer graze their sheep, gather wood for their fires and forage wild food such as berries.

Cyril marched down to Rostherne Mere, a large wetlands area not far from Manchester, with Marie and her brothers in tow. The placid waters below them lay cradled in wooded hills but they could go no further because its shores were privately owned and trespassers were not permitted. Cyril sat the children on a fence overlooking the lake and made them repeat after him: 'The earth is the Lord's and the fullness thereof – down with the wicked landowners!'

When the local vicar bought a coppice (a small forest) and closed the public footpath through it, Cyril took his children to walk where the footpath had been. Outside the new fence he encouraged Marie and her little brothers to tread over the newly made garden-beds. He then had leaflets printed about this 'iniquitous stealing-away of public rights' and circulated them to the community. Eventually the vicar had to provide a new footpath. These incidents gave the children insight into the value of public land and the consciousness that individuals could and should make a difference.

Cyril rose through the ranks to become superintendent, a position that afforded the family free train travel and allowed them to tour widely. As a special lecturer in railway economics at both Liverpool and Manchester universities, his valuable work *First Principles of Railway Signalling* brought him to prominence. In 1910, the Commissioner of the New South Wales Railways offered him an appointment to consult on the reorganisation and modernisation of the existing manual signalling equipment. The challenge excited him but the family looked on emigration with some trepidation: it would be a momentous displacement. They heard many stories of men who had uprooted themselves to take up positions in the colonies only to discover on arrival that no job existed.

In March 1911, the family boarded the SS *Anchises* on a journey towards a far distant corner of the Empire. During the voyage the tropical heat made the milk taste "funny" so Marie gave up drinking it altogether. Soon after her arrival in Australia a teacher described how calves were slaughtered to make rennet for cheese so Marie, already a vegetarian through Ida's influence, gave up cheese as well. She never developed a strong body, perhaps due to so little protein in her diet at this critical stage of development.

When they reached Sydney the family was taken to a boarding house. Marie marvelled that the son of the owners slept on the verandah. She adopted this practice for the rest of her life. The natural features of this strange new country entranced the Byles, as Marie noted,

> Orange and red creepers flamed in glory in the middle of winter; the skies were forget-me-not blue and the sun golden. What was more, the sunshine had a kick to it, as Mother said, quite different from the tender sunshine of the Old Land.

Beecroft, on the rim of Sydney's northwest, was chosen as the place to buy land. Its unspoilt natural bushland and clean air was typical of the exclusive new outer suburbs opened up by the railway boom of the 1890s. Living in a country setting with access to the city by rail was ideal, and so was residing in an area that had no licensed premises. The debate over alcohol in the community was a major social issue. The previous year Beecroft residents, anxious to ensure that no hotel opened in their suburb, voted overwhelmingly in favour of the "no licence" option.

Set among orchards, market gardens and small farms, the wealthier residents of Beecroft built two-storey homes that often had tennis courts, croquet lawns and extensive gardens dominated by exotics. Cyril and Ida preferred the Australian Federation-style design typified by wide verandahs. Each weekend the family visited their 1.3-hectare block at the end of a cul-de-sac to begin the clearing task. The allotment, bought for £200, consisted of a barren sandstone quarry surrounded by native vegetation that dipped down into a gully through which a creek flowed. The locals did not believe that a garden could ever be established on this 'utterly useless' site.

For the house, Cyril used building materials that expressed his "waste not, want not" values: stone hewn from the quarry was used for the basement and, instead of good-quality red or brown bricks for the house, he used common red bricks more suitable to an out-house. As the dwelling was some distance from the street, he reasoned, there was no need to waste money on appearances. In contrast, Ida's artistic talents enhanced the interior: pressed metal sheets lined the ceilings and the curtains had borders she stencilled, her designs inspired by the new environment with Australian wild flowers as the motifs. They named the house Chilworth after Ida's family home in Surrey.

Ida had to manage the chores and cooking herself until they could find a lady-help. She struggled with no family support, and even with assistance, it was a full-time job doing the cooking and housework in the days before electrical appliances. Although Marie described her mother as a superb housekeeper, Ida disliked housework. Her disinterest meant that she gave no domestic training to Marie who grew up without knowledge of cookery, sewing or handy work.

The family had left England at a time when suffragette protests were at their height, whereas in Australia, women's suffrage had been gained in 1903. There was not the same impetus for Ida to become involved politically: instead, her time was occupied with children, home and garden. She longed to have a real Australian baby but Cyril would not hear of it, so channelled her creative energies into the garden. As the barren scene of desolation was transformed into an ordered wilderness, she proved the locals wrong. This magical land was no place for the orthodox garden with trim lawns, neat hedges and wide level flowerbeds, Ida thought. Nature must have her own wild and wanton way if beauty was to flourish. Marie later recalled the beautiful environment her mother created:

A small quarry has been transformed into a lily pond where pure white flowers float amid glossy green leaves on waters so tranquil that they mirror the rocks and trees above. The weeping willow droops its leaves in perpetual sorrow above the lucid depths where the goldfish dart about like fiery rays of light ...'

Rock from the quarry made stonewalls and footpaths, and plants and trees from all countries of the world found a home in Chilworth's garden:

Pines from the snowy plains of Russia, palms from the tropic isles of the pacific, oaks from pleasant England, hibiscus from the antique heart of China. There is probably no land not represented in some secluded corner, and they all grow happily beside the Australian gum.

The approach to the house was along crazy footpaths to the shaded house where wide wisteria-covered verandahs kept out the fierce summer sunlight. In springtime the wisteria was a mass of purple blooms that hung above Marie's bed on the verandah, so that she awoke each morning 'breathing the scented dewdrops on the petals and hearing the birds already singing that life is good'.

Cyril constructed a tennis court on the levelled ground of the old quarry below the house. The children had jolly parties with their school friends on Saturday afternoons while Ida provided sumptuous afternoon teas. Below the tennis court was a forested gully that sloped down towards Devlin's Creek. In the 1920s, Ida and Cyril donated a portion of that land to the Scouts to build a hall in the rustic bushland setting. In 1938 they donated two hectares to the Wildlife Preservation Society as a flora and fauna sanctuary, which became known as Chilworth Reserve.

Each day along with the other professional men, Cyril made the 45-minute journey to the city. His destination was Eveleigh railway workshops in Redfern, the centre of operations for the NSW Railways and the heart of the state's transport system. Thousands of craftsmen and engineers were employed to design and produce the latest in transportation technology, which played a vital role in the state's expansion. After only a short period in his advisory capacity, Cyril was appointed Signal Engineer and given responsibility for planning, installation and maintenance of all electronic signalling in New South Wales. It was a mammoth task. For this he was paid £600 a year when the basic wage for men in 1911 was £125 and half that for women.

The privileges of his position included not only a motorcar with driver at his disposal but a personal rail-motor that had sleeping quarters and an office for use on tours of country districts. He developed an increased sense of importance and at home his strong opinions dominated the family. A large railway clock in the kitchen ensured punctuality of mealtimes and smooth functioning of the household. Despite Ida's insistence on gender equality she progressively assumed the role of wife and mother. Subjugating her own needs, Ida inevitably became dissatisfied and encouraged Marie to pursue a different outcome. As if bequeathing her own unlived life she urged her daughter, 'When you grow up you must not copy me; you must earn your own living.' Marie later reflected, 'At that time I did not quite see how a woman could earn her own living; it simply was not done.'

Her parents' socialist beliefs meant they disapproved of the small private school in Beecroft. Conditions, though, at the local primary school were primitive and there were constant canings. Although her parents insisted to the headmaster that their own children not be punished in this way, Marie was distressed when other children were. Once, after witnessing an angry thrashing of one of the boys, she burst into tears and ran home unable to return for the afternoon's lessons. Her only relief was the weekend bushwalks she begged her father to take them on. These outings provided the happiest days of her childhood, lingering more clearly in her memory than any circus or pantomime.

Puberty brought with it an awareness of her body and a startling change in her mind. A self-admittedly 'unpleasant little girl subject to tantrums', she suddenly developed the conscious awareness of right and wrong. Inner discord afflicted her when she vented anger on her little brothers. From that time on, 'life became a conscious striving for righteousness'. Her parents instilled a strong sense of moral values in their children but this profound change came from within. She was reading everything she could about the Boy Scouts, a movement introduced into Australia in 1908. At the time there was no such thing as the Girl Scouts or Guides but Marie wrote stories about girls rescuing people in distress and doing good deeds every day.

By her last year in primary school she had begun to enjoy her studies and was top of her class. However, when the Department of Public Instruction allocated her to an Intermediate High School in the city, 'my democratically minded parents were wholly in favour of it, but I was not'. A girl in her street attended Presbyterian Ladies College (PLC) at Croydon, southwest of Sydney, and Marie decided she would, too. In the face of persistent requests, her parents were forced to reconsider. Marie's resolve won out. Taking this stand proved to be a decisive turning point.

PLC would be the making of this intelligent and lively girl as it lived up to its promise of the Golden Hope. The Headmaster Dr Marden was devoted to an enlightened education for girls. Before his appointment the main emphasis in the curriculum was on accomplishments and amiability but he scorned the idea that it was some kind of finishing school. The college was housed in a grand Victorian building topped by an imposing tower, a feature of the local landscape. It provided aesthetic surroundings with established gardens and sweeping lawns, an ideal environment for Marie who enjoyed every minute of school life.

In August of her first year at PLC, came that terrible day. Sitting on Strathfield railway station, Marie heard a newspaper boy call out 'War Declared!' Mere schoolgirl that she was, her heart sank into her shoes. Her parent's pacifist stance had made a deep impression. Britain's declaration of war against Germany automatically meant that Australia became involved due to our close ties through ancestry with the "mother country". A large percentage of the five million population were either British-born or first-generation Australians. While the Byles were against the conflict, they soon heard of the horrors of war and of the agonies of those who had lost their sons. Everyone started knitting socks for the soldiers. Marie used to carry her satchel of books on her back and knit as she walked to and from Beecroft station.

Since arriving in Australia the family had holidayed in a variety of beachside locations. In 1914 they visited Palm Beach at the narrow tip of Sydney's northern beaches peninsula. Ida fell in love with the remote settlement and decided to buy land on Sunrise Hill, the choicest site, when there were only two other houses. There was no road access so the building materials needed to be brought in by boat from the further end of Pittwater and then carried up the hill. There were very few cottages in Palm Beach but their owners, some of Sydney's leading doctors, lawyers and businessmen, would go down to the wharf to collect supplies that came by launch. 'Sometimes the meat was walking and sometimes the milk was sour. But everyone was happy', Marie reminisced. The small cottage had a four-metre-wide open verandah on which they lived and slept. Facing due north to the Barrenjoey lighthouse, it looked down upon the still waters of Pittwater estuary to the west and the Pacific Ocean to the east. In winter, the sun rose over a clean horizon like a ball of fire.

> A dwelling gathers its own atmosphere formed from the thoughts of those that live there, and 'Seawards,' as Mother called it, gathered around it the atmosphere of happiness, the laughter and joy …
>
> There were probably sharks in Pittwater but they never prevented us from swimming there. There were sometimes sudden southerly gales and these assisted us to become skilled at handling rowing boats. We scrambled around

the rocks, made friends with the lighthouse keepers, surfed in the ocean and hiked here, there and everywhere …

A born leader, Marie formed a gang of friends from school into the Pirate Girls. A calico skull and crossbones flag flapped on Seawards' verandah as Marie led expeditions to explore Pittwater's isolated beaches and forests. Barefoot, the girls left for their day's excursions dressed in long skirts, blouses and hats, carrying supplies in a small pack. On one outing, the Pirate Girls hired rowboats to have breakfast on a beach across the Pittwater. Half way across the watery waste the buccaneers were in trouble as Marie's boat started filling up. Cold seawater swirled around their ankles as they searched for the missing bung. Marie had to bail frantically with a tin while the other girls rowed as hard as they could towards the shore. When they pulled the boat up on the beach and tipped the water out, the elusive cork was found ensuring their safe return.

In quieter moments, she stood on the verandah and gazed through a tele-scope past Broken Bay at the wide mouth of the Hawkesbury River, across to the rugged coastline beyond. Marie referred to it as her "faery lands forlorn" because it seemed as lonely as the lands in Keats' *Ode to a Nightingale*. She longed to explore the remote Bouddi Headland.

Despite the gloom the war generated Marie maintained a consistent record as an honour roll student and in 1915 was dux of her second year. One teacher in particular made a deep impression. Marie was 'struck' on Miss Constance Mackness because of her 'rather clever, sharp tongue plus absence of corsets'. While all the other girls wore corsets, Ida refused to allow her daughter to par-ticipate in this unnecessary fashion. Miss Mackness taught history at Croydon and, after thirteen years at the school, was appointed Deputy Headmistress. She was truly loved by her girls and her influence became legendary. When PLC opened a new school in Pymble on the north shore, Miss Mackness was appointed Headmistress. Marie was determined to follow. She convinced her parents that the journey by train from Beecroft to Pymble would be no more arduous than the journey to Croydon.

In my third year P.L.C. Pymble was opened, a fine new school standing in its own fifty acres [20 ha] of land and looking very conspicuous and austere from the North Shore Railway line. My especial "strike", Miss Mackness, was appointed Headmistress – not Principal, of course, for only a man was allowed to be that!

The girls at the new school were handpicked for their scholastic and leadership abilities, qualities Marie had in abundance. When Miss Mackness needed a girl to be Head Prefect, the requirement that she had to be a boarder made the choice difficult. Very few girls went on to fifth year to sit their Leaving Certificates. Miss Mackness knew she could rely on Marie and begged Cyril to let her board at Pymble. Her success meant they could develop a close relationship that made a lasting impact on Marie's life. Constance Mackness provided the young girl with the model of a single professional woman sustained by her work and creative pursuits. She presided over the Debating Club and under her skilful supervision Marie learnt to discuss with 'varying degrees of heat and enthusiasm' a wide range of subjects. Her parents' deliberate encouragement of their children's individuality and Marie's natural ability to assert her opinion meant that she took easily to debating. So impressed was Cyril by her force of argument in each debate, he suggested she study law, as he thought she would make a good barrister.

Marie subsequently gained high passes in all her subjects and won an exhibition (a financial grant) to the University of Sydney. There was no question in her parents' minds that this was a suitable course for their daughter. At a time when higher education for girls was rarely contemplated, when many other talented girls were often taken out of school and ushered into either unskilled work or marriage and motherhood, those fortunate enough to gain tertiary education usually settled for women's professions, such as pharmacy, medicine, nursing or teaching. Expectations of following the norm were much greater then, especially for women, but Marie was inclined by birth and instinct to subvert the status quo.

The feminist messages she received from her mother, the unconditional support of her father, and the engaged mentoring by Constance Mackness, meant that Marie developed the self-assurance to envision practising law, a profession still not open to women in New South Wales. She would need every ounce of determination for the struggle ahead in breaking down the walls of the "club": the male-dominated legal profession that looked after its own. Entry into this world of wealth and power was severely restricted and women rarely invited.

CHAPTER 2

The Glory of the Pioneer

1918–1927

WHILE WOMEN had practised law in Victoria since 1905, it
required years of determined advocacy by feminists and women's
progress organisations before the situation was remedied in New
South Wales. Rose Scott, a leader of the campaign for women's suffrage, noted
that women practised law in Victoria, South Australia, Tasmania, Canada,
France and the United States 'and even in British India', but not in New South
Wales. She argued that women's exclusion from the practice of law and other
positions of authority in that state – for example, magistrates, justices of the
peace, jurors, judges, members of parliament and local councils – ensured their
poor social position.

The campaign to allow women to practise law was one that some men
supported, with one generously noting,

> … both branches of the law appear as excellent an opening for the same type
> of celibate women with exceptional talent as any other profession. The truth is
> that the differences between the sexes have been grossly exaggerated by priests,
> journalists and fools generally, and there can be no doubt that at least one
> percent of women are quite as intelligent as any man.

Paradoxically, women were allowed to study law but could not practise.
In 1902 Ada Evans passed all the examinations in law at the University of
Sydney but, despite her representations, no government would change the
legislation permitting her to practise. Despite opposition in some quarters, the
Women's Legal Status Act 1918 (NSW) was eventually passed permitting women

to become qualified barristers and solicitors and practise in the courts. This Act was one of the most significant pieces of legislation affecting the New South Wales legal profession in the twentieth century as it also gave women the right to be elected to the Legislative Assembly.

Ada Evans served her two-year term as a student-at-law and, on 21 May 1921, was admitted as the first woman barrister in New South Wales. She declined to practise however, as she believed that too much time had elapsed. Evans' contribution was nevertheless significant and fulfilled the prophecy of one of her lecturers,

> 'If you cannot reap all the reward of your toil, the greater glory may be yours of sowing what others may reap – the glory of the pioneer.'

In the same year the Enabling Act was passed Marie Byles entered the University of Sydney. Enrolled in Arts in her year were seventy-four women, most aimed for a career in teaching, until marriage, seen to be women's ultimate destiny. Female teachers in public schools would then be forbidden to continue to work. Intellectually energetic women wanting to apply their talents and abilities were often faced with a choice: career or marriage. Marie revelled in student life. She organised debates and was elected to various committees. On the social side, she soon knew all the girls in her year and made some lasting friendships, including with future writers Christina Stead, Dymphna Cusack and Florence James.

During Easter of her first term she accompanied Cyril on her first overnight camping trip to Mt Hay near Leura in the upper Blue Mountains two hours west of Sydney. They stayed a night at the stately Hydro Majestic hotel, and then tramped out along a ridge with views that stretched across the vast and breathtaking Grose Valley. Camping overnight halfway along the route, they climbed next day through tree ferns to the basalt cap and cairn at the top. They looked down the stupendous escarpments to the green treetops of the Blue Gum Forest far below. A highlight was the naming of a flat-topped rock promontory Butterbox Point, after her father pointed out the similarity to this household object.

These outdoor adventures gave Marie a sense of achievement and she soon mastered the Australian bush by using 'brains, and compass and sun and map – if there were such!' Growing confidence in her skills meant she took the initiative and organised bushwalking expeditions of her university girl friends, unheard of behaviour for well-brought-up young women of the period. One weekend they walked from Springwood in the Blue Mountains down to Richmond through the Grose Valley.

On campus, Marie tended to avoid the opposite sex stating, '…being made as I am, I was not one of the mixers'. Nevertheless, the exposure to social interaction between the sexes challenged her to consider her own sexuality. Freud's theories were popular reading and she 'dutifully tried to import sex symbolism into my dreams but not very successfully'. Far more important to her were the writings of Dr Marie Stopes, an expert on sex education, who filled in the gaps her mother had given her (for example, the part men played in procreation). Marie came to the conclusion that, although she was naturally interested in the opposite sex, she felt no inclination to do anything more than perhaps hold hands and that anything further was 'merely silly':

> There were interesting books to read, lectures to listen to, mountains calling to be climbed, worthy causes to be espoused. As for copulation, which we share with the animals, this was merely repulsive.

Sensuality was expressed through her love of being in nature and taking on physical challenges. She was afraid of being attractive and was uncomfortable with her developing female figure. Despite her slight frame, she had large breasts that made her self-conscious. Once, on a strenuous three-day bushwalk with Dymphna Cusack and Florence James along the Hawkesbury River to Windsor where convict history abounded, the young women jumped naked into the icy river just as a boat came around the bend. Her two friends scrambled out of the freezing water and back up the bank, but Marie stayed in rather than suffer the potential humiliation of public exposure.

At university Marie was swept along at the forefront of social change when women were discovering they had greater opportunities to find power through their abilities than their image as women. It was a challenging time and Marie was caught in the social crosscurrent. Traditionally, girls wore their hair long in a plait until they left school when they wore their hair piled up on their head. In defiance of this feminine ideal Marie announced to her parents that she was going to cut her long hair:

> Poor Father was aghast. Next day he braved the ladies haberdashery department of the leading Sydney departmental store and bought some attractive combs. But when he got home my hair was no more. The interesting thing was that when the long hair had been done up in two coils, it was straight. It now developed a wave, and became my one beauty.

As she challenged convention she also re-examined the Christian beliefs of her parents. She concluded that the principles remained but wondered whether Christianity was not after all 'some beautiful dream, the last of the great mythologies and religions which will in its turn die and fade away into the common light of … day.' Acknowledging her 'nascent spiritual interest' Marie joined a society that studied the *Meditations* (160 CE) of the Roman emperor Marcus Aurelius whose writings had become part of the canon of Western classics. Imbued with stoic philosophies they stressed self-discipline, virtue and inner tranquillity gained from the ability to step aside from mental judgements. These ideas accorded with Marie's own inclinations.

While completing her arts subjects, Marie was elected to the board of directors of the Women's Union, among other committees. Her election was no doubt due to her outspokenness on women's issues. This brought her into contact with many other notable women committed to the agenda of equal rights. Their support was crucial to her success during the next phase of her education as she ventured into the male bastion of law school in which Marie was the lone female in most of her subjects. Law was, and still is, one of the most challenging undergraduate degrees with an exceptional workload but the lack of women students was mainly due to it being a conservative profession inextricably linked to the power wielded by the elite. Marie was about to discover what was required to break through the formidable barriers its members had erected.

Classmates were predominantly returned soldiers who had been offered a tertiary education as part of their repatriation. Many of them were 'very brainy and very high-spirited' and became successful lawyers, judges, politicians and company directors, but their behaviour towards her was less than sympathetic. As 'one shy little girl, afraid of young men, in the midst of an uproarious class of over one hundred', Marie faced potential humiliation as her fellow students and even lecturers took delight in taunting her.

There was a precedent in her family for following a legal career. A recent ancestor on her father's side, John Byles, had been a successful advocate, later a judge and a conspicuous authority on commercial law. He wrote a standard text commonly known as "Byles on Bills" found in every lawyer's library. One of Marie's lecturers took fiendish delight in picking out his judgments to read to the class. As soon as he said 'Mr Justice Byles…' the class stamped their feet furiously until the dust rose. When asked whether he did not find a woman student a little embarrassing, the same lecturer replied with a slight lisp, 'She does wather cwamp my style'. This attitude only made her more determined.

In that era laws were designed to maintain existing power structures and generally did not take into account the needs of women or other disadvantaged groups. The common law had been based on traditional values dictating that when a woman married, her status merged with that of her husband and she became a non-person. Men's assumptions about their social superiority were entrenched. The first serious obstacle to Marie's advancement in her profession came when she needed to get articles of clerkship with a master solicitor. Female law clerks were unknown and the door was virtually closed, as most solicitors would not grant articles to a woman. One solicitor exclaimed, 'A girl! Thank goodness I shall soon be out of it!' Another master solicitor Marie interviewed told her, 'We should put you thumping a typewriter.' She later reflected that she would have gained more insight into the law if she had learnt to type, but refused to submit to the stereotype.

Eventually the Stamp Commissioner, who used to live next door to the Byles, persuaded the senior partner of Stuart Thom & Co. to take her on as an articled clerk. This opportunity should have given Marie practical experience in managing legal affairs but she received little proper training. Her time was mostly spent helping one of the typists file letters and running errands. In that regard, she was no different from her male colleagues. The lack of proper training in the articles system was the reason it was later abolished and the College of Law system introduced.

Making use of her spare time Marie exemplified Cyril's nickname for her, 'Mrs Mahabili Pushbar, she who gets things done'. She arranged the building of new accommodation for her brothers, Baldur and David. The tall teenagers had outgrown their 'den', a room underneath the house, and wanted their own rooms. Marie designed a simple structure of two rooms, each three metres square with a verandah two metres wide, and supervised the building. Cyril merely had to pay for it.

During the three underemployed years of her articles, Marie took advantage of this time to explore various philosophies and develop her own beliefs. At university, she threw herself into the production of a journal called "The New Outlook", a forum that allowed her to share her views and engage meaningfully with issues of the day. Hearing a visiting Indian speaker, the President of the Indian Liberal Federation, he impressed her 'as no speaker had ever done'. In an article, she promoted the reform of the White Australia Policy, expressing the hope that it might be modified so that, 'we might benefit from such as he'. The article aroused considerable adverse criticism from other students. In this, as in so many of the causes Marie promoted throughout her life, she was ahead of her time but was prepared to stand up for what she believed.

ONCE WOMEN'S right to vote had been won in Australia in the early twentieth century, feminists focused on creating a welfare state based on the needs of mothers. Their major achievement was ensuring the creation of infant and maternal welfare centres, women's hospitals, children's courts, maternity benefits and eventually child endowment. Marie was so inspired by their work that when she graduated Bachelor of Laws (LLB), she asked Mr A.B. Piddington KC, who had been responsible for introducing child endowment in NSW, to move in court for her admission as a solicitor. Her employers were so shocked by this altogether radical choice that one of the partners suggested she approach a barrister less unorthodox because in the circumstances – Marie being the first woman admitted – 'some questions might be asked'. Not one to succumb to pressure, Marie persisted and Mr Piddington duly appeared in the Supreme Court to perform the duties of a registered practitioner moving a graduate's admission to the legal profession.

On 4 June 1924, the *Sydney Morning Herald* announced:

FIRST LADY SOLICITOR

Miss Marie Beuzeville Byles, the daughter of Mr. C.B. Byles, had passed her examination and would shortly be admitted the first woman solicitor in NSW.

Her admission to practise was newsworthy because of its implications. The New South Wales Law Almanac of 1925 chronicled this momentous event in the history of solicitors in NSW. The newspaper's description of Marie as the daughter of Mr. C.B. Byles had, in this instance, more relevance than the normal cultural assumption that a daughter's identity was determined through the status and position of her father. In the same newspaper that day an article announced that the work of automatic signalling replacing manual signalling had now been brought into operation in Sydney, under the personal supervision of Mr. C.B. Byles. It was a colossal achievement. Cyril was credited with bringing the NSW Railways to a level of modernisation comparable with any railway system in the world. Marie witnessed her father's efforts to succeed at this exceptional feat of engineering and it made a profound impact on her self-expectations.

In 1921, Rose Scott bequeathed to the University of Sydney a prize in International Law for women candidates. Upon graduation, Marie was awarded this prize worth £50. Scott, who remained unmarried, provided this young woman with an important role model of empowered womanhood, of a woman who claimed her authority and spoke openly about the values and principles she believed in.

Feminists, who took every opportunity to celebrate the victories achieved on behalf of their gender, congratulated Marie. To improve conditions for women who were treated in a shocking manner in jails, by police and in hospitals, feminists campaigned to get women appointed to a variety of public offices responsible for their welfare. Women were now being employed as doctors in hospitals, police matrons in jails, as probation officers, police officers, social workers, and finally there was a fully qualified legal officer.

Marie naturally enjoyed the esteem and status she gained from her achievement but reality set in when she was told, 'You can be a solicitor's clerk but you can't practise.' 'I haven't spent all this time studying just to be a secretary,' she thought. Having passed the same examinations as men she refused to be treated like a second-class citizen. Her privileged background and intellectual capacity allowed her the best education of the time for a girl: however, her frustrating attempt to gain articles and lack of success in being employed as a solicitor gave her direct personal awareness of the discrimination women faced in society. This strengthened the strong sense of social justice she had imbibed from her parents. Throughout this period she was sustained by an aspiration to help the oppressed and transform society.

Marie considered an academic career and enrolled in a master's degree in law at Sydney University. Six months later, the dean of the Faculty of Law, Sir John Peden, introduced her to a partner of Henry Davis & Co. who took her on as a law clerk. Given a salary of £6 a week Marie failed to impress, having learnt virtually nothing during her articles. At the end of her first year, when she asked for a rise in salary, Mr Davis told Marie she was hardly worth it.

> I plunged into the depths of despair and for the first time a long lonely bush walk brought no respite from the gloom. I tried to get another type of job but thank goodness I did not succeed; I was fated for law. Mr. Davis gave me a rise after all but it must have been nearly another year before I became his right hand man and a real help to him ...

Though not usually afflicted by self-doubt it took some time for her to gain confidence in representing clients. In one case she managed to get the charges dropped against an old man accused of stealing someone's water tank but he had to hand the tank back. She became expert at serving summonses on people who would not pay their just debts, once making an appointment and actually sitting in the dentist's chair before she could hand him the "blue".

In addition to her law work, Marie returned to Sydney University in 1925 for three years to gain a degree in economics, making her one of the first to have this combined qualification. It is presumed that a feminist critique of economics began in the 1960s as women questioned the traditional economic system that failed to take into account the value of the unpaid work in the domestic setting. Yet since the 1920s feminists had argued on behalf of married women that, as mothers, they performed work of vital social significance. If they had to neglect this role in order to earn their own money in the labour market then families would suffer. Therefore, they argued, women needed some form of financial subsidy to ensure the wellbeing of themselves and their children. Women's organisations debated the virtues of whether women should be entitled to a share of their husband's income, referred to as "family income" or, as British socialists advocated, be paid an income by the state in the form of a motherhood endowment.

Marie's study of economics confronted her with traditional views regarding women's place in society and gave her even greater insight into the forces that controlled their lives. When examining the social theories of nineteenth-century British economist John Ruskin, she argued from the perspective of her gender. Ruskin reinforced the belief that woman's main virtue was as homemaker whom man protects from the crueller realities of life, but Marie protested. If women did not agitate to change laws that discriminated against them who would? Her ardent response to the economist's attacks on women's integrity was intensified by her belief that her mother had become the traditional model of Ruskin's ideal. This person who had once fought passionately for the right of women to realise their full humanity had, Marie felt, taken on the limiting role of 'the self-effacing servant of us all'. Ida was accommodating and tolerant, accepting of others' needs, while Marie's greatest fear was that she would become powerless like her. When Ida meekly submitted to Cyril's 'wholly selfish' refusal to allow her to visit her dying mother in England, Marie lost all respect for her.

Ida's capitulation caused Marie to react against the oppressive forces – just as later she condemned in different ways women who engaged in 'unfeminist' behaviour. Instead, she modelled herself on her father who was a strong, decisive problem-solver. She later declared that she was a 'natural celibate' and avoided any attachment to the traditional feminine identity. At university, there was no lack of suitable role models of women who preferred independence and the life of the mind to serving a husband.

When Marie graduated with first-class honours, her lecturer, Professor Mills, declared that in taking up law, she 'was a loss to Economics'. However she thought she could never have made being an economist because she preferred to engage with people on an individual level rather than trying to solve society's problem en masse through the law of supply and demand or any other generalised economic strategy.

Her legal training was put to good use when she fought a different kind of battle on behalf of the community. By 1927, Palm Beach's popularity as a holiday destination had increased substantially and local hotels were seeking to obtain alcohol permits. They did not reckon on Marie's determination to protect this earthly paradise from alcohol's corrupting influence. She obtained permission from Mr Davis to conduct the case for the objectors. Her success was marred by an incident that upset the committed activist. While gathering evidence from the local residents she visited the house of a managing director of a large city firm who was '… apparently so overcome by my youthful innocence that when he opened the door for me to leave, he took me in his arms and kissed me! I was furious for days afterwards. I was a solicitor; I was not that sort!'

Marie had to fight to be taken seriously as a lawyer. Her later decision to establish her own law practice, the first woman in New South Wales to do so, demonstrated the degree of self-belief she developed to overcome all obstacles.

CHAPTER 3

Pioneering in Law

1927–1928

T O CONTEMPORARY minds, the discrimination women were subjected to before legislative change is unimaginable. Married women were denied the right to own property, to have custody of their children, and did not even own the clothes they stood up in. Although there had been some legislative improvements by the 1920s, the situation for married women under the law meant that feminists saw marriage as a "house of bondage".

Legal studies gave Marie insight into the reality of most women's lives, and how men, often indifferent to the hardships women experienced when forced to support themselves and their children, made the laws, interpreted the law, and supervised the legal process. Her association with leading feminists at university, who, through their work in social welfare, had experienced the iniquitous social conditions many women lived under, motivated Marie to write extensively as a legal correspondent for various publications in the struggle for equal rights.

Throughout the late 1920s and '30s her articles were published in the feminist newspaper *The Dawn* and also mainstream women's magazines and newspaper supplements that canvassed subjects of contemporary interest beyond fashion, cooking and social jottings. The main thrust of Marie's journalism was to inform her female readers of their rights. She always maintained that a woman should not adopt her husband's surname at marriage – 'legally she was not bound to do so'. She could see no reason why a woman should relinquish her identity.

As legal correspondent for *The Australian Woman's Mirror*, she wrote in an article entitled "Who Owns the House-keeping Allowance?" that the money wives received from their husbands was, according to law, 'yours in trust to spend for him and return if you don't spend it'. The moral of all this, she concluded, 'is that legally there can be no reward to you for frugality, and that you may as well spend all you can!' Through her writing on a range of contentious issues, Marie challenged the existing social structures and values by highlighting cases where magistrates and judges interpreted the law to make women's behaviour the issue on trial.

In that era divorce was rare, because it was a nasty business. The plaintiff had to prove fault and the grounds for divorce were many and complicated. Women were often completely dependent on their husbands financially. Any divorced woman was stigmatised and those with children found it difficult to find employment. The legal system often failed to ensure relief for women whose erring ex-husbands defaulted on maintenance payments. Many women, who felt safer confiding the wretchedness of their situation to another woman, came to Marie regarding legal separation or divorce. Her qualities of decency and common sense provided reassurance to many and she worked to ensure just divorce settlements for her female clients.

To save money, Marie did a great deal of her own appearance work on divorce cases rather than brief a barrister. One of her clients was a woman who had attempted to enter Australia from New Zealand but had been barred from doing so on the grounds that she was 'not a fit and proper person'. Her husband accused her of being in love with an Australian Army officer and he did not want her to gain entry as it would mean the break-up of his marriage. The case involved representation to State Parliament as it needed to overturn the ruling in order for the plaintiff to be admitted into the country. Marie also acted for the wife of a leading judge, an influential man who made it extremely difficult for her to get a divorce. This woman was shocked to discover in the divorce court the full extent of the power her husband wielded and his ability to manipulate the system. The plaintiff, a committed communist, instead travelled to Russia to obtain a divorce easily and cheaply for two shillings and sixpence.

This first-hand knowledge gave Marie the insight to dissect the issues relating to many people's married lives. In an article entitled "And They Lived Happily Ever After" published in *The Australian Woman's Mirror*, January 1928, Marie wrote:

> Did they really marry and live happily ever after in the good old days? Or did
> the fairy stories and the novelettes make a vast assumption the falsity of which
> we have not till to-day been willing to face? We do not know; but this we do

know – the tragic ending of the modern love-story is too often 'And they were divorced and lived happily ever after.'

Unlike men, women had to prove cruelty before being granted a divorce. As she described:

> Sydney people will remember a play recently staged … in which the husband wished to enable his wife to obtain a divorce. It was not sufficient for him to make a pretence of 'misconduct'; he had also to knock his wife down in a rose-garden in the presence of a proper number of witnesses in order to add the additional element of cruelty which was also necessary before the wife could free herself from the bonds of marriage.

The one principle of the divorce law that seemed particularly foolish to her was that which stated '… no divorce will be granted if both parties decide that they want a divorce'. Ironically, if both parties have deserted each other, or both committed adultery, then 'these are good reasons why they should be chained together for the rest of their lives'.

After many years of observing the frequently unsatisfactory consequences of divorce, Marie attempted to counsel her clients to reconcile. She invited the couple into her office, and, if they reversed their decision, she would not charge her client. If they decided to proceed, she did.

MARIE'S ACTIVISM was not restricted to asserting the rights of women at home. From the beginning of her career she promoted and supported other women attempting to become established in the professions as dentists, doctors and osteopaths, as well as in law. Her own disheartening experience meant that, when she did find a position in a firm, she took every opportunity to brief the first female barrister to practise in New South Wales. At a time when there were no women judges in the District or Supreme courts women advocates were exotic and newsworthy. On 5 November 1926 the *Daily Telegraph* reported that Miss Sybil Morrison, the only woman practising at the Bar at that time appeared twice in one day instructed by Miss Marie B. Byles and secured a decree nisi for a woman petitioner.

The Bar was the most difficult branch of the profession for a woman in which to establish a practice, because it was virtually impossible to get chambers or briefs from male solicitors. Morrison, from a wealthy family, who did not need to depend on law work for financial support. Attractive and well-groomed, she was well known for her work in the women's movement as Convenor of the

Laws Committee of the National Council of Women (NCW) having prepared papers on the desirability of a uniform matrimonial and divorce law. The NCW, established after the successful campaign for women's suffrage, was an umbrella organisation for a diverse range of women's organisations. Acting as a lobby group it attempted to influence local, state and federal government on issues related to women and children. Through Morrison, Marie was soon briefed by the NCW and became involved in its campaigns for social and political reform. She regularly addressed its meetings on women's legal disabilities and was on the Peace and Arbitration Committee and the Laws Committee.

While Marie had considered becoming a barrister – she had the necessary confidence to act as an advocate and was strong enough to withstand any verbal jousting at the Bar – she weighed up the difficulty of getting established in a field where work was unreliable, against the mundane but steady work of a suburban solicitor. Perhaps the moral issues also influenced her decision, as barristers are expected to take any case presented to them. As well, the Sydney judiciary and police were notoriously corrupt at this time. Against these considerations, she decided that practising as a solicitor gave her the freedom to pursue her outside interests. Distinction in the public domain as an enthusiastic participant in local or international feminist and legal organisations did not appeal to her either. Marie's contribution was to establish her own successful practice and inspire other women in law. She demonstrated that it could be done, that a woman was as capable as a man.

Through the National Council of Women, Marie soon came into contact with Jessie Street, the indefatigable and highly respected feminist who had served as secretary and then founded her own organisation the United Association of Women (UAW) in 1929. Although Jessie was born into wealth and was part of the establishment, her childhood in India as the daughter of a British civil servant gave her an early education in racial discrimination. Married to Kenneth Street, one of Marie's university law lecturers, his position on the Supreme Court bench gave Jessie access to powerful people, but the Streets made an improbable pair, with Kenneth's increasing conservatism and Jessie's socialism. A graduate of Sydney University, she had an intense commitment to social justice and used her privileges to help others. Jessie was a powerful speaker and natural leader who inspired intense loyalty. With its slogan "For freedom and equality of status and opportunity" the UAW grew into one of the most radical feminist groups of the mid-twentieth century. Though the battle for women's suffrage had been won, women still suffered discrimination at work, in the courts, and at home. Over the following decades Street lobbied intensively on equal citizenship for Australian women, writing thousands of letters to heads of federal and state governments.

As honorary legal adviser to the UAW, Marie's commitment to the cause matched Jessie's own and she worked by her side throughout the 1930s. There was much to accomplish. The UAW cooperated with other organisations, such as trade unions, in their campaign for equal pay for women. In the early 1900s, a Labor government had decided to relate the minimum wage to the current cost of living. The basic wage was deemed as needing to provide for the basic needs of a man, a wife and two children. When this principle was adopted as policy, it placed an almost insurmountable obstacle in the way of the campaign for equal pay for women. Legislation provided that women workers, regardless of their skills or family responsibilities, were entitled to only 54 per cent of the male wage. Jessie Street believed that this ensured a pool of cheap female labour, which undermined the standard of living of all workers. The right of any person to sell their labour at the highest price was the very foundation of human liberty. Worse, low rates of pay often forced women into bad marriages, early parenthood or prostitution.

As well as the fundamental campaign for equal pay, the UAW fought for equal guardianship rights, divorce law reform, family planning services, appointments of women to public office and election of women to parliament, among many other causes. Marie devoted herself to changing one of the cruellest laws, that which deprived women custody of their children. Although many rights of women and children were finally being recognised, the fundamental right of a mother to equal guardianship with the father was still denied her. Most married women owned nothing. If they left their husbands they were not entitled to take any of their possessions with them. Similarly they had no claim to their own children. The common law of the United Kingdom gave the father of a legitimate child the sole right to the custody of its person and property and the determination of its education, religion and maintenance. Even after death he still retained his authority for he could appoint a guardian to succeed him and the mother had no more rights than before. As Marie commented:

> It was rather a serious state of affairs that the mother who had borne all the pain and hardship of bringing the child into the world should have no right to bring it up as she wished, and this even if the father was a scoundrel and a drunkard.

Since 1925, the law in England relating to guardianship of children had been fundamentally altered, but the law in Australia lagged very much behind. Marie worked with Jessie Street and the UAW to formulate measures being proposed for its amendment. Her discussion paper, which clarified points of policy, was published as part of the organisation's education and publicity campaign. Marie was included in numerous UAW delegations to ministers – state and federal. Some seventy women's organisations mobilised to change the legislation and finally found success when the *Equal Guardianship of Infants Act 1934 NSW* was passed. Marie proudly declared,

> In 1934 our work bore fruit; the act passed was in line with similar laws in other lands, and few realise that it contained a clause all our own providing that leaving the jurisdiction should not be a bar to granting custody.

Throughout these battles Marie always spoke with the sweet voice of reason but could be blunt and confrontationist when required. Her work with Jessie Street proved fruitful, perhaps because of the women's mutual respect. When Jessie wrote to the prime minister urging action by the Commonwealth Government to implement the Equal Rights Treaty being considered by the League of Nations, she recommended Marie as having the necessary legal knowledge for the task of compiling the required information.

Jessie's son, Sir Laurence Street, a Chief Justice of New South Wales (as were his father and grandfather) recalled, 'My mother was a great admirer of hers. I never met her, but I heard my mother speak of her. I know my mother admired her ongoing commitment as a woman to overcoming prejudice against women in the law.'

Marie could have gained further professional prestige by sitting on various committees related to women's legal rights both locally and internationally. Those opportunities certainly existed as she had the ability and the networks. Social activism gave her a feeling of immense satisfaction and her efforts helped awaken many people to vital issues of the day. But it was never ending, like climbing a mountain, the peak of which remained constantly out of reach. While feminism continued to inform every aspect of her life, Marie's intense desire to climb actual mountains became stronger than any other consideration.

CHAPTER 4

By Cargo Boat and Mountain

1928–1929

UPON THEIR arrival in Australia the Byles family immediately took advantage of Cyril's complimentary rail travel to discover their new country and freely indulge their love of the outdoors. In summer they explored the Kosciusko region and hiked all over the Australian Alps in southern New South Wales. For Cyril's annual winter holiday they went to the Blue Mountains west of Sydney. The chief joys of life, to Marie, were the walking and tramping holidays, especially to the Blue Mountains.

> The train went up imperceptibly, but when the view opened out beyond Wentworth Falls you looked down apparently stupendous precipices and did not look up to any kind of mountains at all but across the gorges to a level plateau skyline. The Blue Mountains are a Blue Plateau, but they provided endless good walking with the two little rucksacks that Father had brought from England, such things being unprocurable in Sydney.

While the Australian landscape served to delight, it never satisfied the family's quest for real mountains. Each year they set out with fresh hopes to a new place, but 'ever and anon fell back unrealised and disappointed'. Afflicted with the 'disease of mountaineering' Marie vowed that if she ever had the opportunity to travel to other lands it would be to the mountains. With a height of only 2228 metres, Mount Kosciusko, Australia's highest peak, was unable to offer the kind of alpine challenges she sought. Once she gained confidence in her abilities as a lawyer and saved enough money, she planned to 'make an orgy of them'. In her research for every opportunity to walk and climb throughout England, Scotland, Scandinavia and Canada she wrote to clubs and magazines in the hope of contacts. After eighteen months of correspondence with the elite Canadian Alpine Club, they accepted her into their annual training camp in the Rocky Mountains.

Customary practice for young Australian women in the late nineteenth and early twentieth centuries was to travel to England and the continent on a grand tour to finish their education, be introduced to society, and perhaps find a husband. The women Marie modelled herself on did not travel to find romance. To them, travel *was* the romance. Victorian women travellers had forsaken cloistered lives to venture by cargo boats to Africa, Arabia and the Far East on voyages of discovery beyond boundaries considered safe for respectable women. Freya Stark, the British explorer and travel writer who authored two dozen books on her experiences in the Middle East and Afghanistan, longed to fill in the blank parts on the map and wrote: 'The beckoning counts, and not the clicking latch behind you: and all through life the actual moment of emancipation holds that delight, of the whole world coming to meet you like a wave.'

Driven by the same desire for emancipation, Marie scoured the Sydney docks in her lunchtimes for a suitable boat to take her on the first leg of her round-the-world trip, with England her first stop. Scorning the luxury of a passenger liner she chose a Norwegian cargo boat. Just when she had started to become really useful to Mr Davis as his managing clerk, Marie booked her ticket and quit her job. Cyril wanted her to remain home until the time she would "go hence", an expression indicating transition to married life, but Marie's destiny did not lie in marriage. Personal independence was the feminist creed and sacrificing the security of marriage was no sacrifice at all for the young adventurer. Resigned to his daughter's choice but forever perplexed at her lifestyle, Cyril wrote her a cheque for £100. With no interest in sentimental farewells from family and friends, Marie soon revelled in the greatest joy of the born traveller, setting out over unknown horizons:

> The last bale of wool had been shipped, the gangway drawn up, and there was
> I alone on a foreign cargo boat with the dream of years coming true, the light
> of Sydney Harbour fading fast and the wide ocean opening out before me.

After her first night on board the SS *Eknaren* she awakened to a deserted deck save the man at the wheel, exhilarated to discover she was '… really alone on the wide sea with the blue sky above, the fresh breeze blowing through my hair, and the spray curling white from the bow.' She was in her element – surrounded by nature.

The opportunity to master the science of the sea was more thrilling than any entertainment offered on a cruise ship. She persuaded the chief mate to take her on a tour of the engine room and to let her take a turn at the wheel. She quickly learnt to navigate with a sextant. In the captain's cabin, table manners were soon forgotten as the finest duty-free liqueurs were served to the five passengers. Wine and whiskey flowed but Marie stuck with limejuice, as a 'concession to the temperamental weakness of one who suffered from a teetotal ancestry'. As amusing as the entertainment was in the captain's cosy cabin, Marie sometimes escaped to the solitude of the starlit decks:

> Those wonderful tropic nights were more intoxicating than the Captain's beverages – the rich dark, blue-velvet sky hung with stars of piercing brilliance, the sea alight with glimmering phosphorescence, the balmy breeze … and the infinite ocean rolling eternally onwards …

How she pitied the unfortunate tourists on the passenger boats, where the lights of the saloon challenged the light of the stars and the music of the orchestra drowned the sad and solemn music of the sea. On a passenger boat, man made the music and dancing but to Marie, alone on the bow of the cargo boat, the music of the waves and the dancing of the moonbeams were the life of the universe.

For the first three weeks in England Marie made headquarters with her uncle George Unwin, a publisher, and conscientiously visited all her relatives. She had already met her mother's first cousin, Stanley Unwin, when he had visited Australia on a round-the-world trip in 1913 (who co-founded the George Allen & Unwin publishing house in 1914). Marie attended the wedding of the prettiest of her cousins and watched her 'sacrifice herself on the altar of Aphrodite. It was very sad, but it gave me an opportunity of killing two or three relatives with one stone.' Although she enjoyed her relatives' company, she found the social side of her visit trying: 'I am not affable by nature and the strain of assuming affability all day long for twenty-one days, with no Sunday holiday, nearly caused a mental and physical breakdown.'

Most Australians went to England almost as a pilgrimage to the centre of culture, but Marie felt it her duty not to do the regulation cathedrals and ancient buildings. Nor was she at all interested in attending any of the conferences that could have advanced her career, such as those of the National Council of Women 'and the other high-brow societies to which I belong …' The main attraction in London for her – and the only thing she professed to like – were the law courts, the 'shrine of English Law'.

The most profitable time spent in London was shopping for mountaineering equipment. Impressed by the testimonials of some Everest expeditioners, she ordered a pair of the best climbing boots that she came to cherish and named Feroce, Latin for "bold". She bought snow goggles, maps and an ice axe she named Felice, "friend", which her life would soon depend upon. After purchasing a large amount of camping equipment, she headed straight for the mecca of walking and climbing clubs in England, the Lakes District in the west of Cumbria.

As the steam train drew her towards this spectacular region, Marie exclaimed, 'Mountains at last!' These towering, impregnable heights possessed the charm of grandeur combined with accessibility, so different from those to which she was used. Compared with the rugged, relatively unmapped Australian landscape, these hills were domesticated with footpaths and landmarks everywhere. Above all, there were maps!

She expected to be intimidated by the English people's aptitude for walking but found the members of the Cooperative Holiday Association's walking club quite dilettante in their approach. Eight hours or 15 miles (25 km) a day were considered quite sufficient and two long days together were never done. Marie made friends with a Scottish boy who believed that each day his feet must climb at least one mountain 3000 feet (1000 m) high and walk at least 20 miles (33 km) along the level. His endurance was similar to hers and together they climbed a full range of peaks throughout the region. Despite her small frame, Marie had strong legs, and her strength and stamina had developed through continuous outdoors activities. Sheer determination and love of a challenge took her higher and further than others with greater physical endowments.

For English women interested in outdoors pursuits it was the fashion to wear knickerbockers, woollen trousers that buttoned below the knee, with long socks. They gave the wearer freedom to sit astride their bicycle or pony or to climb mountains. Marie adopted this attire during her travels. On her last night with the walking club she was asked to give a fireside talk on Australia from the point of view of the rambler. With heavy irony she called it, 'a rambler's paradise', as she described the prevailing conditions for bushwalkers in the 1920s:

> … there were no mountains, no water, no footpaths, and no maps, so that a person tramping in the Australian bush was like an explorer in untrodden country, with the ever-present possibility of gloriously perishing and leaving

his bones to bleach on the hillside undiscovered for generations to come. I then topped it off with a few well-chosen snake yarns.

Marie headed north to Scotland after having her boots nailed in a manner proper for real rock climbing. Through the train's window the desolate moorlands held a fascination for her. The breaking storms made the Highlands wilder than she had often pictured them to be. At Glencoe she joined up with the Scottish Ladies Climbing Club for her first official rock climb. Although it was a bleak day all went well until the path ran out. The leader unroped and went off on a reconnaissance while the rest of the party were left standing on two very narrow ledges with a great drop below. A snow blizzard swept up against the mountain as Marie's teeth chattered and her knees knocked together. With each gust she felt her legs might give way under her and she would be hurled over the edge of the cliff: 'For the first time I understood how people lose their nerve; instead I clapped my hands and tried to sing "There's a Tavern in the Town", which was the first appropriate thing I could think of.'

With growing confidence Marie climbed glaciers and mountains in Norway's Jostedalsbrae, the largest snowfield in Europe, and then headed for Canada and the high peaks of the Rocky Mountains. In Banff, she made her headquarters at the Canadian Alpine Club's clubhouse situated in the midst of a spruce forest with splendid views of mountains and a river valley. With 150 other enthusiastic mountaineers she signed up to undertake the club's rigorous training camp. To share her tent was a Miss Gardiner, who Marie was impressed to discover was the daughter of a well-known English mountaineer.

After a couple of days of fitness training they were driven up to base camp where Marie erected the tent she had bought in London for alpine camping. Its small size attracted scorn from the other campers, but she thought their tents large and ungainly. Real cowboys dressed just like in the movies brought up their provisions and a bear rampaged through the camp dragging the contents of their bags into the forest. Marie soon discovered that mountain climbing was judged by very austere standards among certain members of the club and wondered if she had ever, properly speaking, climbed a mountain at all. Nevertheless she applied for the graduating climb that if accomplished would entitle her to full membership.

After breakfast at 5 am her party set out through the dripping undergrowth and up the smooth ice of a glacier. They took to the snow slopes and finally reached a narrow ridge of bare rock that led to the summit. The guide, pointing, said: 'If we go up that, I expect it will do as a graduating climb.' To Marie it looked as if he were pointing to a perpendicular wall. But she found it to be good solid rock 'with some thrilling moments but otherwise it was easier than some of the rock climbs I had done in the Scottish Highlands'. On the summit they congratulated themselves on having bagged a virgin peak but then saw a tin with the names of the people who had climbed it in 1911 and named it Mount Thompson. On their next climb they did the Dome that overlooked the camp. To get to it they went up beside the Lake of the Hanging Glaciers, named for the glaciers that hang from the mountains all around and continually drop large blocks of ice into its opaque green waters, dotting them with miniature icebergs.

Every evening after the day's climb the campfire brought the internationally diverse group together as they sang songs, told outrageous stories and listened to prepared lectures. After comparing windburn they went to the noticeboard and entered their names for the climbs of the following day and then went off to their beds made of fragrant spruce boughs to dream of mountain peaks to come.

The club established a camp for experienced climbers 24 km away up a valley, and Marie brazenly put her name down. The nonexistent trail to the camp tested all her bushman skills. The hot sun had melted the snow so rapidly that the trail was a continuous stream and the meadows had become a lake that had to be waded knee-deep through. When their small party reached the camp in an open valley they found the head of it blocked by a gigantic glacier flowing down from three peaks: the Commander, the Eastern Guardsman and the Western Guardsman. That night Marie slept rough on stones instead of spruce. In the morning the one-eyed cook made them flapjacks and then Marie, Miss Gardiner and a guide set out for the summit of Mount Commander.

They climbed over slippery rocks, dashed under melting glacier waterfalls and then onto the snow-covered glacier that was split in all directions by small but treacherous crevasses. The Swiss guide, acting like he was lord of the mountain, delivered lectures on what would happen if they let the rope sag even a few inches. He had an attitude that treated amateurs as 'merely worms whom it was their misfortune in life to trail over rocks and snow'. When the guide turned to reprove Marie for letting the rope come within a few centimetres of the snow 'he did it with an air that I was just about the greatest idiot the Lord Almighty had ever miscreated'. She scorned asking him for help as he strode on oblivious to their difficulties and hesitations but grudgingly acknowledged that he was a first-rate guide and his spartan methods were doubtless good for their souls, saying: 'Anyhow, I learned more about mountaineering from him than I did from any other one person.'

Standing on top of Mount Commander the party was about to make their descent when to Marie's delight the guide suggested they climb the Western Guardsman as well. Up they went and when they discovered on the summit that it was a virgin peak, she was ecstatic:

> Now virgin peaks over ten thousand feet are not picked up every day … The view from the top was particularly fine … The view from any mountain-peak is fine, but to feel that yours are the first eyes that have seen it is, for the mountaineer, the nearest approach to heaven on earth.

ON HER return journey, Marie stopped in California where she visited her grandmother, Cyril's mother, who was old and miserable and not very welcoming. She was glad when her uncle and aunt took her to live with them in Beverley Hills. She was less impressed with the movie stars she saw in restaurants than the modern conveniences that made Chilworth seem primitive. She marvelled that Los Angeles houses had a gas and electric heating system that circulated hot water to the kitchen, the laundry and all the bathrooms. Her relatives found it hard to believe when she told them that in order to wash the dishes at home they first had to boil a kettle, and when they wanted to warm the bath water, they had to light the chip heater.

> California houses seemed to me like homes in Utopia; you pressed a button and, hey presto! The thing was done. Indeed, they were fitted with every imaginable device for encouraging laziness.

Her uncle's house was centrally heated with the flick of a switch. It had a washing machine where the only manual labour required was to fill the tub with hot water then press a few buttons. On Sundays, Marie dutifully accompanied her grandmother to church. This was the same one attended by the movie star Mary Pickford, whose husband, Douglas Fairbanks, would drop his wife outside and read his newspaper in the car until the service was over, then drive her home again. But in 'the land of the almighty dollar,' Marie was shocked to discover that the noble word "solicitor" had degenerated to mean a person who solicits people to buy real estate. From then on, she called herself a lawyer.

Her uncle kindly put his car and a driver at her disposal allowing her to escape civilisation. Springtime in the nearby desert meant masses of brightly coloured flowers and cacti in all conceivable shades of green. Out of the flat desert floor arose the awe-inspiring San Jacinto Range towering 2750 m in height. Palm Canyon provided an oasis with water and shade from the glare of the sun under tall graceful fan palms. At a ranch selling dates Marie hoped to buy them fresh but was offered only the dried variety. She insisted on getting a ladder to pick them from the palm trees herself. Trudging along a sun-scorched trail through the Sierra Madres, she only just made the bus back to town in time to catch her boat home.

IMMEDIATELY ON her return to Sydney, Marie left for New Zealand and the last lap of a perfect holiday. From Christchurch, she headed for the historic Hermitage Hotel nestled among the imposing white peaks of the Southern Alps, fired with a desire to bag as many of them as possible. The more experienced climbers warned her that New Zealand's mountains were climbs for men only, but she ignored them. At the peak of fitness, she was ready to test herself against the terrain. At 157 cm and slightly built, Marie did not have the physique of a mountaineer, but what she lacked in size she made up for in spirit.

She was unable to explain why she and others like her were willing to suffer the tortures they were exposed to under the blazing sun or icy wind, the thrill of clinging fearfully to treacherous rocks with a precipice below, or the dull pain of toiling up endless snow slopes before reaching a more actively painful stage of the ascent:

> All I know is that we do these things and suffer them gladly, that mountaineering means the exercise of every muscle of the body with a constant alertness of mind, and a consequent state of physical and mental exhilaration, and that, when we stand upon our mountain peak and see the snow-clad ranges stretching out as far as the eye can reach, we are filled with an ecstasy nothing else on earth can bring.

Excited about the prospect of extending herself, Marie hired two Norwegian guides, Alf Brustad and Arne Larsen, and planned her expedition. The guides introduced her to another woman climber who wished to join their party, Marjorie Jones, who, at 153 cm and 35 kg, was even smaller than Marie. Together they set off on a venture that would, Marie later reflected, demonstrate 'the enormous resources that lie behind our normal physical strength'. Their objective was the flattened cone-shaped Malte Brun at 3199 m but, after a four-hour hike up the mighty Tasman Glacier, their progress was halted by a blizzard. For three days the party was marooned in a freezing alpine hut. When the snowstorm subsided the guides deemed the summit too dangerous, as the fresh snow would make the rocks slippery. They packed their rucksacks and started down the Tasman Glacier now half covered in snow, making crevasses a source of danger. Marie was devastated at the failure of the expedition.

> It seemed to me to be the greatest loss I had known. If Calais were graven on Queen Mary's heart when she died, Malte Brun would be graven on mine. As we hopped down the crevassed Tasman Glacier there seemed to be no interest in life, and the shadow of Malte Brun fell upon me with a gloom nothing could pierce.

About halfway down the glacier, Mount Cook emerged from the mist, the setting sun making a halo behind its snowy crest. With an elevation of 3763 m it was the highest mountain in New Zealand – its Maori name, Aorangi, means Cloud Piercer. Remote and inaccessible, Marie dared not hope that she would ever reach the top of those jagged and forbidding rocks. When Alf suggested they climb up to Haast Hut, 2134 m up the side of Cook, she eagerly agreed. Marjorie opted for a hot bath and civilised dinner at the Hermitage Hotel while Arne accompanied her down to phone his girlfriend. It was arranged that Marjorie and Arne would leave the Hermitage very early the following day and go right through to Haast Hut allowing them time to have a rest before their departure for the summit.

Marie and Alf stayed the night at Ball Hut. In the morning they began the steep climb up to Haast Hut. Just below it, Alf pointed out the historic site where Freda du Faur, the first woman to climb Mt Cook, had bivouacked in 1910. This fearless mountaineer, daughter of early Australian explorer Eccleston du Faur, had climbed all the most difficult mountains in New Zealand. Perched so high, Haast Hut commanded a view of the whole of the Tasman Glacier from its head to where it breaks down and becomes the Tasman River. Marie wrote of her impressions, 'All the mountains overlooking the glacier are also visible, so that you get a bird's eye view of one-half of the highest Alps in New Zealand.' Inside the hut were two men preparing to leave the next morning for the summit. Grasping the opportunity Marie decided, with Alf, to join them.

Shortly after 1am the party left the hut as the silver moonlight bathed the snow-clad slopes with an ethereal mystic splendour transforming the landscape into a fairyland. For several hours they plodded through the soft snow as the sun rose above the ranges like a great ball of fire touching first one peak then another with the deepest crimson glow. The red flames spread down the white mountainsides until they reached the crevasses at their feet and then burst into blue flames filling the crevasses with an intense deep-blue fire. In ten minutes the unearthly blaze faded away into the light of a bright and clear, cold day.

In contrast, the next stage was torment. Eating a hasty breakfast, the party prepared for a quick ascent of the treacherous Linda Glacier. Avalanches periodically swept down from the icecap of Cook. With the prospect of death before them their little group hurried as quickly as possible. Above the glacier were some steep ice-slopes where steps had to be cut requiring tremendous effort. It was heartbreaking work and it seemed as if they could not possibly reach the summit 'for already it was noon and we had been on the climb for eleven hours'.

At long last they reached the summit rocks and removed with relief their heavy, steel-spiked crampons that provided secure footing on the slippery ice. Crawling up the peak was painful work as a piercing, raging wind threatened to push over the slightly built women. Marie's party reached the top at 3.30 pm where they stood shivering in the icy blast. With her ice axe firmly planted, she looked over the 1200-metre precipice and delighted in the victory – the monarch of the mountains was theirs at last. With a hurried shaking of hands, two photographs and a hasty glance at the most 'superb panorama imaginable', they started the descent, the worst Marie had ever experienced. The wind increased in ferocity with each step, so fierce that she needed to lie on her side feeling her way down the interminable slope. Her side became black and blue and her left arm ached till it hurt to touch, but it had to be done. Unable to provide her with physical support Alf gave the moral support she needed to continue the perilous descent. The sun set below a whirlwind of clouds as they reached the Linda Glacier with only half their journey home completed. With the aid of only a dim lantern they reached a crevasse and found that a snow bridge they had used in the morning had collapsed. Fortunately it was a small crevasse. They risked it and jumped each in turn while anchored to the rest. At 2.45 am, 25 hours and 40 minutes after they had left, they made it through the hut door, 'to the inexpressible relief of those who were waiting for us with fevered anxiety'.

After ten hours of sleep Marie declared she was ready to do it all again. While Arne and Marjorie slept, she lay outside the hut 'drenching myself in the beauty of the view. Below, Tasman, like a white snake, basked peacefully in the sunlight.' Shortly after midnight, she prepared breakfast for the others. When the last echo of their nailed boots died away, Marie was alone with the moon-blanched mountains and the quietness of night. The profound depths of the Tasman Valley lay at her feet and the hills around were wrapped in the mantle of eternity. For a long time she sat on the low wall of the hut drinking in the beauty and watching the sun disperse the mists below. It was a day of perfect peace and calm.

> The serenity of Nature brooded over all things, making them one with the Spirit and Wisdom of the universe, and in the murmuring among the mountain-tops I heard the ocean of beauty gently surging round the world and tuning it to harmony with itself.

Marjorie and the guides returned triumphant soon after dark, having had a perfect day. The climb made Marie's mountaineering reputation. At the Hermitage telegrams of congratulation flowed in. It was the culmination of a year of unalloyed delight. She was twenty-eight years old and felt that life had just begun.

CHAPTER 5

The Law of the Living World

1929–1932

ARRIVING BACK in Sydney in February 1929, Marie was determined to establish her own law practice. Although Mr Davis would have happily given Marie her job back, she feared she would stay a lowly clerk forever. With the self-confidence of having successfully surmounted so many challenges on her voyage around the world, she had a strong urge to control her own life. She also wanted to redefine perceptions of women's capabilities. When women first sought the right to practise law, the stereotype was raised against them that they did not possess the same rational faculties as men and were unable to retain confidences. New stereotypes then formed of women being unable to manage money or handle the criminal (i.e. disputive) side of law. Women lawyers faced a challenge to succeed in a profession where they were not welcome and little encouragement was given to those attempting to establish a practice.

To place her situation in historical context, in the fifteen years following the passage of the *Women's Legal Status Act 1918 (NSW)* only nine women were admitted as solicitors and two as barristers. Women reported being treated like idiots when interviewed for legal jobs. Many gave up their attempts and looked for work in business or other professions. Those who gained a position were mostly employed in family law firms run by a father or brother, or as legal officers in government or quasi-government departments.

With an attitude common to high achievers who focus on the desired outcome, Marie turned a blind eye to prejudice. The result was, she declared, 'that I never met it and everyone both in the profession and outside it was very decent to me'. Instead of looking for office space in the city like most solicitors, she took the radical decision to establish her practice in Eastwood, the largest town between Strathfield in the west and Hornsby in the north, and only a short train ride from Beecroft. M.B. Byles & Co. was one of the first suburban legal practices anywhere in Sydney and the first in Eastwood. But office space was almost impossible to find. The local real estate agent convinced her to take a partitioned-off section of the foyer of the Duke of York Theatre for fifteen shillings a week. Built just two years earlier the theatre boasted an orchestra and a Christie organ that accompanied the silent movies.

With £40 from her mother and an office table, three chairs and a small safe from her father, Marie created the rudiments of a professional workspace. Outside the theatre on the main street she proudly erected the brass plate her father had given her. Mr Sommerville, the real estate agent, introduced her to his bank manager and she sat down and waited. A well-meaning friend warned her that she would never succeed if she did not wear make-up and dress more expensively, but Marie had never worn make-up and her dress was plain, but neat and clean. Her professional manner made the strongest impression and created confidence in prospective clients. When meeting a client for the first time she drew herself up to her full height and faced them with a penetrating look that immediately communicated her competence.

Marie needed to rely on her own brain to handle any business that presented. One client might be bankrupt and she would have to know bankruptcy law. The next client would have a completely different issue. No one person can know everything about each field of law; every circumstance is different and a solicitor has to understand how the law applies in varying circumstances. Being very bright, confident and personable, she clicked with the bank manager, Mr Lloyd, and was soon consulting clients referred by him. Marie gained a reputation for completing the work thoroughly 'and, most importantly for a solicitor, promptly'. In government offices she became well known for wanting things done quickly. Some officials resented her hop-to-it approach but she achieved the desired results. And her work stood up to the closest scrutiny. On one occasion, when having dealt with a matter with the Registrar of the District Court he told her, 'Next time, Miss Byles, you need not come back yourself; you can send your clerk.' She did not tell him that she had no clerk to send.

Bookkeeping was her biggest headache. She found a text that explained the rudiments and kept her own accounts until she could afford a bookkeeper, although she needed an accountant to explain the intricacies of trust accounts.

Taking it for granted that a client's interests always came first she was scrupulous in ensuring that there were no debits in any client's trust account. To avoid bad debts, money was collected from a client before anyone was engaged on their behalf. The barristers she briefed appreciated this as she always had the money to pay their fees immediately.

Conveyancing was a profitable area of business in the 1920s as Sydney's population increased prompting rapid suburban growth. With a second-hand typewriter, though no typing skills – she had refused to learn when working for others – Marie managed to type transfers on the appropriate forms that were just too wide for her portable. Her perfectionist nature and controlled demeanour were suited to the pedantic general work of a suburban solicitor: conveyancing, probate and administering estates – work that required patience and an eye for detail. During one case that involved a land dispute, Marie took the opposing barrister out to the site and measured it out with a twelve-inch ruler.

The Public Trustee of South Australia sent probates to her for re-seal in NSW, work that was consistent and provided a steady income. Through this and the referrals from the bank manager she managed to cover the rent at Eastwood and a pokey office in the city for work that needed to be done in the divorce courts, the probate office and the Registrar General's office. When the Great Depression hit with full force soon after, she noted, 'working up the practice was a downhill, not an uphill struggle'.

Throughout the Depression years, Marie worked with Jessie Street and feminist organisations to change legislation. She supplemented her meagre income through her journalism on women's legal rights and bushwalking, enticing her readers with descriptions of spectacular locations accessible from Sydney. 'All the same,' she wrote despairingly, 'time naturally hung heavily on my hands.' Describing herself as 'that curious entity, a young woman lawyer', Marie was a forerunner of the twentieth-century phenomenon, the single professional woman. While she obviously found satisfaction in her work and outdoor pursuits there is one moment in her written reflections where she allows a glimpse of something missing.

> Sydney's winter skies reminded me most uncomfortably of the forget-me-not blue eyes of a young man I had met; even though I was certainly not in love I used to get an unpleasant feeling of misery and envy when I saw young couples fondling each other's wrists. Lack of work can play havoc with even sane people.

To Marie, sanity was her independence. In her terms, if you did not have a focus on work, the implication was you would lapse into the insanity that caused people to look for closeness and connection in relationships. Marie equated intimate relationships with the unhealthy model of her parents. While her journey around the world by cargo boat had allowed her to have an adventure that challenged her physical abilities, that environment was emotionally safe. She did not need to develop close connections with anyone. Compromising her independence was not an option.

Her thoughts were temporarily redirected when Constance Mackness, her former headmistress, suggested she write up an account of her travels. Miss Mackness was also a published author having written the first two of ten books while at Croydon PLC: *The Gem of the Flat* recalled her happy childhood among the goldfields, while *Miss Pickle* was based on her teaching experience. Miss Mackness proofread the 300-page manuscript, corrected bad grammar and made invaluable suggestions. Dedicated to her, *By Cargo Boat and Mountain, the unconventional experiences of woman on tramp round the world*, was printed in England in 1931 by a publisher who specialised in travel books.

DURING THE lean years of the Depression, bushwalking occupied most of Marie's spare time. Immediately on her return from overseas she had joined the recently formed Sydney Bush Walkers club. With them she enjoyed an exhaustive schedule of bushwalks throughout the state. The SBW was an offshoot of the exclusively male Mountain Trails Club that had strict entry requirements suited to its founder Myles Dunphy. This legendary bushman had a patronising attitude to women; he believed they did not have the endurance for extended walking trips in the trackless Australian bush. His usual load, weighing 30 kg, included a heavy canvas swag, an axe to chop firewood, and a rifle. Regardless of the respect the new generation of bushwalkers held him in, and though grateful for his efforts in drawing maps that filled the void of this terra incognita, they had no wish to emulate his approach. They preferred to enjoy an uncomplicated recreational experience with the pleasure of mixed company, while carrying a lighter load.

The SBW club meetings were rowdy events and these energetic young people enjoyed their newfound camaraderie. Bushwalking gave them the pretext to be in the great outdoors all weekend doing whatever they liked, out of their parents' sight. Many came to meetings just for the social occasions and to plan their next expedition leaving the Silly Bush Walkers (as the serious members were derisively called) to take on the responsibilities of running the club. Lectures were organised to educate members about the geography of the land and the skills required to survive in it. The bushwalkers had a healthy respect for the Australian bush, a place where it was easy to perish from dehydration if unprepared, as had happened to some boy scouts. With knowledge they gained from each other and formal training in first aid and search and rescue skills, their confidence to interact with the sometimes-threatening but alluring landscape increased. To ensure all walkers made it out successfully, a leader was appointed for each walk – he or she conscientiously planned the expedition from start to finish.

Although impressed by Marie's lantern-slide show of mountains she had climbed around the world, what really made an impact on the other members was the latest purpose-designed outdoor equipment she took delight in flaunting. Her much-envied Bergen rucksack purchased in Norway was copied in canvas by various club members. One man in particular took a professional interest in her European-designed gear. Frank "Paddy" Pallin had been actively involved in the scouting movement in England and had made his first lightweight tent out of parachute material. As an immigrant to Australia he despaired that opportunities for outdoor adventure were not matched by the supply of suitable equipment. In the back room of his home he began making his own gear using a domestic sewing machine. When he was laid-off from his desk job due to the Depression, Paddy took the opportunity to turn his passion into a business. He created items to order for his friends in the bushwalking clubs and tested them extensively in the field before modifying and improving his designs.

Paddy Pallin launched what became Australia's most successful bush-walking and camping equipment chain. Advertising himself as the Complete Outfitter for Walkers, his cane-framed rucksack was specially priced to bring it within reach of modest purses. The steel-framed version, modelled on Marie's Bergen rucksack, had straps of tanned leather that retained 'its velvet softness under all conditions'. Clientele gradually increased to the point where Paddy could establish his own shop in George Street in Sydney's CBD and take on an assistant.

The SBW journal, *The Sydney Bushwalker*, provided a valuable advertising medium; soon his venue became an informal meeting place for the bushwalkers. He provided a complete set of military maps with tracing paper and pencils for those who wished to trace out a route free of charge. As "Paddy-made" light-weight equipment enabled them to climb higher, further and faster, his business along with the whole bushwalking movement thrived.

Virtually every weekend the Bushies, as the club members called themselves, hiked through the heat and dust, or the wet and mud, as the god of weather ordained. The Depression era was a boom time for walking clubs as hiking offered a brief respite from the burden of poverty or the fear of unemployment. It required very little expense to participate, just a packed lunch and train fare to escape to the countryside. The luxury of paying for one's own entertainment disappeared after the stock-market crash of 1929. During the Depression "mystery hikes" organised by the daily newspapers were a novelty that drew thousands of people who had never previously shown interest in walking in the countryside. This was a passing phenomenon. The SBW was the focus for serious bushwalking activity in Sydney. Equality at work or in the home did not exist for most women, but in the outdoors, where survival depended on cooperation, women were respected for their skills and accepted for their personal attributes as camping companions.

The Bushies were a bohemian group of free-spirited artists and intellectuals from a variety of backgrounds drawn to a closer connection with nature by the environmental concepts of American architect Walter Burley Griffin who had come to Australia to design the new capital city, Canberra. Many lived in Castlecrag, the suburb in Sydney he had designed, which brought the native bush into the domestic sphere. They showed little respect for the conventions of the day in their behaviour and dress and their uniform of light shirt and shorts, even in winter, made them conspicuous – especially in mixed gender groups. Casual attire was then uncommon in public and the conservatively dressed townsfolk and respectable tourists looked on in horror as they strode by in country towns. The women in particular were targeted for their shamelessness, as skirts were de rigueur at all times. When they wore shorts in the train they risked being laughed at and ridiculed for having robbed their brother's wardrobe, which they often had. One solution was for the women to reveal their costumes only after they had travelled in respectable clothing on the train to their destination and been safely absorbed into the bush.

Marie preferred the comfort of the knickerbockers she had become accustomed to throughout her travels overseas. These modified trousers were all the rage with the liberated young women of the 1920s in Great Britain and Canada. 'To my heterodox mind it seemed a waste of energy to carry a frock all day long in my rucksack to avoid hurting the feelings of my fellow-countrymen.' She became a common sight walking the scenic pathways around Sydney Harbour in this unusual attire. Once, while driving with her parents to Watson's Bay, Aileen Fenwick, a young female law graduate, noticed Marie walking in her knickerbockers with a tweed cap and a big stick and declared, 'Oh that's one of the Sydney lawyers, Miss Marie Byles.' Her mother remarked in horror: 'Don't tell me they look like that!'

For Marie and many others who had to work the usual five and a half day week it was not until Saturday lunchtime that they could leave the city. Each weekend after work they would race home, snatch a lunch and their rucksack, and then meet at Central Station. With shouts of 'Whoopee!' as the train moved out, small groups went in every direction to visit new locations or old favourites: Royal National Park and Era beach in the south, Kuring-Gai Chase in Sydney's north or the Blue Mountains to the west.

The bushwalkers with whom Marie spent almost every weekend and holiday were a stoic breed. Facing the elements, rising to any physical challenge without showing weakness, they explored the often-unchartered areas of wilderness. Marie, who Paddy described as 'not very strong physically, but very strong willed and strong spirited', could exist on minimal supplies carrying under a kilogram of food per day – mostly nuts and raw food. Her lightweight backpack, sleeping bag, and a Paddy-made tent that weighed only 1 kg, allowed her to be self-reliant as she hiked into the roughest country. At 5′2″ (1.57 m) and seven stone (44 kg), her size was a continual sorrow to her but makes her outstanding exploits even more remarkable. Marie set a daunting pace as leader and allowed nothing to distract the group from achieving their destination. She described one excursion to the southern end of the Snowy Mountains:

> There were three in the party … and we all saw eye to eye on the desirability of going to bed early, of getting up before dawn, of wasting no amount of precious daylight on cooking and as little as possible in eating, of expending no energy on carrying superfluous gear in heavy packs and generally of the necessity of reaching our objective, the summit of the rather remote Mount Bimberi, in the short three days we had at our disposal.

Despite the hardships willingly endured Marie took each opportunity to escape her clients' complicated problems and the immense amount of paperwork endemic to a solicitor's practice, to where her professional persona dissolved into the misty, moonlit landscape of an ancient valley. These outdoor adventures were more than merely recreational for Marie; her intimate relationship with nature sustained her spiritually.

Writing prolifically for the *The Sydney Bushwalker*, she expressed frustration that her skills were inadequate to convey the profound association she felt with the timeless land:

> There is something in the contact between the human being and nature which is very hard to explain, but as you lie on Mother Earth and look up at the

stars, the life force seems to bring a new health to your tired limbs and worried mind. And then you wake to the first bird calls and watch the smoke curling upwards and the billy boiling for breakfast. When you start in the morning the mist lies in the valley, and in the dew-lit sunshine every blade of grass carries rainbow lights of diamonds, and the cobwebs are gossamer cradles of filaments of silver thread. And then the long day follows, scrambling down gullies and round the spurs of the mountains, twenty miles or more, and perhaps three thousand feet in rough country down and up again.

No, I am not a genius – I cannot make it live again. I only know that if you love it, then whatever the pains, and however tired you may be in the office the next day, you will do it again and again.

One weekend she travelled with a friend to re-discover a route said to exist from the Grose Valley to the plateau east of Mount Hay. They stayed at the picturesque town of Leura in the upper Blue Mountains overnight, and then very early on a cold winter's morning, climbed down the steep escarpment and breakfasted in the pristine Grose Valley. They found the pass up seemingly impregnable cliffs and arrived back triumphantly on Sunday evening. These 'mild bushwalking adventures' she wrote, 'were among the happiest days of a fleeting life. No storms marred their harmony and beauty.'

That is until a headline in the *Sunday Times* on the 8 September 1929 announced: "Bombshell: Signal Chief's Unexpected Move". Cyril's employment had been suddenly terminated. It was an agonising time for the family, as he would not reach retiring age for another year. Marie was not emotionally equipped to deal with this crisis; nobody in the family was. Within a week she had her parents packed off to stay with relatives in New Zealand. Cyril's fellow officers saw him off at the boat. As Ida was being presented with flowers and fruit, one of them said to her, 'We love him.'

Marie notes that her father was certainly beloved by those over whom he ruled as his 'kindness and faithfulness to them were beyond question.' She never learnt the facts behind his dismissal, but her father's autocratic manner had caused continual conflict with his superiors. Reflecting on this period, she compared Cyril to one of Shakespeare's great tragic heroes, a man of tremendously fine character spoiled by one defect:

He was utterly straight and honourable. His word was his bond, and he never prevaricated. He was utterly dependable and every task he undertook was done thoroughly. Hard work never deterred him and if more work were put upon him he would go out of his way to get more still.

45

But he had one defect: self-centeredness and love of power. He recalled nostalgically the time when he first had an office of his own and people under him to whom, like the Centurion of the Gospels, he could say 'come here' or 'go there'! This made it impossible for him to see the point of view of his superiors or even of his equals in business and social life, and less still of his wife.

Marie tried not to judge her father but her own character, both its positive and negative dimensions, owed much to him. She, too, had extraordinary energy and the drive to achieve works of substance but, often lacking in empathy, was similarly brusque and direct in her dealings with others, unaware of how easily she upset their feelings. For example, Cyril was a non-smoker who would not permit smoking in his presence. Although common today, his dogmatic attitude caused some ill feeling among high-ranking officers and government visitors. Marie, too, forced her friends to abstain from their vices while in her company.

The misery contained in her parents' letters illustrated how unsuccessful her strategy had been. They soon returned to Sydney and Cyril applied to be re-instated as an adviser to his successor who had been his Chief Assistant. He resumed duty on 19 December, but the arrangement proved unsatisfactory and three months later he retired permanently. Cyril and Ida intended to return to New Zealand when their house was sold; however, because of the Depression, the house did not sell and their move did not eventuate. After a fall, Ida had an extended stay in hospital. Cyril visited her five days a week to read to her, ostensibly ministering to her needs. In reality, he was bereft without her. In the living room of Chilworth was a round stained-glass window with the enigmatic motto: "Sooner or later, near or far, the strong have need of the weak." This homily accurately described the dynamics between Cyril, with his inflated sense of self, and the gentle woman he had dominated but had come to entirely depend upon emotionally.

While her mother was hospitalised, Marie was forced into the untypical role of housekeeper for her father and brother David who had recently returned from the UK where he had been on a scholarship to study electrical engineering. Her youngest brother Baldur was no longer at home. As a recent graduate of Forestry he was touring Europe on a scholarship conducting field assignments for the Forestry Department.

Marie had few clients but, no matter how adverse the conditions were at home or at work, she always found money for trips into the outdoors. In December of 1930 she booked Bett's Camp, a rough weatherboard cottage in the high alpine country near Mt Kosciusko, to share with a group of friends. Baldur, who had recently returned from Europe, would join them. After Christmas with their parents, Marie and Baldur travelled by train to Cooma and then by bus to Jindabyne. Inspired by the exhilaration of the bracing upland air of the Monaro tablelands, they decided to leave the bus early and hike the remaining 25 km via the Thredbo River. When their friends arrived, the party trekked towards the summit of Mt Kosciusko but a snow blizzard forced them back. The next day they climbed the nearby Mt Townsend (2209 m) that, to Marie, commanded a far finer view than the higher peak. For Baldur – who had travelled through the UK, France, Corsica, the Canary Islands, Lebanon and Turkey studying commercial plantations – the magnificent view from Australia's highest plateau of range after range extending to every horizon, was an epiphany.

> As we looked down on the treetops far below, Baldur knew he had come home. All his travels in Europe had never given him a view over such virgin bush-lands as these; he told himself that this would be the land of his future labours.

A serious and determined man, Baldur committed himself to the preservation of this vast, ecologically sensitive area. On horseback in the summer of 1931–32, with minimal departmental resources due to the Depression, he undertook a six-month environmental study of the Snowy Mountains region. The area, 140 kilometres long and 25 kilometres wide, comprised the steep mountainous catchments of the Murray, Snowy, Murrumbidgee and Tumut rivers. His task was to examine in detail the basins of the streams that came together to form the Murray River for indications of damage to the vegetation and soil structure.

The remote, uninhabited country was once covered with forests, but repeated burning by cattle graziers had destroyed tree growth so that cattle could feed on the grass that replaced them. Until his expedition, little scientific research had been conducted in the area. Baldur's exhaustive 34-page report to the Commonwealth Forestry Bureau in Canberra (23 May 1932) condemned the graziers' land-management practices and the damage done to the fragile ecosystem by cattle grazing. Although Baldur did not recommend expelling the graziers, his report became 'the first shot in a long fight to break their hold on the alpine pastures of the Snowy Mountains'. Baldur's recommendations for effective control of this area subsequently formed the basis of a plan that the NSW government adopted for an alpine national park. Its reservation is recognised as being the true turning point towards natural landscape conservation in New South Wales. (Named by the Polish explorer Paul Strzelecki in 1840, the correct spelling of Kosciuszko's name, with the z added, finally replaced its Anglicisation in 1997).

Baldur's interest in the region became a lifetime involvement. In 1944 he was appointed a foundational trustee of the park representing the Forestry Commission. Exhibiting the same qualities of determination and integrity (some would call it arrogance) of both his father and his sister, he quickly gained a reputation for resisting the pressure to promote vested interests. With his conservation agenda firmly in place, Baldur played a key role in pioneering modern national park management. He not only epitomised scientific rigour and the highest conservation ideals but, like Marie, had a spiritual sensibility that enhanced his contribution as a trustee.

In his paper *Snow Gum – the Tree*, written at the climax of the battle between Kosciusko State Park and the Snowy Mountains Authority in the 1960s, Baldur embodied the ethos of nature ecologists. He argued that, although the Snow Gum had never earned dividends for timber companies, it made a contribution to conserving soil and water:

> We cannot appreciate anything fully until we understand it, until we pick up its wavelength so to speak, until we learn to think the way it thinks …
>
> So, if we wish to appreciate this particular Australian tree we must try to understand its point of view, realising that it is a living organism like you and me … We must try to understand its manner of living, its philosophy of life, its place in the world of natural things and the spirit that keeps it going in spite of great adversity.

Baldur rose to be Deputy Chief of the Resources Branch of the Forestry Commission, and in 1973 was awarded an honorary degree of Doctor of Laws by the Australian National University in acknowledgement of his services to national parks. Just before his death in 1974 he received an OBE for his services to conservation.

BY 1932 Marie was the only one left at home: Baldur had embarked on his environmental study of the Snowy Mountains region and David had been commissioned to build a hydroelectric power station to supply electricity to the town of Batlow in Tumut Shire. Her parents were on an extended visit to New Zealand and had leased the main house, so she had moved into the bungalow her brothers had occupied. It had an unlined shower recess and no hot water but Marie, who was in the habit of taking cold showers, was undaunted. If she wanted a hot bath she could ask the tenants or go to a neighbour's house.

To store her food and keep it cool she made a "bush safe", a portable pantry, by improvising from whatever materials were at hand, but in the humid air of Sydney it was of little use and the butter turned to oil. Previously uninterested in learning the domestic arts from Ida, she had to make up for her lack of training and taught herself to cook, sew and do "handy work". Self-sufficiency was an art that everyone developed during the long Depression and bushwalkers were more adaptable than most.

Aside from her law work, Marie undertook a two-year course in geology at Sydney Technical College to add to her appreciation of the natural environment. She found it the most absorbing subject she had ever studied. Geology exposed the underlying structure of the landscape and the excursions into the field gave her insights over and above the aesthetic aspects of bushwalking.

As self-dependent as she was, Marie keenly felt the separation from her parents after a year's absence. She attempted to persuade them to return by creating an album of her best photographs of Chilworth. She added amusing captions about the house in the primeval forest on the edge of an ancient quarry that everyone had deserted 'except the daughter and a possum which came on the verandah'. Her entreaties were successful. At the end of 1932 Cyril and Ida returned taking a flat in the same building as David and his wife Babette in the nearby suburb of Normanhurst. Cyril proceeded to have his former workshop at Chilworth converted into a small two-roomed cottage where he and Ida could then live.

Marie took little notice of the gradual deterioration in both her parents. She was too absorbed in work and her efforts on behalf of the conservation movement, in particular her attempts to reserve the coastline area around Bouddi Headland, her "faery lands forlorn".

CHAPTER 6

Bouddi Natural Park

IN 1788, on his first foray outside of Sydney Harbour in search of suitable agricultural land, Governor Arthur Phillip explored the region to the north around Broken Bay at the mouth of the Hawkesbury River. Broken Bay also has two inland waterways – with Pittwater its southern branch and Brisbane Water its northern branch, as they are known today. Aboriginal people living in small bark huts were encountered in many of the bays.

From 1825 settlers arrived by sea and occupied the foreshores of Brisbane Water close to the ocean entrance. Hardys Bay was one of the first to be established to service the farmers along that stretch of inland coastline. Vineyards were soon established with wine sold by the gallon. Ferries were the main transport running between Hardy's Bay and Woy Woy, the closest town with road access to Sydney. The completion of the railway in 1889 through Gosford at the furthest reaches of Brisbane Water meant increased development of the area for holidaymakers. The infertile soil on the Bouddi coastline, however, deterred any serious attempts at settlement; its exposed coast was unsuited to small boats and there was no road into this rough, inaccessible region. In 1876 it was set aside as a coal and shale reserve and reserved from sale in 1884.

WHILE STILL at university, in 1923, Marie convinced three of her old Pirate Girl gang to accompany her on an expedition to the rugged Bouddi coastline. Arriving by ferry at Hardys Bay, they navigated their way up the long steep hill behind aided by map and compass, and a tomahawk to tackle the rough terrain. Her audacious plan required them to carry canvas groundsheets and quilts for overnight camping, just enough food for their survival – and guns. Of this she wrote:

> Esther, 'the handsome he-man', carried hers ready to hand on her hip and loaded. It was a gigantic Colt automatic fit to frighten the most wicked villain. Myself, I had merely a revolver. As leader of the party I knew it was my duty to protect the others in time of peril but I did not really like this instrument of destruction.

From the top of the hill, densely covered with pink-skinned Angophora eucalypts, ancient cycads and abundant double grasstrees, they climbed down a steep fern gully onto the secluded crescent-shaped beach where the only foot-steps to have previously left impressions were the Aborigines, fishermen who arrived by boat, and shipwreck survivors. The rusted boilers of the SS *Maitland* wrecked on a nearby reef were tragic reminders of the twenty-four passengers and crew who drowned when the steamer floundered helplessly on the rocks in 1898. Elated at their success, the young women took off their skirts and danced on the sand in their bloomers. Swimming in the gentle waves of the protected half-moon bay, Marie looked back at the magical landscape with its long sweep of beach and steep forested green hills; her intense emotional connection was confirmed. The historic opportunity to protect and preserve the area came a decade after that youthful adventure following the formation of the Federation of Bushwalking Clubs of NSW.

The Federation was established in 1932 when the bushwalkers' beloved Blue Gum Forest in the Grose Valley of the Blue Mountains came under threat. The subsequent campaign to save the forest galvanised the bushwalking fraternity and turned their recreational pastime into a cause. In 1931 a party of bushwalk-ers had discovered a local farmer ring-barking the impressive 60-metre-high stately trees on land he held the lease on in the valley. They were so alarmed they persuaded him to stop until they could raise the money to buy out his lease. After some clever negotiating with the committee set up by the bushwalkers, the farmer, Clarrie Hungerford, agreed to relinquish the lease for the price of £150. The committee's representative managed to bargain him down to £130 with a £25 deposit payable immediately and the remainder due by the end of the year.

Although worth only about $15–20,000 in today's terms, it was a daunting sum in the middle of the Depression. Raising the money required the bush-walkers to mobilise the public through an education campaign on the need to preserve the forest in its pristine state. Lantern-slide images of the forest were made for presentations to bushwalking clubs and other groups, and donations began to flow in. Profits from the SBW annual concert raised £11 and the Blue Gum Forest Ball, a grand affair at the Hordern Pavilion in Sydney, raised a further £27. Thanks to some wealthy benefactors, sufficient money was obtained by the deadline enabling the committee to pay Hungerford and receive the title deeds.

When Myles Dunphy took the deeds to the Lands Department to present it as a gift, its officers were staggered by this unprecedented gesture. Never before had the Lands Department received such a gift. Dunphy's only request was that the sixteen hectares of forest be gazetted as a Reserve for Public Recreation to be managed by a trust. The reserve was declared in September 1932 and a trust duly appointed. The bushwalkers were justifiably proud of their effort to retain such a magnificent forest for posterity. This was the beginning of a movement that would grow in the decades to come.

Myles Dunphy and others in the SBW devoted to conserving the natural environment discussed the many other areas that needed protection. They realised these efforts were beyond the capacity of the club's members. They approached all the small groups of experienced walkers and campers they knew and persuaded them to form clubs that were then amalgamated into the federation that led the conservation drive. The general downturn in business during the Depression gave Marie the opportunity to devote her legal skills to the cause closest to her heart. She offered her services as honorary solicitor and later served as its secretary, and then president. Her peers in the legal profession were bemused by her exertions on behalf of a landscape they perceived as uninviting. They questioned her sanity in undertaking expeditions into unmapped territory that required strenuous physical exertion, hauling a pack and sleeping on the ground. Marie cultivated her eccentric reputation and her legal training was invaluable to the Federation, as she could confidently argue their case. Myles Dunphy held Marie's solicitor's mind in the highest regard:

> Marie was a person you could not bluff, not that you wanted to, but you had to be dashed careful how you talked to Marie because you knew she had a mind that weighed the odds all the time … she could stand up in front of a magistrate … she had that demeanour, that knowledge of the law …

His opinion was formed through long years of working together on causes that mostly united them, but could also divide them. For now, their dedication and commitment were aligned to the same ideals. The bushwalkers were conscious of the massive destruction of natural habitat taking place and the ecological significance of wilderness. At every opportunity they petitioned the Lands Department that was impressed by their knowledge of the virtually unexplored areas and willingly accepted suggestions on places of value to reserve. This gave Marie the chance to protect the Bouddi Headland that she had loved since childhood.

Driven by a sense of quasi-ownership Marie mounted an insistent campaign. In one article for the *Sydney Morning Herald,* published in 1934, she pointed out that the area was perfect for creating a public recreational reserve. In her zeal she wrote that the Federation was seeking its dedication, when few of its members had even heard of it. Her quest became to persuade the Federation to put Bouddi on their agenda. In this attempt she took a group of the members for a bushwalk through the area and out to the headland to show them the view of the bays and the ocean. Unfortunately, they were not impressed, or pretended not to be. At the next Sydney Bush Walkers' annual camp, Marie was humorously presented with a lengthy scroll Deed of Gift of Maitland Bay, giving her title to the place in return for her noble efforts to have it set aside as a national park. She reported:

> They spoke disparagingly of the clear fresh drinking water that takes so much finding, the glorious grassy slopes for camp sites that do not exist, the day-and-night flying of imperial-sized mosquitoes, the sleepless nights, the surfless bay and, in short, the whole doggone place.

But their jesting resistance was not enough to thwart the realisation of her dream. She assigned her law clerk to search titles at the Lands Department and make copies of maps and plans. With characteristic persistence, Marie eventually convinced the Federation to make Bouddi the first major cause it espoused. They issued an invitation to the Lands Department to send a representative to inspect the area. The Department in turn requested the Federation to send a deputation to escort the Gosford District Surveyor, Mr Barry, on an inspection tour.

In the train on the way there Marie and her companions excitedly discussed the best way to show him around the area. They turned up at the appointed meeting place with their business-like rucksacks ready to take Mr Barry by the hand. But they had underestimated him. He arrived ready for the task with his lunch in a handkerchief tied to his waist-belt and led them through the roughest bush. After they walked throughout the entire area the group stood on a prominent lookout to view the narrow stretch of coast. Marie told Mr Barry, 'All the eye can see, I want kept as a park.'

He was easily convinced of its value and even offered to include a wider area than she had originally hoped for. He realised that it was essential that this strip of valuable coastline be left unspoilt. With an additional subdivision arranged for fishermen's shanties, the whole area was a bushland reserve almost before they knew it. As a result of this expedition, 263 hectares were duly reserved on 5 July 1935.

The Federation was invited to nominate three trustees to act alongside three from the local council. Marie was appointed honorary secretary. The first recorded meeting of the trust took place at the Gosford Town Hall in 1936, although most of the subsequent meetings were held on the beach at Maitland Bay. They nicknamed the shire council's first representative "Mr Steamroller" because he rode with iron will over all their proposals. To the horror of the bushwalkers he wanted roads and improvements all over the park. But when it came to discussing a name for the reserve it was he who suggested inclusion of the term "natural", so Bouddi Natural Park it became. Bouddi (pronounced 'boodie') is the Aboriginal name for the most conspicuous feature of the district, appearing on maps as early as 1828, the northern headland of the bay where the SS *Maitland* was wrecked. The name means "heart", and accurately expresses Marie's deep connection to the place.

After having successfully reserved the area the trustees then had the problem of managing the park. With no government funding, all the work on tracks, water supply, campsites and so on had to be done with voluntary labour. Marie took it upon herself to organise working bees among the Federation's members. To everyone's surprise, the first one, held at Maitland Bay in May 1940 before World War II had really started for Australia, was a huge success. Sixty people turned up armed with tools to make paths that provided, 'possibly the finest scenic half day's walk within easy reach of Sydney'. A corrugated-iron tank was floated in by boat to supply the campers with water. On subsequent working bees after the war up to 120 people came to clear the tracks and plant trees in an effort to regenerate the forest.

Given Marie's practical relationship with the outdoors, organising these major events was not a daunting task but her relentless enthusiasm was jeopardised by an inherently autocratic approach. Perfectionism was brought to everything she did and exacerbated the need to do things her way. Every task was thoroughly prepared for and prioritised – she knew who was coming and when. Marie arrived well before the others to work out exactly what needed to be done and where trails had to be made. When the volunteers arrived she divided them into groups with explicit directions about their tasks. To one of the worker "bees" writing in *The Sydney Bushwalker,* Marie's behaviour was reminiscent of a dictator:

> The Intelligence. Stand erect with awe and respect. Where would we be without the Intelligence? Where, indeed? The President of a well-known club was allotted the task of keeping up the lines of communication and, as those working away from the headquarters toiled, they lived in constant fear of this euphemistic Gestapo …

The volunteers had given up their weekends and did not appreciate the level of discipline required to complete tasks to Marie's high standards. Complaints, however, were made in a good-natured fashion; in the same article she was likened by one of the "convicts" to the governor of a penal colony.

> The First Fleet arrived on Friday night and landed at Killcare … and were not expected to go more than 'dead slow' in the new colony before Sunday … With the arrival of the multitude of minor offenders on Saturday afternoon, the site of the settlement began to seethe with people … The tents grew in two, more or less parallel rows with a street between … the largest congregation of tents I have seen for a long time … indeed it outgrew the available camping space and at least one satellite township had to be commenced in a neighbouring valley.

In the evenings the bushwalkers congregated on the amphitheatre of beach around a blazing bonfire sharing songs and reminiscences. All enjoyed themselves immensely and the campfire was the best they had ever attended. But the bees' insistence on enjoying the social occasion did not deter Marie from keeping them on task.

> After pleasure cometh pain! … Saturday night's signs of growing democracy must have irked the autocratic Governor so on Sunday, at an early hour, she once again very firmly seized the reins of government. But every detail of the numerous jobs which had to be done and adequate chain-gangs to perform them had been arranged meticulously. Clearing tracks, mending tanks, planting trees, making fireplaces, erecting signposts, repairing fences were a few of the tasks which were carried out with speed increased by the knowledge that the sooner it was over the sooner one could relax. Every previous colonising

venture seems to have failed miserably on account of some unthought-of difficulty but not Bouddi.

Working bees were an annual event organised by the Federation and held each May. Marie was notorious for booking people up eighteen months ahead. If she asked someone whether they were coming to the next working bee and they had an excuse, she would inquire, 'Well, what are you doing on this particular weekend next year?'

THE WAR years decimated the ranks of volunteers able to commit time and effort to the maintenance of natural areas. Many of the bushwalkers served duty overseas and many died. Gordon Smith was one of the SBW's "Tiger" bushwalkers, an elite group that covered vast distances each day in order to reach their ambitious goal for the weekend. Before the war, Smith, a giant of a man, was the Australian roadwalking champion; he died on the Sandakan Death March. Charles D'Arcy Roberts, one of the foundational trustees of Bouddi Natural Park, died while a Japanese prisoner of war on the infamous Burma Railway in August 1943. On Bullimah Spur, a high ridge near Maitland Bay with a view over the ocean and Broken Bay, Marie had a plaque erected to Roberts' memory in a ceremony that included his parents and the local mayor. The plaque is positioned on a rock and faces the ocean, its inscription describing the origin of the outlook's Aboriginal name Bullimah, Home of the Great Spirit.

Her friend's death inspired Marie to write *Above Bouddi Headland*, revealing her more gentle nature.

> A Sabbath calm drops from an azure sky
> As soft and sweet as flowers of love in mist.
> And cradled in that calm, a pink-starred moor
> Drops to a tranquil silent sea, sun-kissed.
>
> A perfect scene whose peace is absolute,
> And nothing knows of all the hate and war,
> Which tear the ruined hearts of shattered men
> Upon that sapphire ocean's far-off shore.
>
> Oh man! Who first of living things found eyes
> To see a beauty never seen before,
> Find thou the sight to see the strength of love,
> Find thou the vision of a further shore.

DESPITE THE Trustee's protests, rutile mining was forced on them in the 1950s at Putty Beach, just south of Maitland Bay. The northern end of the beach had immense dunes with pure sand like a snow slope, rich in heavy minerals including rutile that contains titanium dioxide, used as a base for paint. The mineral's value had increased on world markets and mining it deemed a national necessity. Marie was incensed by the mining operations that ruined a tall rainforest behind the beach and destroyed the sand dunes allowing the sea to subsequently wash away part of the beach and foreshore. Although she had resigned from the trust by then she wrote complaining that mining had destroyed the rainforest and the best campsites, and left a desert. She was outraged that the Mines Department had the rights to virtually any land in New South Wales and that the trustees had no option but to submit. The mining company undertook to restore the land to its natural condition afterwards, but of course they didn't, Marie complained. Disastrously, they planted the South African bitou bush that threatened native flora and spread throughout most of the coastal region of NSW. Marie's activist's voice was undimmed when she wrote:

> If I had my youth back again I should use it in getting the Mining Acts amended to take away the autocratic powers of the soulless, ruthless, money-making miners. What about the Federation placing the amendment of the Mining Acts top of its agenda?

BY THE time Bouddi Natural Park came under the control of the newly formed National Parks and Wildlife Service in 1967, additions had more than doubled its size to 530 hectares. Dedication of the area as a state park meant there was security of tenure and restrictions on exploiting its natural resources. The trust was reconstituted as an advisory committee with the job of seeing that old proposals were continued and new projects were in the best interests of the management. It was disbanded in 1985. By the time Bouddi was renamed a national park in 1974 its area had expanded to 800 hectares.

Today the park consists of 1532 hectares and Maitland Bay is at the heart of a 300-hectare marine extension to protect the marine life and shoreline ecosystem. One of the first of its kind, the marine extension park was created in 1971 and includes both the seabed and the waters beneath. Several oceanic seabirds have homes there including albatrosses, shearwaters and little terns. Migrating southern right whales and humpback whales as well as dolphins have been observed in the marine park.

On top of the plateau that ends at the cliff-top overlooking the Pacific Ocean are indicators of Aboriginal ceremonial sites, dozens of rock engravings up to 20 metres long depicting fish, whales, kangaroos, birds and shields on the flat, exposed Hawkesbury sandstone. The middens of discarded shellfish on the beaches confirm that this place was an important source of food for the Garingai and Darkinjung people, and for trade.

It was due to the foresight and resolve of Marie Byles that Bouddi Natural Park was declared in 1935. Her zeal as a campaigner and publicist convinced key decision-makers to reserve this superb area at the southern-most tip of the Central Coast of NSW.

As Judge Don Stewart, head of the Coastal Zone Inquiry into the protection of the coastal environment, wrote in 2007 regarding the 'almost obscene' development of our headlands and foreshores, 'Governments at all levels have allowed self-interested development to continue unabated on almost every eastern seaboard headland from Queensland to Victoria.' Today the park protects the only undeveloped strip of coast between the major population centres of Sydney and Newcastle.

In recognition of her contributions to the environment the Nature Conservation Council of NSW established the Marie Byles Award in 2006. This award is given annually to a group that has initiated an outstanding new environmental campaign and demonstrated strong commitment and passion for conservation of the environment.

The Bouddi Coastal Walk from Putty Beach to Maitland Bay is a three-kilometre track that follows the same pathway Marie encouraged volunteer bushwalkers to create on their working bees. On The Scenic Road at Killcare Heights, Marie Byles Lookout is one of the most popular in the area. It gives commanding views across Broken Bay to Barrenjoey Head with its lighthouse standing sentinel over Palm Beach and Sunrise Hill where Marie used to gaze across through her telescope from Seawards' verandah.

CHAPTER 7

Bagging Virgin Peaks

1932–1938

IN 1932 while the Depression was in full force, Marie managed to afford an articled clerk 'the excellent Mr Leonard Giovanelli'. Although there was little to learn as transfers of land and houses had all but ceased, Leonard felt fortunate to have this position; all his friends were having trouble finding work. Leonard was prepared to tolerate their good-humoured ribbing for working under a woman boss, as he could continue his legal studies while earning just enough, ten shillings a week, to support himself. One of the first things Marie said to him was, 'There are plenty of good solicitors, but you've got to be quick.' She expected Leonard to do the right thing by the client at all times. He witnessed Marie's distress when she acted for a retired surveyor who had given all his money to a solicitor to invest who had taken him down for the whole lot. She was shocked that a solicitor would violate the professional code; to her, moral integrity was worth far more than money and defrauding a client unthinkable.

A partner to share the workload was a relief for it also meant that she could do more bushwalking without worrying about the office. Leonard soon proved he could shoulder the responsibilities when she returned a day late from a horse-riding adventure at Kosciusko, having lost track of time. Aside from the substantial benefits of having a male business partner, Leonard's surname proved to be another bonus. Eastwood then was semi-rural and the local community around Macquarie Fields included many Italian market gardeners who had settled in that fertile area. Marie was a convenient choice for them and Leonard's Italian name (although he was born in Australia) also helped attract those clients. In the early days of immigration, if members of an ethnic group were happy with the service they received from a professional, they stayed loyal and recommended her or him in their community. Even though they came from a traditional patriarchal society, Marie's Italian clients were unconcerned that their legal practitioner was a woman. What was important was that she had gained a reputation for being reliable and trustworthy. One client, Mr Scaramuzzi, whom Marie got along well with, brought a lot of clients to the office and interpreted for his friends who did not speak English. During the Depression, Marie happily accepted fruit and vegetables in lieu of payment.

It was at this stage that the only known episode of an intimate personal relationship surfaced in Marie's life. Although she had declared herself to be a natural celibate, she became emotionally attached to her close friend Dymphna Cusack. Ellen Dymphna Cusack, also known as Nell, was a younger student at university when Marie took her under her wing and included her in her social group. Marie opened up the big world to the young convent schoolgirl, although as Nell noted, if you were a friend of Marie's it was 'at the expense of giving up all your vices, like lipstick'.

On holiday at Seawards, Nell lay in bed while Marie and the rest of her family were early risers. Marie once bribed her with breakfast in bed if she would compose a poem on Mt McKinley in the Rockies to accompany an article she had written for the *Sydney Morning Herald*. At university Nell studied arts and gained a diploma of education but was apprehensive about where the Education Department would post her. Marie described the unfortunate sequence of events:

> At the beginning of 1928 we had a large Palm Beach party. Nell Cusack got the wishbone of the chicken [and] hugged the wishbone to her bosom and said aloud 'Please, dear Lord, don't send me to Broken Hill!' When she got home there was a telegram saying that the Department of Public Instruction had allocated her to Broken Hill. She was a superb teacher but her health had never been robust and the dust and heat of Broken Hill's out-west mining town broke it completely.

After two years in the 'hell on earth' of Broken Hill, Marie lent Nell the money to take a cruise to Ceylon (Sri Lanka). On her return in 1935 Nell accepted Marie's offer to stay with her in the bungalow at Chilworth while she taught at Parramatta High School. From her experiences in Broken Hill, then the centre of the Australian mining industry, Nell had developed a keen sense

of social and economic justice. She was also on the verge of an international-
ally acclaimed career as a playwright and author. Later, with Florence James
– another university friend of theirs – she wrote *Come In Spinner*, the runaway
bestseller about the American troops in Sydney that focused on, 'the lives and
loves of women in wartime'. In the 1950s and '60s she also became a significant
figure in the peace movement on the world stage.

Although smaller in stature than Marie, Nell was no lightweight. Marie
found in her marked personal and intellectual qualities equally matched by her
free-spiritedness. Nell was entirely the opposite of Marie, able to express feelings
in ways that she could not. At 33 years of age, she had a bohemian streak and
experienced, according to her biographer, 'a lively, at times controversial, romantic
love life'. In their frequent camping holidays, Nell happily posed bare-breasted for
Marie's camera. In one photograph, a topless Nell immersed herself in the roots
of a giant figtree.

As they shared the confined closeness of the bungalow, Marie was confronted with previously repressed feelings, aspects unknown in someone so
self-controlled. She developed an intense emotional attachment to her friend.
Marie craved closeness and love, but having no experience of intimate relationships, her feelings were too intense and too complicated to express in a way that
allowed for understanding between them. She became neurotically obsessed
with Nell, and her behaviour became increasingly demanding. Confused by this
dramatic change in her friend's manner, Nell felt suffocated. She finally lost
her temper, precipitating a break-up. She later said that she found it too difficult to cope with Marie's 'very emotional attitude' towards her. Interviewed just
before her death, Nell adamantly attested that 'Marie was not a natural celibate',
although she refused to elaborate on the 'very painful circumstances' that led to
her adopting this belief.

With her emotional defences down for the first time in her life, did Marie
suffer a breakdown when Nell responded disapprovingly to her advances? With
her chronic need to control others, had she attempted to force Nell into a sexual
relationship? Although there is no indication of lesbian affairs in Nell's history,
perhaps Marie gained the impression that she might be open to one. At this
stage, at the peak of Marie's involvement in the feminist struggle, it was not
uncommon for women in the movement to have lesbian relationships. One way
to escape the oppression of men was to turn to their own sex, to people who
valued and respected them in ways that men, in that era, generally did not.

Whatever drove Marie's behaviour, the outcome was that she exposed her deepest feelings to another and was rejected. She never admitted to the pain this caused. Marie would go on to have many close relationships with women who admired her and enjoyed being swept up in her active, creative world but she never again allowed herself to be vulnerable or to feel such a strong emotional attachment. As well as her own problem with intimacy and expressing emotion, she had the additional burden of society's homophobia. The danger of living openly as a lesbian was powerfully demonstrated in September of that same year, 1935, when Marie's friend, the mountaineer Freda du Faur, the first woman to climb Mount Cook, suicided.

This event came some years after the death of Freda's lover, Muriel Cardogan, of a broken heart. Their love affair had been conducted under conditions of extreme duress due to the social attitudes that made having a normal relationship impossible. While they were living in England, Cardogan suffered symptoms of stress and mental disturbance and was forced to undertake a cure for her "inverted hedonistic persuasion" (i.e. lesbianism). Later, both women were subjected to a version of psychiatry's controversial deep-sleep therapy. As du Faur's biographer noted, 'Strong intelligent and independent women were thought to gain particular benefit from it.' Muriel had been forced to separate from Freda in an attempt to remove her from her lover's influence, but died on the boat voyage back to Australia. Six years after her lover's death, Freda gassed herself at her home in Sydney. As her executrix, Marie defended her client's decision to bequeath her estate to two young friends from family members who questioned Freda's sanity when making her will. Marie scathingly remarked:

> I suppose cynical people might suggest that mountaineering was also a sign of an unbalanced mind! In the end … I compromised the action. This was the first time I had come up against the rapacity of relatives and I was genuinely shocked.

If more was needed to convince her of the need for discretion regarding her private life, this tragic sequence of events removed any doubt. Grief-stricken at the loss of her friendship with Nell, Marie channelled her emotional energy into the quest for mountaineering challenges. Despite the ongoing Depression, she combed the *New Zealand Alpine Journal* to discover which mountains in that climbers' paradise were still virgin. She had sufficient funds to justify writing to the best-known guide in New Zealand, Frank Alack, for his advice. Frank recommended the peaks at the head of the unvisited Mahitahi Valley reassuring her that they were uncontaminated by the foot of any climber. Marie invited

Marjorie Jones, from her 1929 Mt Cook party, to accompany her on the expedition. When Marie boarded the small boat from Wellington on a stiflingly hot Christmas Eve in 1935, her androgyny was an asset she used to her fullest advantage. While men were allowed to sleep on deck, women were not: 'Being a bushwalker I merely spread my sleeping bag on the hard boards in the shadow of a lifeboat and fell asleep, pretending to be a boy!'

Marie was privileged to be able to travel to places her heart desired and not just as a tourist, but as an explorer–geographer fired with desire to add to the world's knowledge. After six years in mountainless Australia, Marie again experienced the ecstasy of feeling snow and ice beneath her feet as, with the aid of Frank Alack, she climbed and named a number of virgin peaks in the Southern Alps. Her party flew into the lower Mahitahi Valley and reached Mueller Pass at the head of the valley on New Years Day. They established camp and, over the next week made at least eight ascents, most notably the heavily glaciated Mt Fettes (2451 m) and Mt Strachan (2561 m) in the Hooker range, a first ascent. Others included two 2200 m peaks at the head of the Zora Glacier, Mt Butzbach (2080 m) in the Bannoch Brae Range, and Crystal Peak (203463m). They climbed Crystal Peak on a perfect afternoon allowing them to take photographs and further their knowledge of the region.

In recognition of her abilities as a mountaineer and contributions through mapping these previously unexplored areas, Marie was given full membership of the elite New Zealand Alpine Club.

THE DEPRESSION was still in evidence in 1936 but M.B. Byles & Co. accumulated enough business to move into larger, more suitable office space. The real estate agent, Eric Somerville, convinced Marie to take two rooms in his new building conveniently located opposite the Eastwood railway station and having the advantage of street frontage. On Tuesdays, she closed Eastwood and conducted her business from the city office at 4 Castlereagh Street, a short stroll from the law courts. On Saturday mornings she alternated with Leonard to mind the city office.

She also engaged her first stenographer, fifteen-year-old Pearle Pitcher. Pearle, who was bright, bubbly and quick to learn, had previously worked her way up to the staff manager's office in David Jones, Sydney's major department store. Not only did she equal Marie's standards of efficiency, most importantly her spelling was reliable and able to compensate for Marie's chronic deficiency in this regard. Spelling was critically important in legal documents – when a mistake was made, the whole stencil on which a contract was typed had to be redone. Pearle was more than happy with the working conditions and had good relations with her employer whom she later described as 'the original feminist'. Marie, who never wore make-up, objected to Pearle doing so. She told her that she 'had this lovely skin and this lovely face and not to ruin it with that stuff'. Pearle had to wash it off until Marie's friends convinced her that she was being too strict.

In the same year, Marie enjoyed one of her most memorable bushwalking holidays in the Warrumbungle mountain range with her SBW bushwalking friend Dot English and Dr Eric Dark, husband of Eleanor Dark the writer. Eric was president of the Blue Mountains Climbing Club, facetiously known as the "Katoomba Suicide Club", due to the perilous climbs they made on the sheer escarpments for which the Blue Mountains are famous. Having already scaled one of the rocky peaks in the Warrumbungles, he aspired to make a second. They travelled to Dubbo in the central west of NSW by train then hired a car and drove across the flat western plain. On the horizon arose a small range of spectacular rock spires, pinnacles and walls – some of them 450 m high. Marie's geological training enabled her to appreciate this unique volcanic scenery. Immediately upon arrival, however, she admitted that she was out of her element because she was not a rock-climber. Dot's natural ability and adventurous inclination became quickly apparent as she scrambled about barefoot on the rocks. Although she had no experience with roped climbing, Eric enlisted her as his partner to climb Crater Bluff, the most highly prized peak in the range. Tied together by ropes, they edged along scarcely perceptible ledges of grey, lichen-covered rock. After a life-and-death ascent, the brave pair managed to reach the summit. Next day they brought up their companions by ropes they had left to share the view of the huge, hollow crater that had a dozen or so magnificent, rugged peaks rising out of it. Impressed by the unique area with over 120 bird species, the party persuaded the local farmer, who held the lease, that it should be reserved for public recreation. A proposal to the Lands Department was made as soon as Marie returned to Sydney.*

Complete opposites, Dot and Marie were unlikely friends, but their love of outdoor pursuits gave them a bond that transcended their differences in age and temperament. On occasion, Dot stayed at Chilworth where she poured over Marie's books on mountaineering while Marie scoured maps of New Zealand looking for the whitest, therefore least-mapped, portions of the Southern Alps.

*This later resulted in an area of 3360 hectares being withdrawn from the Crown Lease in 1953 and reserved as Warrumbungle National Park.

In expectation of again standing on previously unclimbed mountain peaks, Marie ordered a new pair of climbing boots from London. Her passion fired Dot's imagination. Before long she would follow in her mentor's footsteps by climbing the highest peaks in New Zealand and return year after year to lead tours of beginner climbers from Australia, many of who had previously ended up as casualties in the deep crevasses.

In March 1937, Marie set off again to New Zealand's Southland region to traverse the Hollyford River from its source to Lake McKerrow, a distance of 65 km. Her guide, Kurt Sutor, met her at the bus. Kurt had climbed mountains since childhood in Switzerland and was now guiding at Mount Cook. Camping in rough cattlemen's huts along the way they followed the dry shingle riverbed up a muddy track, 'curtained, roofed and carpeted with ferns and surrounded by the exquisitely lovely bush common to the West Coast.' Another guide, Tom Cameron, blazed their route and left food for them at various points and then met up with them at McKerrow Hut. Lookouts provided Marie with compass sights to many of the surrounding peaks for the purpose of mapping some of the roughest country in the Western Otago, a region containing some of the highest peaks in New Zealand. On their one clear day, her party successfully climbed four virgin snow-clad peaks. The scale of the mountain range was breathtaking. Covering over 22 km of snow, ice and rock, Marie considered it to be the best holiday of her life. But the climbing had not been as difficult as she had hoped. She was compelled to plan a more ambitious challenge.

Back in Sydney, she poured over maps looking for white spaces that denoted unclimbed peaks; not only in New Zealand but also in countries further off that had 'far higher virgin mountains to be climbed'. She met a well-travelled businessman who inspired her by saying, 'If you want a fine place to go to, the loveliest spot in the world with some of its most charming people, is the Yunnan Province in the south-west corner of China.' Fired with an ambition to mount an expedition to climb Mt Sansato, the region's highest virgin peak, she read voraciously about what was to Westerners an unknown and unvisited part of the globe.

In order to learn of the countries the expedition would pass through on their way to Yunnan, she wrote to the authors of the books she had read, asking for their opinions and whether they approved of her projected walking trip through the province. She met with the Chinese Consul in Sydney who was 'most anxious to help'. He would arrange the necessary permits and 'write to his friends in Yunnan to assist us at every point'. The only dissenter was

Mr Harding, the ex-British Consul for Kunming, the province's capital. Marie felt he disapproved of the pioneering spirit 'that had made the British Empire what it is'. He met with Marie and spent the evening showing her all the difficulties she would encounter if she tried to take a mountaineering party to southwest China. She challenged him with, 'So you don't think I'll ever get up such an expedition? "Frankly, I don't" was his reply. So whatever previous doubts I had had, there was now no alternative but to get the expedition up.'

The ex-British Consul underestimated this diminutive woman with the piercing blue eyes; telling Marie not to do something only made her more determined. She contacted the missionary, Mr Andrews, whom Mr Harding had mentioned lived at Lijiang, the main town near the foot of Mt Sansato. He turned out to be 'the embodiment of helpfulness'. So began the reading and research from books, letters and articles about the country, the local tribes, the difficulties and the dangers, that occupied all her spare time for the next two years. The expedition required voluminous correspondence to gain first-hand information from local missionaries, as well as visas and special permission from military authorities to travel into remote areas. Marie made the travel arrangements for all the expedition members and sorted out the hire of transport, interpreters and porters throughout their journey into China. As well she had to arrange the purchase of clothes, climbing equipment, cooking equipment and food, with quantities carefully calculated for the needs of each member of the party.

Most exasperating was her uncertainty over which prospective members would make a definite commitment. If they were to do any serious mountaineering, their financial assistance was essential. Marjorie Jones kept changing her mind, as did various New Zealand mountain guides. Marie was disappointed that Dot English, who she regarded as 'the best climber I have ever met', dropped out due to fear of seasickness and disease in Asia. The only confirmed member was Dora de Beer. Marie had met her while climbing in New Zealand in 1929. She called upon Dora, then living in London, to arrange the purchase of mountaineering and camping equipment. In March 1938, with a need to make definite arrangements, Marie wrote to her in frustration:

> I know the whole expedition is mad, and I only want people who don't mind being mad to come, but it is dreadfully awkward when they won't make up their minds whether to be mad or not. If we all go in for it ready for what the gods send, I think we shall carry it off, and whatever happens won't it be frightfully interesting …

Planning a route for an expedition is a complicated process where a range of factors need to be taken into consideration: time of year with its anticipated weather, capability of the group, accuracy of maps, nature of the terrain, denseness of vegetation, flooded rivers and so on. Unlike most expedition leaders, Marie also needed to factor in the impending war. The most direct route to Yunnan was through French Indochina (as Vietnam was then called), but news about the Japanese invasion of northern China with an army of occupation became more and more disturbing. In April she wrote to Dora: 'Things are in a dreadful state, enough to make one despair of progress, but I do not think they will interfere with us.' While she predicted another Dark Ages with the worsening war situation: 'I do not think this will stop us from climbing mountains in Yunnan, especially as the Chinese seem to be winning and taking the war further north.'

One month later, with the increased threat of war in Europe, she wrote to reassure Dora that the missionaries in Yunnan 'cannot see how the War could possibly reach that far – there is nothing to fight for there, they say.' As a precaution, Marie switched over to the alternative route she had planned, through Burma. They would arrive in Rangoon where the town of Myitkyina, inland from the capital, would be the jumping-off point for the mule-trek into China.

One crisis after another made preparation difficult and Marie questioned whether it was worth the effort. She was occasionally overwhelmed by feelings of utter desolation at the enormity of the undertaking. Her main fears were the Japanese advancing south and west, bandits proliferating as a result of the war, rumours of typhoid and cholera epidemics, and the impending rainy season. No one ever travelled during the rainy season, but it seemed there was no alternative if they were to arrive at the mountains at the correct time for climbing.

Less than a month before departure she was frantic with worry. The New Zealand team members, either Marjorie or the two guides, she was unsure who was to blame, had announced to local newspapers that they were heading off on an expedition to China. They even named the actual mountains they aimed to climb and the dangers they might encounter, including wild animals and bandits. The resulting publicity proved a nightmare. Marie was afraid that if the Burmese authorities found out, it could jeopardise the expedition. Her insurance company sent a cheque refunding the amount of the premium.

The *Sydney Morning Herald* had agreed to print stories of the expedition Marie would file along the way. This gave her another £50 towards expenses. She acted quickly and took their journalist into her confidence explaining, 'how the success of everything depended on saying nothing about mountaineering'. In return for his cooperation, she gave him an interview for an article that would appear after their departure. While he insisted on getting all the sensational details like wild animals and bandits, Marie was able to disguise their reason for visiting Yunnan, as the Chinese would refuse permission to climb in the area if their real intention was revealed.

Publicity brought another concern: that her clients might disappear once they knew she was leaving for an extended period. Leonard Giovanelli, who had only recently qualified as a solicitor, was to be left in charge of the office. With the Depression coming to an end and business increasing, Marie couldn't afford to lose the hundreds of pounds caused by her practice falling off due to all the fuss. The stress made her so sick she could hardly struggle through the final arrangements and her chronic stomach problems flared up. Suffering unpleasant nausea she supervised the export of 10 cases of groceries through customs. By the time the New Zealanders arrived in Sydney, she was ready to depart, confident that all possible contingencies had been taken care of. As the transcontinental train bore her west across the country to meet the boat that would take the party to Rangoon, Marie could relax enough to enjoy the fascination of the Nullarbor Plain.

Walking through China

Sydney Woman Realises Her Dreams

This month, Miss M.B. Byles, a Sydney solicitor, sailed from Fremantle as leader of a party of three women and three men on a walking tour from Burma to the 'loveliest spot in the world', Yunnan province in China.

Miss Byles said: 'After centuries of world exploration there are still fascinating, little-known places to which one can go and steep oneself in the mysteries of a new country.'

In this *Sydney Morning Herald* article of 19 July 1938, Marie introduced her fellow expeditioners: Marjorie Jones was an amateur botanist, 'well known in New Zealand as having more major peaks to her credit than any other amateur climber'. Dora de Beer, on her way from London to meet them in Burma, was a member of the Ladies Alpine Club of Great Britain and an active member of the Royal Geographical Society. Chief guide was Kurt Sutor, 'born into one of the most aristocratic families in Switzerland'. Mick Bowie was well known as the chief guide at the Hermitage Hotel, Mount Cook. While all the other members were between 30 and 40 years of age, Frazer Ratcliff was the youngest, in his early 20s. 'I know he is simply out for adventure, but he has been unwavering in his keenness from the moment he threw in his lot with us' reported Marie. 'This is the spirit that will go a long way towards taking us there.'

Although understandably nervous about what might eventuate on their expedition into the unknown, she relished the adventure:

> Half the glamour of the expedition is that it has to face dangers and difficulties. We will not court them – but they will be there. Bears are probably the worst enemies we have to watch for. There are also giant pandas, which one of our party has a great ambition to catch. In Burma, there are tigers.
>
> As bad as the wild animals, are the wild men – the bandits. They are still at large, and travellers are appreciated as possible sources of silver. Unfortunately our money has to be changed into the weighty silver currency of China, and somehow we must hide away enough to take us there and back.

Undeterred by the potential obstacles faced in an unknown country she was unable to explain what drove her on except by alluding to the British heritage she still identified with:

> When you ask why I want to do this, I scarcely know myself, except that the urge may contain something of that customary pioneering spirit of our nation which, rightly or wrongly, has led to its expansion over the ages.

Uncertainty accompanies any expedition where information concerning conditions to be encountered may be missing, vague or unknown. If Marie felt a certain apprehension, she did not reveal it. Perhaps the thought of failure never entered her mind, but success in mountaineering is never guaranteed. Conditions at high altitude are unpredictable, delays inevitable and disappointment always a possibility.

CHAPTER 8

The Black Dragon

1938

DISASTER STRUCK when the party arrived by boat in Rangoon, the capital of Burma. The Chinese Consul confiscated their passports and explained that the Chinese visa would not enable them to proceed into the interior. An official in Rangoon informed her that the riots between the 'Mahomedans and Burmese Buddhists were very bad in Mandalay' and her party would probably be stopped from going further. Apparently some American missionaries had just been turned back. There was a chance entry would be granted, but they wouldn't know for 24 hours.

While they waited for news, the party visited Shwe Dagon Pagoda, the most revered shrine in this devoutly Buddhist country. The 100-metre-high glowing, bell-shaped shrine is coated in real gold and precious gems. Inside, the pagoda radiated a palpable atmosphere of serenity, despite the presence of an actual human skeleton kept to encourage reflection on the transience of life. A local guide explained Buddhist beliefs and Marie was impressed to hear that Buddhists did not pray but only meditated, as Buddha is not viewed as a god but as a man who had achieved full enlightenment. A confirmed atheist, she found her first exposure to Buddhist teachings a mystery. Nevertheless, as they viewed scenes from Buddha's life painted on the walls, Shwe Dagon Pagoda gave Marie the impression of a 'being in the midst of a great universal tolerance'.

Their passports were returned and they steamed up the Irrawaddy River through rice paddies and a horizon scattered with bell-shaped pagodas. Grey skies of the monsoon hung over the landscape as the paddle steamer continued on its way. When the boat journey came to an end, they caught a train to Myitkyina. For two nights and a day, it sped over the wide, flat plain of the Irrawaddy River. On the second evening the guard kept the train waiting while they ate dinner in town. 'In this country a white skin gets you almost anything except low prices!' Marie wrote to her parents.

At Myitkyina, the starting point for their mule-trek into China, she had to sort out the staff they would take on the expedition – an interpreter, a cook and two servants – then negotiated with the mule contractor. Marie had not anticipated that her legal training would come in use, but after a couple of hours of haggling found herself seated at her portable typewriter drafting 'an anything but simple contract for mule hire'.

The party, wearing pith helmets and carrying umbrellas for shade, crossed the wide, muddy river in a dugout canoe. Eleven miles over the other side it was goodbye to civilisation as they left the road and took to the track across the sparsely populated jungle-clad hills between Burma and China. To get to their destination at the most propitious time for climbing they were forced to travel through the rainy season, the worst possible time for a trek through tropical jungles. Their route took them through parts untouched by Westernisation where habits and customs had not altered much 'since the days of Marco Polo'. At Sadon, there was no wheeled traffic to disturb the peace in the villages of bamboo huts. Telegrams had to be sent by helio, a system using mirrors to flash sunlight in Morse code. Marie filed her next report for the *Sydney Morning Herald* from there.

A Sydney Woman In The Wilds Of Burma

Last month, Miss Marie B. Byles a young Sydney solicitor, left Australia to undertake a hazardous walking tour through China … Now, from the last outpost of British rule, where a tattered Union Jack waves bravely from the moss-grown fort, Miss Byles sends the first of a series of articles about her adventures …

'…We have 15 mules, 11 for ourselves and four for our servants and muleteers. We have also three riding ponies between the six of us. They are very small ponies, and it looks rather like the Charge of the Light Brigade when the men mount the poor little things. But they are most admirable beasts. They walk along at a steady three miles an hour, like the mules, without being led.'

After Sadon the steep rocky track became worse. When the muleteers started to drop out with malarial fever, the party was left to do their own unpacking.

The track went over the 2500 m range separating Burma and China, where only a stone marked the border. There the scenery changed completely. The jungle vanished from sight and they looked over grassy hills to 'breathe the atmosphere of an ancient land where stone footpaths have been worn down through the ages by the tramp of bare feet'.

Out of consideration for local custom, the party wore the Chinese costume of tunic and long pants. But on the strenuous climb through the mudslide hills they quickly reverted to the Australian bushwalker uniform of shorts and shirts. As they ate their lunch in the marketplace a crowd formed staring at the strange animals with pink knees.

The party crossed an 1800 m pass and encountered one of the camps guarding the countryside against bandits. The monsoon rain made progress slow but the scenery was consolation. Passing under wild apple, pear, plum and peach trees, they finally arrived in the quaint and beautiful town of Teng-Yueh. Going ahead to pay respects to the British Consul, Marie wanted to ask about the best temple in which to stay. Humbly sending in her passport, she wondered if her name might possibly be somewhere in the consular records, only to discover they had been expected. The consulate was the temple they could park in.

The region they passed through skirted the southern end of the Heng Duan Shan mountain range, a series of north-south parallel gorges at the eastern end of the Himalayas. This unique geological formation was created when the Himalayan mountain range, being forced up through pressure from the Indian plate, buckled at the eastern end. The monsoon rains travel up these steep gorges from the Indian Ocean, creating lush tropical rainforests of spectacular botanical diversity. Yunnan Province was unknown to the outside world but since the 1920s English botanist-explorers had come in search of exotic plant species, of which 3000 were to be found only here, to satisfy the European mania for ornamentals. The Chinese, however, were discouraging travellers into the interior. Kingdon Ward, the British botanist, had recently been prevented from pursuing his collections in the region.

The scenery was breathtaking on the next leg of the journey with no day the same. Terraced rice fields on the sides of every valley were seas of waving emerald tended by blue-clad peasants. Mud was everywhere, as were pigs, and slowed their progress. Their rubber-soled shoes slipped on the liquid manure and the baggage was immersed in it when the mules got stuck. So far they had not met any bandits, but there were signs of their presence. Another mule train up ahead had been attacked and the servants refused to travel at the rear for fear of being targeted. At each town they discussed whether to ask for a military escort and met groups on the road that had taken that precaution.

Marie feared not the bandits but, because of her short stature, being mistaken for a Japanese. The Japanese Army had invaded Manchuria in the north in 1931 and controlled a vast amount of Chinese territory but was stalled in the centre of the country as Nationalist troops defended the rugged terrain. When she filed her next report Marie acted as a war correspondent in the area:

Through Chinese Bandit Country

It was not until we reached Hsiakwan that we saw any evidence of the war, but from there to Lijiang its existence was obvious. There were many soldiers about, photography was prohibited, goods were expensive, and worst of all, missionaries had warned us to keep all maps out of sight lest we be mistaken for Japanese spies.

In wartime China, maps and mapping were strictly forbidden. They had heard stories of people losing their freedom or even their lives because of them. Marie's Leica camera was an essential tool to illustrate her newspaper articles. Photographs could be taken unobtrusively outside towns but the prohibition of maps was a problem. They were essential to the success and safety of the expedition; without them it was not worth continuing their attempt to climb in a foreign mountain range.

In early September, the party left Hsiakwan and turned off the road to head north alongside a lake. On the other side the hillside was a vast cemetery with graves that dated back 500 years and more. The local Naxi women, descendants of the people who had occupied Yunnan before the Chinese overwhelmed them, rowed them across the lake covered with tiny white and golden waterlilies. Marie's research had drawn her attention to the Naxi people – their women appeared to be the dominant sex and enjoy a unique status; when a man married he adopted the name of his wife. Though the custom did not prevent the man from making his wife the bearer of all the burdens, Marie noted: 'They certainly earned the daily bread while the men stayed at home and played with little children.'

The local English missionary, Mr Andrews, told Marie that the Naxi women carried blocks of stone weighting 54 kg each for the making of his church. And she saw women carrying home from market huge flooring boards or a new piece of furniture on their backs. Among them walked a small group of men carrying baskets that, to her indignation, contained 'a vegetable or an egg or so.'

A missionary explained the women had to keep their husbands in all essentials and often in opium, 'so that they were really slaves … Whatever the position, there was no doubt that the women did the work and held the purse strings, and were far too busy working to act as servants. All the servants we took to the mountains were men.'

Outside Tali they succumbed to a military escort because there had been robberies in the previous days and bandits had been killed. Escorted by two soldiers armed with rifles they finally approached the ancient town of Lijiang, the closest town to the Sansato Massif, a mountain mass about twenty-four kilometres long that dominates the country for miles around. As the party walked under the arched entranceway they passed caravans of ponies loaded with tea on this ancient route for tea convoys. Down narrow alleys lined with walled family compounds, they passed houses of primitive simplicity roofed with green tiles and little dragons to scare off demons. Water from the melting snow-capped mountains spilled out of the Black Dragon Pool at the edge of the town into channels that flowed through the streets, crossed by stone-arched bridges.

The first stage of the expedition was supposed to take six weeks. They arrived in Lijiang on 19 September, five weeks after they set out from Rangoon – good going, Marie thought, considering they had travelled during the wet summer season when the Black Dragon, as the locals called the monsoon, reigned in the heavens.

This expedition and the subsequent book she intended to write would place Marie in the same class as her female heroes, such as the adventure travel writer Fanny Bullock Workman who climbed in the Himalayas in 1906 accompanied by a surveyor from the Survey of India. Her book *Two summers in the ice wilds of the eastern Karakoram* was illustrated by his highly professional maps. Marie was confident of her own surveying skills having had considerable experience in mapping parts of New Zealand's Alps; the New Zealand Alpine Club had accepted her maps for publication. Were this expedition to be successful, Marie would be the first Australian to establish an international reputation in mountaineering. If fame and glory motivated her, they were within touching distance.

JADE DRAGON, Snow Mountain is the local name for Mount Sansato, the southern-most glacial mountain in Asia. Dragons are a symbol of auspicious power in Chinese folklore, associated with the weather as the bringer of rain in this rural, water-reliant land. According to legend, the Black Dragon descends at the time of the autumn equinox to its home beneath the rivers where it slumbers through the bright cold days of winter. The Black Dragon took on mythological proportions as it continued to reign over the mountain Marie had come to conquer. When Mt Sansato emerged from the rain clouds, this glimpse of their destination was ominously short-lived. Almost immediately the clouds returned to obscure it from view.

The interval between the rains ending and winter beginning, the optimum period for climbing, was short. In April and May avalanches of tremendous volume pour off the mountain and rocks are loosened. In June the rains return and last until the end of October. In November winter starts with freezing winds and rocks coated in snow. Desperate to be on the mountain when the window of fine weather opened in October, Marie's frustration grew when none of the rest of the party seemed to share her sense of urgency. She had engaged professional guides to make these decisions and felt she had to trust their expertise.

A week went by, a week not of perfect weather but good enough, Marie thought, to have gone out to prospect sites for base camp and a higher climbing camp. Then there was a burst of perfect weather and Mount Sansato rose into a clear blue sky. The guides, Kurt Sutor and Mick Bowie, agreed it was time to stir and set off to establish base and middle camps. Another week passed before the rest of the party, including porters and servants, left Lijiang on 5 October, 'With the mountains standing out boldly in the clear blue air, we set out on the great quest'. It was a thirty-kilometre walk over a flat plain to get to the mountain range. They passed through a limestone gorge and emerged onto flat grasslands patterned with pines and spruces just as clouds began to gather over the mountains.

Base camp was sited on flat land 250 m above a wide, open grassy valley to the east of Mount Sansato. It was between the two best possible approaches to the mountain, from the south and the east. Once camp was established, they could appreciate the beauty of their surroundings: meadows starred with blue flowers and surrounded by bamboo thickets, dark fragrant firs and trees in flaming reds and yellows. Nearby a crystal-clear limestone spring gushed from the mountainside, and collected in hollow logs where they rigged up a hot bath.

Fortunately, the missionary, Mr Andrews, Marie's main source of practical and logistical support, was determined they should be comfortable in base camp. Although scornful of his 'sissy' luxuries, under the domination of the monsoon rains, she was thankful for his thoughtfulness. A marquee tent served as the living room and men's sleeping quarters and for the women, a tent two metres high. Each tent had a table and chairs as well as a charcoal fire. Marie was determined to enforce the motto of the Sydney Bushwalkers in this idyllic camping ground:

> Burn and bury all your rubbish and your tins,
> And hide your bottles as you would your sins.

The tins were in such demand that there was no need to worry about them lying discarded and the cook reassured her that the rubbish would be cleared up perfectly.

The second night was clear and moonlit, but after dawn, the clouds returned and the rain fell.

> Now, the Black Dragon is the Deity who presides over the weather, and he has decreed that before the wet season departs there will be 'nine rotten days' … believe it or not, no sooner were we comfortably in camp than it rained a solid nine days with hardly a break …

The rains did not prevent them from prospecting a route to the mountain and visiting the proposed site of middle camp. From base camp they went north up the hill behind, crossed the valley below the Geepa Glacier and made middle camp under the southern side of the glacier, 4500 m above sea level. Marjorie led the way and then Marie, as the others came up by degrees. None of the party experienced any ill effects from the higher altitude after having walked continuously for so many weeks.

The moon shone in a clear night sky but soon after dawn the next day the mists gathered. Regardless, the two professional guides set off up the mountain with the porters and guides. The following day Marie and Marjorie made ready to join them at middle camp. Kurt and Mick felt the effects of the altitude slightly and advised them to go up and get used to it, even though the weather was not good enough for climbing. That evening, after they returned to base camp, it began to rain again. It teemed down on the tent roof and rained solidly all the next day.

To keep warm, Marie lit a fire in front of her tent to dry their clothes and used this time to improve her Chinese language skills with the help of Tai, the interpreter. Her vocabulary soon reached the 'presentable' number of about 400 but the non-English speaking Chinese suffered unintended insults from her mispronunciations. Meantime the three women went for short walks on the partly fine days while the men hunted, but there was little animal or bird life. Seed collecting was Marjorie's favourite pastime. She spent a lot of time sorting them and putting them into packets. One day Marie went with her up the hills opposite the mountain, where they passed some nomad Tibetans and their yaks camped on a meadow beside a clear running creek.

Always intrigued by other cultures, Marie returned the next day with Tai. As they approached the camp a huge Tibetan mastiff rushed out to attack them and had to be restrained by one of the men who dragged the huge beast to the ground. They were invited to join the Tibetans for a meal of walnuts and cream cheese with brown sugar and seats were placed for the guests around the fire. Marie discovered they traded Tibetan butter, carpets, and yaks for a livelihood.

It continued to rain and then, as prophesied, the rainy season ended on the tenth day and the Black Dragon departed from the heavens. The morning dawned fresh and clear with the snow-clad mountains standing out against the clear blue sky. On 25 October, the first day of fine weather, Kurt and Mick went up to the high camp with Wang, the sturdiest of the servants. A tiny man no bigger than Marie, Wang was nearly overwhelmed in the windproof suit and large mountaineering boots as he carried the heaviest load. He returned with news that the high tent in open alpine land was completely buried in snow and had to be dug out.

The next day Marie and Marjorie went up to assist with the excavation accompanied by Wang and a Tibetan porter carrying supplies. By 3.45 in the afternoon the sun had sank behind the rocky peaks and a deathly chill settled on everything. Gradually the light of day faded into a pale snow-lit night. The thermometer registered −9.5° to −6.6°C. There was little chance that the feeble autumn sun would melt the snows. The lateness of the rain had made a difficult mountain even more difficult. The high altitude caused slight headaches and breathlessness to some of the party and Marie felt that a few days at 5000 m was essential before they could hope to reach 6000 m. At night they drank hot Horlicks Malted Milk, a nutritional supplement, then snuggled into their eiderdown sleeping bags designed for alpine conditions, while the billy of water froze beside them. The next day they returned to completing the work of excavating the tents.

Kurt and Mick took two of the Everest tents up for an even higher camp from which they hoped to reach the summit. Marie and Marjorie then followed them up the Geepa Glacier with more gear. To Marie, it was 'a superb glacier whose upper parts were guarded by towering rock peaks, standing like sentinels or pillars of heaven.' To the north, the awe-inspiring peak of Mount Sansato with its serrated knife-edge of rock and ice towered above their camp. As she described it, 'The whole stupendous mountain ridge seemed to me like the wing of a great white dragon piercing the blue.'

When the guides decided it was time to make their move, it was to her great relief. Two little Everest tents were placed in a snow-filled crevasse high on the Geepa Glacier that looked down over deeper crevasses to the valley and range beyond the blue hills. The next morning, Monday 31 October, it blew a gale as they set out for their attempt on the peak. Muffled up to their eyes in wind-proof Everest suits over many layers of woollies, Marie and Marjorie joined the guides while Dora remained at camp to organise stores and dry their clothes. Marie's feet soon lost all feeling; she feared the possibility of frostbite. They had to climb on a rocky peak plastered with loose snow but the rocks lay at a steep angle and most were unstable. They found it difficult to kick steps in the soft snow and equally difficult to find footholds or handholds on the rock. It was soon clear that the mountain was impossible. It had taken an hour to climb up thirty metres; the descent was even more agonising. It took almost two hours:

> Poor Kurt Sutor sat on the top and belayed Marjorie and me down, cursing, no doubt, at our slowness and refusal to trust the rope and be let down foot by foot by him.
>
> Frozen and numb, we dropped down on to the glacier once more, realising that even in perfect weather, of which we had had none since the rains departed, the peak would be impossible until next summer's rains should have cleared the rocks of snow.

The Black Dragon had granted a burst of perfect climbing weather in September while they were in Lijiang but the party had failed to utilise it. They realised they had missed an opportunity that would not recur for another year. Marie was bitterly disappointed.

> Alas! It was the end of the hopes and plans of two years, the months of labour and the aspirations of the past ten years. No one else seemed to care very much; but then no one else had hoped and planned as I had, and no one else knew the weeks and months of work, the difficulties that had risen up, one after another, till the very fates seemed against me – as indeed, perhaps they were. To the others it all seemed so simple and so easy to get where we did that they could not care very much if we failed. But to me, when I realised the lost fine weather at the end of September was the loss of the mountain, the weariness of life seemed a burden too heavy to be borne.

Despite her low mood, 'the Honour of the British Race' was at stake. Marie organised the party to climb a 4900 m peak above middle camp. For the first time they saw the imposing Sansato Massif spread out around them with its four main peaks.

> But, oh! Those peaks! Those knife edges of rock and ice enfolded one within the other. How could one even approach them, let alone climb them? I have seen mountains in Norway, Canada and New Zealand, but never anything to touch the icy inaccessibility of those virgin dragon queens whose serrated and ice-covered rock-ridges bristled like giant walls protecting them.

The futility of the expedition was now apparent; nevertheless, Marie was unwilling to accept full responsibility for the consequences of choosing an objective in defiance of the advice she had received.

They shifted camp to the head of the next valley. From there they climbed through the steep forests and made camp at 4500 m in a sheltered glade with a frozen stream falling from one limestone basin to another and a glorious view across blue hills towards the rising sun. The professional guides were sceptical when Marie and Marjorie decided to climb a 5500 m peak with two of the servants Wang and Magato, the local Naxi mountain guide, who were both eager to climb to high altitudes. Mick and Kurt thought the two experienced women climbers could make it but it was sheer madness to take the two new hands, as they did not even have the right equipment. When they made the summit they photographed each other with legs dangling over the edge, the Yangtze River more than 3000 m below. After a 'gloriously happy day of laughter and pidgin-Chinese', Marie and Marjorie decided that for the remaining three weeks they were just going to enjoy themselves. They climbed three more peaks up to 5500 m and Magato proved to be a skilled climber, soon mastering the use of rope and ice axe.

One day Marie went off on her own with Magato to obtain geographical information for a map she was making of the area. Alone for the first time in months, her despair surfaced. As she sat miserably among the sky-blue gentians in the meadows near a lake and looked up at the ancient glacial moraine above, she was stricken with the anguish that every mountaineer feels when, after much planning and effort, they fail to achieve their objective. 'What I had striven for and desired above all lay dead. I should never climb the mountain or feel again the touch of its rough limestone rocks.'

It was a relief for the others to have time apart from her while she was in this mood. Dora wrote in her travel diary, 'A heavenly peaceful day – no Marie!'

The party then visited the Yangtze River gorge where the huge river narrowed down between towering walls of rock and flows through mountains 5800 m high. Marie, Marjorie and Mick left the peaceful mountains in a race to catch their boat at Haiphong. They travelled through Kunming, where they were liable to 'be bombed by one side, and seized as spies by the other'. En route they had to leave four cases behind as they squeezed into a bus full of ammunition from Burma. Marie noted considerable changes the impending war had caused during the three months of their journey:

> Bandits had been banished from the road. Aerodromes and drilling grounds were being rapidly constructed. The inns were packed with soldiers at Hsiakwan, the terminus of the bus from Kunming.
>
> In two days the bus carried us from a roadless ancient China with old traditions including even foot binding, to Kunming, a city rapidly becoming modern with coloured electric road-traffic signals, radios, men and women sitting at the same table and using knives and forks ...

Over the following years the Japanese bombed the railways and bridges she had travelled across. Newspapers were eager to publish Marie's full-page articles of this area so strategically close to Australia. It was one way at least, that she could profitably use her experiences.

CHAPTER 9

Ahimsa

1938–1941

FOR MANY years Marie 'had been compiling the requisite of my dream cottage'. In 1937 she looked around for land to buy in Cheltenham, the next suburb to Beecroft.

> Eventually I found what seemed just right. It was over ten minutes walk from the station so that there would always be a walk, right in the midst of bush-clad hills which were a reserve, and out of sight of other houses. I took my sleeping bag and slept out on some flat rocks to get the "feel". The stars were superb.

On her next visit she saw a survey peg so rushed to the Lands Department and paid the deposit on a Conditional Purchase of £60, for the two-hectare block on Crown Land. Before she left for China, she supervised the architectural design of the house and its construction by a builder she employed. And it was not an easy job. She had difficulty getting the water main down and materials had to be carried up to the site 15 m above the end of the cart track. One morning when she went to inspect before going to work she found the workmen had made a tombstone inscribed 'Here lies Bill Smith, done to death carrying bricks for Miss Byles fire-place'. However, all was finished for her to move in to just before sailing off to China.

On her return in December 1938, her new house provided much-needed sanctuary to recover from the worst setback of her life.

> The new little cottage was a great delight … and of all the places at which I have stayed during my travels only the bungalow at Binsar in the Himalaya

hills, with its vision of snow peaks, could compare with the beauty of the bush-lands seen from my own cottage.

Its unique location – next to a vast nature reserve that extended along the peaceful Lane Cove River – reproduced the idyllic circumstance of Chilworth: at the end of a cul-de-sac, facing an expansive area of bushland that would never be built out. The land sloped down to a creek that curved around its border on two sides, with fern-covered banks. Across the creek, eucalypt-covered hills rose to a high ridge in a crescent-shape that ensured Marie's view was of the natural world. Native trees and wildflowers covered the land and in the belief that nature was to be shared with everyone, she resolved to maintain public access.

The sandstone and fibro house reflected her extremely practical nature – she preferred not to spend effort or money on maintaining its appearance. Imperative in the design was the four-metre-wide verandah that faced north towards the reserve. This was where she would live and sleep. A habitual early riser, Marie loved to wake to the first sounds of the coming dawn and watch the landscape quietly emerge with the soft light. To her the verandah was the most important aspect of the design; it was there she entertained and held lantern-slide nights for friends, sharing the pictorial record of her journey through some of Asia's most remote and exotic regions. Photography was a passion since childhood, and she later added a darkroom to the outside laundry.

There was a small living room with a fireplace for winter nights and a bedroom for occasional guests. Double sliding glass doors allowed the living room to open up to the verandah, inviting the outside in, dissolving boundaries between living space and the magical vista of trees – banksias, casuarinas and pink-skinned angophoras – that surrounded the house. A frangipani tree was planted directly below the verandah and would grow in the years ahead to a height where the sweet scent of its flowers reached Marie as she sat reading, writing or entertaining.

The main feature of the living room was the high bookshelves that accommo-dated her collection of books that continued to grow as her interests expanded. Exotic items brought back from Asia decorated the house: a Tibetan rug in red, blue and green for the guest bedroom, and in the living room a Chinese rug depicting a picturesque sampan in sail covered the oiled wooden floorboards. As soon as she could afford it, Marie bought a refrigerator and installed a hot water service, luxuries she had never had before. An unenthusiastic cook, her modern electric stove would get some use but no more than necessary. The utter simplicity of the house was exactly what Marie wanted and spoke eloquently of her lifestyle. She had little interest in creating a glamorous house with beautiful decorations – aesthetic value, to her, lay in the setting.

Returning home one afternoon, Marie found a black cat that purred so furiously that he seemed to be singing 'Laudate Dominum', a Catholic hymn. Despite his potential threat to native birds, she let him stay. His company was appreciated for the next seven years and gave her a deeply needed source of affection. When he died she reflected, 'I had loved old Laudate and his glorious purring.'

Each weekday she walked to the station carrying a sharp-pointed stick in order to pick up any discarded rubbish. This helped establish her rather eccentric reputation with the locals. During her six-month absence from the office, Leonard, Pearle and a new stenographer, Ruth Milton, had managed capably. Ruth was good with figures and quick to learn. Before long, she took over the accounting duties and quickly rose in Marie's estimation. But her employer's constant demands were exacting. Ruth, years later, recalled, 'She just told me what to do and I did it and I was running around so quickly doing everything. She was one of those people who got on with the job and you just had to do it.' Pearle staffed the city office while Ruth stayed in Eastwood. On Fridays they swapped around so both became familiar with the work at hand.

A new setback loomed as restrictions brought on by the war effort made life difficult for everyone, homemaker and businessperson alike. Leonard Giovanelli enlisted at the beginning of the war and staff became unprocurable. Marie was philosophical, 'Like other solicitors, I returned to doing my own search and registration work. None-the-less the practice grew.'

MARIE SPOKE little to her intimates about her disappointment at the failure of the China expedition; instead, writing proved an expressive outlet. Intended as a guide to the next party of adventurers who might attempt to follow in her footsteps, she compiled a full and thorough account of the expedition to Mount Sansato. If the expedition had succeeded and the book about it had been published, Marie would have become Australia's most famous mountaineer. Her account, however, would never be read, although an excerpt was printed in the *New Zealand Alpine Journal* in 1939. In it she gave useful logistical information to those perhaps inclined to bag a high mountain peak of international significance. She ended mournfully, 'Now let another party go and succeed where we failed, and if this information we have gathered helps them to triumph I shall feel we did not go in vain.'

Failure is an inevitable part of the human condition, but it triggered a crisis of meaning in Marie's life. With persistent application she had achieved virtually every goal she set herself and valued her unique status as a leader in many fields. Gradually, an awareness grew in her that what she truly desired was far more elusive than any material success, and much more difficult to attain.

> Whether this absurd suffering had anything to do with it, I do not know, but apparently what Eastern people would call 'ripening karma' took effect, and on the return to Australia in 1939 there developed a strange interest in moral and spiritual values, things for which, as a university student in the early twenties, I had a supreme contempt.

Until this time Marie had been a confirmed rationalist. If during a discussion someone had suggested that people might be swayed by these values, she dismissed the idea as nonsense. Through disenchantment with worldly attainments, her aspirations began to shift. She started reading widely on topics that had previously held no interest for her, particularly Carl Jung's psychological concepts. Marie explained this new change of consciousness that came at the age of 38:

> According to Carl Jung, the great change of life comes about the age of 35 to 40, the middle of life. From puberty until then the natural attitude is an endeavour to make one's individual place in the concrete world of outward things. After the zenith of life the natural thing is both a turning inward to the psychic life and also a turning outward to the universality of all …
>
> It is a fact that, while there are schools for teaching us how to earn a living and make our way in the material world during the first half of life, there are no schools for training us for the second half of life and showing us how to look inward to our own psyches and outward to the Universal, and so fit us for that second half of life, and death which is the greatest of all adventures.

On a scorching hot day in March 1939, she and another couple of bushwalkers tramped through bushfire-swept country. On reaching a river they put on swimsuits. After cooling off she sat on a shady rock in the middle of a pool and read. 'Of all unlikely books I read *Peace with Honour*. This book tipped the balance.'

In 1934, A.A. Milne, of *Winnie the Pooh* fame, wrote what became a classic for Christian pacifists on the abolition of war. In *Peace with Honour* Milne prophetically declared that the next world war would destroy civilisation. Having been brought up a pacifist, Milne's writing triggered an interest in pacifism and religious belief in Marie.

Coincidentally in a second-hand bookshop she picked up a copy of the *The Song Celestial*, Sir Edwin Arnold's translation of the *Bhagavad Gita*, and read this classic of Indian spiritual literature in a sitting. It made a profound impact on her: 'How could such sublime wisdom be crammed into so small a space? I had never heard of it. Whatever was it?'

The *Bhagavad Gita* is an episode of the Mahabharata, an epic description of the ancient world, and contains a depth of metaphysical consciousness befitting what is considered to be the world's oldest surviving religious culture. The Sanskrit poem relates a philosophical dialogue between Prince Arjuna, who had been cheated out of his throne by his cousin, and Krishna, the Supreme Deity, who was acting as his charioteer. A great battle is pending between the armies of the two cousins and Prince Arjuna, a fabled bowman, is poised to lead the attack. The *Gita* influenced many great and independent thinkers, among them Henry David Thoreau the nineteenth-century American naturalist and practical philosopher who advocated a simple, principled lifestyle in accord with nature. He declared that each morning he bathed his intellect in the 'stupendous' philosophy of the *Bhagavad Gita* and was struck by the profundity of its wisdom, 'in comparison with which our modern world and its literature seem puny and trivial'. The *Gita* also struck a chord with Marie. Previously oriented to outward goals and profoundly ignorant of the inner workings of her mind, these philosophical discoveries came with the force of revelation.

As often happens when a personal shift like this occurs, people came into her orbit who could point her along the path. Someone told her that her ideas were rather like Mohandas Gandhi's. Up until this time Gandhi had been little more than a name but she read all she could about him and soon discovered that the *Bhagavad Gita* was his daily reference. Each night at his Indian ashram his followers recited verses from the *Gita*. The battlefield where the epic story is set represented the human heart according to Gandhi, who tried to embody as best he could Lord Krishna's definition of the 'the man established in wisdom'.

While books satisfied intellectually, they did not satisfy spiritually. Marie began questioning her model of the world. Impressed by the deep sincerity of the local Congregational Minister the Rev. Frank Wheaton, who was known and liked by her parents, Marie found herself being drawn to hear him speak. Her account of this unprecedented step shows the deep inner conflict she must have been experiencing while not even being aware of it. On the one hand she felt a pull to explore the spiritual dimension: on the other, her belief system was saying, 'no, no, this is nonsense'.

> And then, oh horrors! I found myself slinking into Mr. Wheaton's church like a dog with its tail between its legs and hoping to goodness that no one would see me. No member of a respectable family beginning to engage in the sly grog

traffic could have been more afraid of being found out. But Cheltenham was not a large suburb and the rumour soon spread, 'Did you hear the latest? Marie Byles has gone and got religion!'

It is ironic that such an independent freethinker was terrified of what people would think. From her verandah, Marie looked over the bushland and heard the silence of the night and the first birdcalls of morning while pondering the process that was unfolding: 'There was something behind all which I had not known before, something that the deep sincerity of Frank Wheaton also seemed to make known, something that could not be put into words and yet was very real. What was it?'

While aware of being in harmony with a force greater than her own, talk of a 'loving heavenly father' did not convince someone with a natural dislike of religious terminology. It did not suit her agnostic mentality, she preferred Jung's explanation that the psyche has come to life of its own accord. Eventually, she found an intellectual explanation in Julian Huxley's *Essays of a Biologist*.

> This, to my mind, is what actually happens when people speak of communion with God. It is a setting, and organising of our experiences of the universe in relation with the driving forces of the soul or mental being, so that the two are united or harmonised. There is a resolution of conflicts and attaining of profound serenity, a conviction that the experience is of the utmost value and importance.

She had found a way of comprehending the process that was unfolding, although it would take her many more years to understand what the psychological change demanded for its development.

WHEN WAR was declared in September 1939 Marie joined the peace movement, believing war was an unacceptable way to resolve conflict. Her involvement included financially supporting pacifist organisations and activities, writing articles for *The Peacemaker* journal published by the Pacifist Council of Australia, and giving talks on pacifist figures of historical note. Compared with the war news screaming out from the daily newspapers, Gandhi's weekly journal *Harijan*, distributed to his followers throughout the world, was a tonic of peace and sanity that she absorbed.

Mohandas Gandhi was a lawyer when he began his life of social activism. The reputation he gained was based not just on ability, but his insistence on truthfulness. If he found his client lying, he would get up in court, apologise, and refuse to represent the client further. He never handled a case unless he was dealing with truth in spirit and letter. Gandhi's example guided Marie in her own law practice and confirmed her moral objectives in a profession where commercial values usually took overriding significance.

> In our social and business life most people take it for granted that petty fibs do not matter if they seem to be helpful to oneself or to others. To stick to facts, which are a part of truth, was like stepping from a shaking quagmire on to firm, hard ground. Brought up in the surroundings we are in, this truthfulness cannot be acquired all at once, but by persistence it did come …

Gandhi believed that money was not the first objective of work, but only a sideline. To him the ethic of service to others comes before service to oneself. The less interested Marie became in making a high income, the more firmly established financially the practice became. The little city office became too small and she was forced to get a larger office on the opposite side of the street. As her reputation for honesty grew, banks recommended clients who discovered that her word was her bond. Another reason for her success was that she followed Gandhi's example in acting as a conciliator who encouraged parties to negotiate a settlement rather than take an adversarial position that inevitably led to court.

Inspired by Gandhi's ability to lead non-violent protests challenging India's ruling power, Marie named her property Ahimsa, after his core principle.

> Literally it means non-killing, but Gandhi said that it took him into realms infinitely higher, that it means that you may not injure anyone even in thought. For example, if you do not like a person, you do not want him removed, even by divine agency. And, of course, it covers non-injury to the bushlands as well as to people. You cannot love a person, or the bush, at will, but you can avoid injuring by deed, and eventually by thought also.

To Gandhi, ahimsa was the quality of love in its purest, all-embracing form. For those who are not saints, who struggle to forgive and forget, practising ahimsa could transform the forgiver and lighten the heaviest heart. This was a turning point in Marie's life. Gandhi had given her something that could, when practised, change life's inherent conflicts into the peace of mind she was seeking.

Gandhi's endorsement of a lifestyle of voluntary simplicity and asceticism required no adaptation for Marie, as her abstentious parents had brought up their children with similar values. Throughout her life she never drank alcohol or smoked, and remained vegetarian. She lived frugally, ate sparingly, grew organic vegetables using her own waste as compost and recycled as notepaper every envelope her office acquired. Gandhi's radical celibacy also resonated with her but his celibacy was attained through constant struggle, whereas Marie believed hers was naturally endowed. Perhaps this is how she rationalised her relative position in society. Perhaps the "celibate" label also enabled her to avoid delving into her own personal truths, about either her sexuality or the difficulty she had with emotional intimacy.

Throughout the 1940s, she corresponded with Gandhi and spoke often to pacifist groups on his progress in the struggle against British rule. She viewed with concern the ups and downs of his health as he fasted in non-violent protest at the extreme behaviour of both the British and his own countrymen. She also gave talks on Aldous Huxley and reviewed his books in *The Peacemaker*. Huxley was an avowed pacifist who, although medically unfit for military service, registered as a conscientious objector during the Great War. During the 1930s in the build-up to World War II, Huxley actively crusaded on behalf of pacifism. He believed that the only winners in war were the bankers and industrialists.

In his great spiritual work *The Perennial Philosophy*, published in 1945, Huxley described saints and enlightened ones who had, through a process of "dying to self", experienced deeper knowledge of the Self and the Kingdom of God within. This concept, meaning ego dissolution, made a deep impression on Marie, as would a similar phrase Gandhi used "reducing self to zero". She believed, 'It was the very basis on which his life's work rested and without it the best endeavours and noblest causes would fail.' Gandhi believed that only through the dissolution of his ego could he be an instrument of peace.

THROUGH HER pacifist affiliations, Marie came into contact with The Religious Society of Friends, colloquially known as the Quakers. More a spiritual community than a church, their silent meetings opened her to the value of silence and 'stilling one's own thoughts and desires'. Strengthened by a community that held the space for spiritual reflection, her inward journey progressed and deep feelings began to surface.

Poetry offered Marie a way to connect with an emotional self that had not previously found expression. It provided an outlet for the passionate, complex feelings she experienced towards human relationships and the fragility of nature. Through verse she expressed her deep yearning for the divine. Mystics such as St Theresa of Avila, who experienced profound spiritual ecstasies, gave inspiration and 'being one with the light of the infinite' became Marie's goal. Although she wrote about love, it was love in a spiritual form, the 'Love-Soul of mankind' that flowed forth.

In a poem, *The Quaker Meeting*, Marie writes,

> Oh love! Which flows through all we know
> Flow through our minds, and make us one
> Banish our selfish hopes and fears
> And make the love of all, our sun.

Although she was tapping into a higher consciousness, Marie eventually acknowledged her discontent:

> The verse that sang itself on to paper shows agony of pain, sublime heights of joy, and an understanding and spiritual discernment which often afterwards made me despair because, over many years that followed, I seemed to progress no further. It is one thing to glimpse the truth; it is quite another to absorb it and live it in actual experience from moment to moment.

Increasingly, she immersed herself in the study of Buddha's teachings, finding a philosophy that was complementary with Gandhi's and the Quakers' beliefs. But it gave her something these two paths did not – a deeply felt experience of meditation.

THE WAR might have enhanced her need for a spiritual belief, but Marie was at heart a pragmatist. She soon found practical ways to confront the evils the war produced. At the beginning of World War II many Jewish refugees, fortunate enough to escape the disintegration of their communities in Europe, found themselves at the other end of the world. In Australia with their different appearance, thick accents and heavy, dark clothing, they were treated with suspicion. Because of the perceived fear of foreign invasion, refugees were subject to a law that insisted they sleep at the same address every night and report to the police station regularly. These people had limited options to discover their new country so, in September 1939, Marie enlisted the help of Paddy Pallin in creating a bushwalking club that accommodated the needs of these often very competent walkers who were unable to go on overnight camping expeditions. In contrast to the Sydney Bush Walkers, this new club, prosaically named the Bush Club, had no qualifying requirements and walks were chosen that were within reach of Sydney.

For Marie and Paddy the basis for the club's existence was that there should be no physical test for membership. A whole family – husband, wife and children – could join. Members needed only to have a genuine love of the bush, a desire to protect it and a willingness to extend the hand of friendship to any bush-lover. In fact, among those who joined the club were eminent rock climbers and skiers from Europe – capable of passing any physical test. The Bush Club gave these Europeans the opportunity to familiarise themselves with their strange new environment. As a result of the founders' inclusive beliefs, the club became very cosmopolitan. Membership filled with names foreign to Australian ears: Raubitschek, Spiegel, Souhami, Heilpern, de Freitas, Mautner, Bergman, Hein, Fried, Jaeger, Schoen, Roehrich, Weisz, Zueller, Landauer and Herzer. Marie gravitated to these Jewish intellectuals because she enjoyed their stimulating discussions. But their group soon came under suspicion. On one occasion, a new member, from the Department of the Interior, joined the walk fully equipped with new gear. It was the only time he walked with the club, giving rise to the suspicion he was checking up on what all these aliens were up to.

One of the early members was Dr Rudi Lemberg, an eminent scientist who had been a professor at Heidelberg University. As the Nazi shadows fell on Germany he had seen that the future for the Jews under Hitler was annihilation. He was not afflicted with the political blindness of his academic colleagues who refused to believe the situation was that dire. Reluctantly, as he thought that the move could quite conceivably end his scientific career, he accepted a position as research scientist at The Royal North Shore Hospital in Sydney. Germany's loss became the New World's gain. In 1959, after a distinguished career, Dr Lemberg was made a Foundation Fellow of the Australian Academy of Science simultaneous with his election to the Royal Society.

On their arrival in Australia, Rudi Lemberg and his wife joined the Sydney Bush Walkers. They enjoyed its campfire comradeship for many years, until the war descended. Suddenly people with German names, even Jews, were suspected of being spies; not necessarily voluntarily, perhaps through being blackmailed by German authorities holding their family hostage. As the Japanese threat to Australia's north intensified, the entire country felt the imminence of invasion. One SBW club member with a military background campaigned to reject all applications by foreigners (labelled "friendly enemy aliens") to join the club. Although it was not a unanimous decision and incited heated debate, membership for a German friend of Rudi's, whom he had sponsored to Australia, was refused. He decided not to stay in the club. Having met the Lembergs through the Quakers, Marie invited them to join the Bush Club.

Marie and Paddy gave lessons to the new members on survival in the Australian bush and compass and map-reading instructions to upgrade their skills. Rudi gave his assistance, agreeing to act as contact officer for the search and rescue section and also gave lectures on nutrition after their club meetings. Paddy soon became immersed in war work and Marie was left to carry on alone as leader. Meetings were held at various members' houses, including Marie's, and her city office was used as headquarters for members wanting to pick up their schedules. Most walks explored the many nature reserves within Sydney's metropolitan region, while others went further afield. She took delight in introducing the recent arrivals to Bouddi Natural Park, even though the travel time would mean a late return.

It was in 1941 while leading a Bush Club tour through Bouddi that, as Marie wrote, 'Fate now took possession of the arena of my life.' In the group was a young boy who had been sent by his club-member parents. They had provided him with a whole chicken for lunch, presumably to share. Instead he ate it all himself and became sick. Rudi and Marie were the last to leave the picnic spot. When they realised the boy was unable to walk, Rudi carried him out while Marie shouldered the boy's pack as well as Rudi's and her own. She hurried ahead hoping to catch up with those in front before they reached the railway station. The path from Maitland Bay up to The Scenic Road is long and steep, especially under such a load. As she strained uphill against the weight of the heavy packs something went wrong with her right foot. 'It had always been a very skinny foot, but in strong climbing boots it had support; in sandshoes it had none.' What gave way were the structural supports within her foot, the ligaments and tendons. The ligaments were overstretched and the bone structure weakened. It must have been extremely painful as she continued the long climb. At this stage, Marie did not realise that the damage she sustained would be permanent.

Injury was the worst fate to befall a bushwalker, something she had always dreaded. Once when climbing on Mt Kuring-gai in 1937 with her friend Kath McKay, a rock gave way and Kath broke her ankle in the 20m fall down a steep slope. Although she bore the injury with a smile, Marie felt that she could never have done so: 'to lose one's feet for walking, no, no, I could never do so.'

There is often a precipitating event, some illness or disability that can turn a life from the outward to the inward journey. Marie had already begun focusing on the spiritual dimension, but the injury made that reorientation more pronounced as her great loves, bushwalking and mountaineering, were denied her.

CHAPTER 10

An Adventure in Loneliness

1941 – 1945

ALTHOUGH IT hurt to walk, the pain was not bad enough to prevent Marie from taking a long-cherished holiday at Kosciusko. Used to solitary walking, and even camping, this would be, 'an adventure in loneliness, a whole week or more alone.' Ever since childhood, she was confident and strong enough to stand alone, but this reference to loneliness perhaps indicates that her sojourn had more to do with the dark night of the soul.

Twenty years previously, she had read H.G. Wells' *Modern Utopia* and it had left an indelible impression. Utopia was ruled by a voluntary nobility of men and women who spent at least a week every year alone in the wilds without matches, maps or compass, with only the sky above their heads at night. Marie admitted that she was not as hardy as those Utopians and packed matches, map, compass and tent – as well as food, but rejected a book that that she had looked at longingly, *Some Sayings of the Buddha*. Though this particular book seemed appropriate to take into the wilderness, 'for did not Buddha discover truth while sitting alone in the forest?' she returned it to the bookshelf.

Standing on Strathfield station, Marie put aside her worries about leaving the office in the care of her staff over the Christmas holiday period. Thinking it might be the last holiday she would get for the foreseeable future, she ignored the propaganda in the newspapers about the unpatriotic people who went holidaying at Christmas. Earlier that month, on 7 December 1941, the Japanese had bombed Pearl Harbour naval base in Hawaii and knocked out the main American battle fleet. This signalled the beginning of their sweep throughout the Asia-Pacific. Many Australians feared invasion but Marie refused to react with the same level of anxiety and sank into her compartment's bunk in an untroubled slumber. The next morning she rode in a hired car with other passengers to the Kosciusko Chalet at Charlotte's Pass and stayed overnight. At lunch the next day, she was forced to defend her plan to camp alone:

> At the Christmas dinner table… weird and wonderful reasons were invented as to why I was going; they ranged from nudism to yoga. In the end I persuaded them I was not even a poet, but just a trifle mad, and I was allowed to depart in peace.

Dropped at the track leading to Blue Lake, Marie hefted the heavy load of groceries in front balanced by the pack on her back and began the five-kilometre walk along the rough, steep track. By the time she made it to her destination, the distance seemed much further. Finding a place to camp out of view of the main path, she pitched her tent beside the still waters of the small, deep lake formed by glacial activity. She boiled a billy of tea on a tiny campfire surrounded by frozen beauty with snowdrifts coating the gaunt rocky hills above, even in midsummer. Her strategy to avoid war news by escaping into nature was immediately effective. Looking up into the night sky, she wrote in her diary, 'It is a calm heavenly evening and the spirit of love is abroad – all burdens have faded away …' The first night was cold and she awoke several times, catching sight of the Southern Cross turning over. The sun rose at 5 am promptly, just as her old school motto flashed upon her:

> So here hath been dawning another blue day
> Think, wilt thou let it slip useless away?

Stretched before her were sixteen hours of daylight that she had to let slip 'uselessly' away – she had seldom tackled a more difficult problem. After lunch she dozed and hoped that something of the peace and joy of the hills would return with her so that when people or events disturbed her, she could remember the quietness and calm found there. For the most part the holiday was uneventful although her writing shows a gradual shift in perception:

> … things emerged from the ground, the air, the sky that I never knew before, and there was an increasing thrill in little things – the porcelain blue edges of the tiny white flowers starring the moss green banks of laughing brooklets, and adventure in noting that they varied their petals from five to seven.

The world and the horrors of the war receded further and further from consciousness. Marie reflected on her insignificance as 'all of history passed before me like a cinematograph film to a god on Olympus'. The hills around her with their knowledge of the last Ice Age took no account of wars or empires – Roman, Spanish, British, German and Japanese. The only element that persisted and seemed to grow in her awareness was the 'slender plant of human kindliness and helpfulness, and this persisted despite all that was against it'. Towards the end of her retreat in the wilderness she posed an intriguing question: does one learn anything new from being alone with Nature? She thought not.

> One gets from Nature only interest on the capital one takes to her; one gets no fresh capital. But if one gets nothing new one does get something very old and an art the modern world is losing, the ability to sit still and leave Nature to follow her own way.

THE LONELY holiday at Kosciusko had been 'wonderfully purifying and illuminating'. Marie returned feeling, 'recreated, cleansed and renewed mentally and spiritually and with an overwhelming love of humanity – if only because I had done without the human species for so long'. While she had been among all the things she loved, nature and walking, all the things that so inspired and uplifted her, they also revealed how limited she was physically.

Inquiries were made among her acquaintances about what could be done for her feet. She heard only of an operation for the bunion that had developed from her collapsed arch. Kath MacKay, the friend who had broken her ankle climbing with Marie some years before, recommended a doctor: a Dr Hertz had set her ankle and saved it from being amputated, and then managed with a second operation to make it fairly straight. While her parents did not like the idea of an operation, they realised that Marie had made up her mind and Cyril gave her a cheque towards expenses. Both feet were operated on and Cheltenham friends, Keela and John Dey, invited her to stay with them for a month to recuperate. Keela escorted Marie from hospital and, on arrival at Cheltenham railway station, went to fetch a wheelbarrow to transport her to the house. Although John was a solicitor, very few people owned cars in that era, especially those in the bushwalking movement who preferred to use their feet.

When she left the hospital Marie took it for granted that in due course the feet would be all right. And when she said goodbye to the doctor she added jokingly that she would send him a telegram from the top of Mount Everest! However, the operation was not a success. The big toe on her right foot was left sticking up. Even though she tried to weigh it down with heavy books, it refused. Dot Butler used to bicycle over to Ahimsa and massage Marie's feet. However, her training in physiotherapy did nothing to rectify the problem. Later, Marie discovered the same friend who recommended the operation also knew an osteopath who could have reduced the inflammation with manipulation. She regretted bitterly that her friend had not recommended the osteopath instead of the surgeon.

By May 1942, her feet were sufficiently improved to arrange another working bee at Bouddi Natural Park. She managed the long walk in to Maitland Bay, but her big toe was sticking up alarmingly. With the limited medical technology available at the time, the doctor could do nothing more, and the problem became chronic. The condition worsened until she was walking with a bad limp. The experts she consulted about arch supports and specially made shoes provided no relief. It caused her great pain to acknowledge that her feet would never again allow her to bushwalk in the manner she had. At the age of 42, she could have expected to enjoy many more years of an active lifestyle. She later wrote that the unsuccessful operation,

> … took away the things in life most treasured. The need for spiritual and moral values to give meaning to life became doubly necessary, more especially as the body went steadily downhill and there followed about thirteen years of ill-health and suffering, both physical and spiritual.

IN 1942, Pearle left to enter the army and marry; staff was almost impossible to find but Marie was fortunate that a replacement, another 'jewel', found her.

> Over the years I have been wonderfully blessed with staff of the very first class. There have been ups and downs, of course, and there have been a very few who, much to our relief, have left of their own accord. But by and large the girls and women have been nearly perfect and they have risen to my idea that a clerk always shares my responsibilities and takes some of the burden of management on her shoulders. Without such wonderful women to depend upon the practice would not have been possible.

Well ahead of her time in office management practices, Marie introduced a flexible scheme of permanent part-time employment for her all-female staff. By arrangement of a regular timetable they negotiated between themselves, clerks and secretaries organised their working hours to fit in with domestic commitments. Trained to handle responsibility, they became highly skilled paralegals with Marie delegating specific areas to each person: conveyancing, divorce, leases, bookkeeping, litigation, estates and probate. While she expected maximum effort from everyone, she was very generous in return, rewarding loyalty with above-award salaries. When the business started to make a profit, she instituted the practice of profit sharing in the form of a quarterly bonus to all staff. With this approach she gained their devotion. Over the years, staff members became like family to her. June Taylor started, aged sixteen, in 1946. She used her first quarterly bonus to buy a pushbike to help her get to work. Marie came to regard her like a daughter. As a vegetarian, she did not like buying meat from the butcher and used to send June down to buy meat for her cat, a stray she had adopted. June fell in love with the butcher boy and married him. When she was twenty-five, she left to have a baby despite Marie's stern admonitions against over-population, an issue she felt strongly about. Returning to work after five years, June stayed for the next twenty. Many staff members stayed with M.B. Byles & Co. their entire working lives.

Staff members were encouraged to nominate a charity that a proportion of their quarterly bonus could go to, although this did cause some adverse reaction. Marie also began a charities account where a percentage of the profits were spread around various conservation and community groups. Not a day went by when a letter either of request or thanks came in. She donated her services as honorary solicitor to a range of community groups including: women's organisations, conservation organisations and later on, Buddhist organisations. Deciding that she needed only a certain amount to live on, Marie paid herself a small wage, enough to keep body and soul together. About her philosophy she wrote: 'I never made a fortune; I am not one of those who have this ability; besides, I have never wanted to for there are more interesting things to be done.'

DURING THE war years, barriers to women entering the legal profession in New South Wales weakened marginally due to the acute manpower shortages. In the period 1941–1950 only 48 women were admitted, an average of just over three a year. For women, wartime public service meant employment in the legal profession at a time when private practice was not easily secured. To provide each other support, from 1941, women lawyers in Sydney began meeting informally at the Feminist Club in King Street. Their aim was to develop a network of support to compensate for their exclusion from the men's clubs. Male practitioners were advantaged by social contact within the club system, where they met and made new clients. Male networks extended to community groups, sporting bodies, clubs, associations and organisations covering a wide range of activities.

A woman's opportunity for contact was far more restricted. The common meeting ground for most women provided little client potential: church activities and community welfare projects. Women were excluded from most organisations – even the Rotary Club did not allow women members, and neither did the University Club. Women lawyers were unable to enjoy the same benefits as their male counterparts through relaxed social encounters and, as a minority group with no formal structure, remained outside the mainstream professionally. It was this lack of opportunity and need for stimulation and support from others in similar situations that prompted women lawyers to meet in order to share legal problems, hear guest speakers and join in discussions relevant to the legal issues of their time.

As a long-term advocate for women's advancement Marie was involved in these meetings from the beginning and spoke with great conviction. Considered a legend by the younger women, she was highly respected for having established a successful practice on merit, showing it could be done. Most of the women felt that membership of an association would give them strength to survive in a hostile environment but, while Marie contributed to these informal meetings and was willing to support individual women who were interested in law, she adamantly resisted the idea of an association for women lawyers. Her attitude was that lawyers were lawyers. They all did the same examinations and all had the same attributes, so why create a specific entity when they were part of the one legal profession? Despite, or because of, the challenges she had overcome throughout her career, Marie maintained an expectation of success. She *knew* she was going to be successful and was void of doubt. To her, identifying as marginalised went totally against the grain.*

The success of her law practice meant that she had no need for the networking opportunities the association offered, but she actively mentored young women who needed support. Typical of these was Margaret Crawley who, as a student in her second year of Law at the University of Sydney in 1947, was frustrated by her inability to obtain articles. With the war over, the returned servicemen accounted for a renewed difficulty for females to qualify with articles – in Crawley's year there were 400 male students to nine women. She applied to 72 law firms only to be blatantly informed, 'We don't employ women!' She later reminisced, 'In those days it was very, very hard for women to become articled; firms did not want women.' Fortunately a mutual friend, a judge, mentioned Crawley's predicament to Marie who, after an interview and the usual formalities, took her on for three

---

* The Women Lawyers Association of NSW formed in 1952.

years of articles. Through this, Marie ensured her place in posterity as the first female master solicitor to a female articled clerk in Australia.

Perhaps if Marie had not been so determinedly opposed to joining an association of women lawyers, she could have benefited from the emotional support it provided. While her obsessive personality helped her excel professionally, it was this aspect most likely to cause psychological stress and exhaustion. Seeking insight into the cause of her physical and spiritual suffering she immersed herself in the writings of Carl Jung, the Swiss psychiatrist with a unique approach to psychology, who asserted that the real patient was not the individual, but a dysfunctional Western civilisation. Having read widely of Eastern philosophies that emphasised the importance of balance and harmony, Jung warned that modern people relied too heavily on science and logic. Instead, he believed it was beneficial to integrate spirituality and awareness of the unconscious realms. In order for Westerners to be cured of their inner discord, he claimed they needed to bring their subconscious into the light of consciousness by contemplating dreams and visions. He espoused that understanding the archetypal forms and symbols represented in dreams could lead to resolution of the underlying disharmony. Out of curiosity, Marie began waking in the night to record her dreams. After about six months, there was a sudden flash of understanding on a series of them. She learnt there might be a connection between her physical ailments and her subconscious state that had been deeply disturbed by the war.

> It was most humiliating to accept the revelation, for it showed what Jung calls the shadow-side, that I was a superb fool, that with my infinitesimal intellect I was worrying about how I could make the post-war world a better place to live in than the First World War had done, in other words, that humility was badly needed. The result was that the nausea disappeared within twenty-four hours. The great change of middle life demands the ending of 'I' and 'mine' and 'me'.

This was the beginning of her acceptance of the connection between the psychological and the physical: 'The festering sore between conscious and unconscious had been lanced and there was relief physical as well as mental.' Some time later she had a startling vision that she interpreted as the cross of suffering from which sprang the wings of victory.' Although this vision represented an opening of awareness, of itself it could not heal 'the darkness of the spirit'. Until it could be actualised in physical reality, it was merely a step in the process of transformation of consciousness.

The natural world gave Marie respite from her inner torment. Her reverence for it is illustrated in her reflections on a memorable visit to the Blue Gum Forest in the 1940s.

> When I was sitting there alone among the wild violets and ferns and looking down the aisles of the tall blue and white tree trunks, with impregnable cliffs towering above, I had the experience of one of those sudden glimpses of Eternity when everything fades away and lives no longer of itself but only of God. Many poets have sung of these moments. But again, it is quite another matter to live daily life amid Eternity as well as time.

Her sensitivity to nature inspired a vision of pure wilderness. Having for some years edited the NSW Federation of Bushwalking Club's annual journal, the *Bushwalker*, Marie contributed articles that outlined her changing beliefs about wilderness, beliefs that soon needed to be defended against other conservationists, in particular, Myles Dunphy. In 1932, Dunphy had formed the National Parks and Primitive Areas Council to advance the cause of national park reservation in New South Wales. Primitive areas, now referred to as wilderness, are defined as the 'last substantial remnants of the ecologically complete environment that once covered the earth.' Although his plan for a Blue Mountains National Park was Dunphy's main priority, a primitive area in the Alps with sections in NSW and Victoria was almost as desirable and should, he declared, have been done years before.*

At this stage, Marie and Myles held fundamentally different cosmological views of the world. Dunphy's initial experience of wilderness had given him a passion for the outdoors that he wanted to share with others but, according to his biographer Peter Meredith, he was at heart a recreationalist who earlier in life carried a gun on his explorations ready to shoot or bludgeon to death all venomous creatures that might pose a threat to humans. Marie, however, had by 1941 immersed herself in the study and practice of Buddhism. She believed passionately that nature had intrinsic value and was not merely for the use of humans. In the 1940s this inclination made her seem especially eccentric.

As secretary, and then president in 1947, of the NSW Federation of Bushwalking Clubs, Marie actively influenced its members to recommend that the Kosciusko primitive area discourage human intervention. She made a

---

*This plan came to fruition in 1959 when Blue Mountains National Park was gazetted including 63,000 hectares. In 2000 it was included as part of the Greater Blue Mountains World Heritage Area.

withering criticism of elitist, imperialist relations with the bush in an article published in the *Bushwalker* entitled "What Is a Primitive Area?"

> Recent discussions about the Kosciusko primitive area have revealed a definite cleavage of opinion as to what a primitive area should be.
>
> The minority opinion regards a primitive area as a place where nature-lovers may go freely in order to see the wild life in its natural state. It is to be educational, and therefore of use to human beings. It is asserted that a primitive area would serve no purpose if human beings were not to have the pleasure of seeing it. There is also the important point that perhaps the only way of keeping the wild life is to educate mankind to appreciate and enjoy it.
>
> If it is once admitted that a primitive area exists for the pleasure of human beings, then it automatically follows that facilities must be given for human beings to go into it. Perhaps roads and motorists might be excluded, but tracks, huts and pasture grounds must be arranged.
>
> … However, the vast majority of bushwalkers have ruled that a primitive area must be for the wild life, which shall flourish there, not for our pleasure, but for its own. After all, why should man in his arrogance say that primaeval lands are of value only in so far as they subserve his ends? Is not this the vicious old profit motive coming out in another form?
>
> … Cannot man for once admit that there are other things beside himself with rights, and that he is not the only being in the universe? The majority of bushwalkers say he can and should. Human beings will not be excluded from the primitive area but no facilities for entering it will be given, and the flowers may blossom and the kangaroos and wombats enjoy their lives there, whether any one sees them or not.

It was a debate that would take decades to resolve and provoked outrage in Dunphy, devastated by the 'first and only serious setback in his conservation work'. Was Marie suggesting that his beloved bush be used for the purpose of atoning for the environmental damage inflicted by humankind throughout history? Dr Geoff Mosley, a leading conservationist, states that Dunphy regarded the action of the Federation as a major betrayal. He had, Mosley believes, no comprehension that nature had rights.

This ideological conflict was symptomatic of Marie's shift in consciousness. It was not only Buddhism that formed her opinions on environmental protection. She was connected to a growing worldwide movement of environmentalists who promoted the protection of wildlife and wild country. This gave her the

Marie's parents Cyril and Ida Byles.

"Chilworth" the Byles family home in Beecroft, an Old English village-style suburb in Sydney's northwest (1912). Marie's bed was on the verandah (at left), under a wisteria vine.

Marie (front left) and parents with brothers David (centre) and Baldur (right).

Marie's crowning glory, before the haircut.

Seawards beach house on Sunrise Hill, Palm Beach, with view over to Bouddi Headland.

The Pirate Girls on Barrenjoey headland, Palm Beach (1919).

Marie walking to Mt Hay near Leura in the Blue Mountains, NSW (1918).

Graduating in law from Sydney University (1924). Cut short, her hair developed a wave, 'my one beauty'.

Palm Beach party. Marie in front (right), Nell Cusack behind her (1928)

Nell Cusack, 'a Dryad among the roots of an old Fig tree'.

Marie with group of Sydney Bush Walkers.

A cuddly encounter while bushwalking.

Maitland Bay and Bouddi Headland, on the southern tip of the NSW Central Coast.

At the wheel of the SS Eknaren, the Norwegian cargo boat that took Marie to Europe – more fun than a passenger ship. (1928).

Canadian cowboys in the Rockie Mountains (1928).

The day Marie first went on 'The Ice'. Her companion is dressed normally (for the time) in a skirt in a skirt, Marie in knickerbocker pants (1928).

Marie with guide, Alf Brustad, on the summit of Mt Cook during a blizzard (January 1929).

Marie and Marjorie with guides Alf Brusted and Arne Larsen, after the conquest of Mount Cook (1929).

Baldur surveying the High Country from Mt Townsend (1932), 'this would be the land of his future labours'.

*Snow Gum –
Southern Alps,
New South Wales.*

*Mr Barry
from Gosford
City Council
appreciating
Bouddi's natural
assets. Marie told
him, 'All the eye can
see, I want kept as a
park.' (1934)*

*Bouddi Natural
Park working bee
(1941).*

Preparing to embark up the Irrawaddy River, Burma (1938).

Mule train and porters.

Expedition members outside the temple they camped in that night.

Marie typing an article for Sydney Morning Herald *while village children look on, intrigued.*

Dora de Beer in local costume and Marjorie Jones in usual bushwalking oufit, Lijiang.

Black Dragon Pool, Lijiang (picture postcard perfect).

Marie eating with chopsticks, delighted at mastering the technique.

Sansato Massif, Yunnan Province, the goal is in sight.

Marie and friends on Ahimsa verandah.

Ahimsa, Marie's basic fibro house in an ideal setting in Cheltenham.

Ahimsa sign, welcoming all.

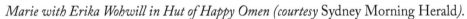

Marie with Erika Wohwill in Hut of Happy Omen (courtesy Sydney Morning Herald*).*

Meditation group at Leo Berkeley's house. Leo on seat at back (left) with Marie and Natasha Jackson in front of him (1949).

Sr Dhammadina with group at Leo Berkeley's house (1952).

Ven. U Thittila with members of the Buddhist Society of NSW visiting the Vihara land in Pennant Hills (1956).

When the sun was shining in winter Marie preferred to work on the front steps of the office in Eastwood (1940s).

Berangie Chambers, Marie's new office building, under construction in Eastwood (1956).

Marie's kuti at Maha Bodhi Meditation Centre, Mandalay (1957).

U Thein, Vipassana meditation teacher.

Marie (under umbrella) and Sarana travelling by bullock wagon to Sagaing Hills, Burma (1957).

Marie showing respect for Burmese monks.

Tenko San the founder of Ittoen community.

Marie performing "takuhatsu", roadside service, with members of Ittoen community (1963).

Enjoying Ahimsa's peaceful surroundings.

Marie lived, worked and slept on Ahimsa's verandah. On the wall is a notice declaring her life was not to be extended artificially.

strength to stand up to a powerful figure like Dunphy, known as "the father of conservation" in Australia.

The struggle to maintain Kosciusko's integrity as a wilderness or primitive area was a battle that Marie was prepared to put time and effort into, but her drive to achieve outcomes created conflict. Coming on top of an ever-increasing workload, her community work tested her resources. From 1946, 'the strain and tension got worse'. In a state of physical, emotional and mental exhaustion, she was headed for burnout.

When the pressure overwhelmed her, Marie took the train to Kiama on the south coast and stayed with bushwalking friends and kindred spirits, Rae and Peter Page. Since the war, the Pages had lived an alternative lifestyle on a small farm near the top of the mountain at Jamberoo, inland from Kiama. They grew their own food and Rae bred goats that provided milk and cheese for the locals who drove from as far as Kiama to collect it. They also built cabins they rented out to their bushwalking friends. The view from their house on the side of the mountain at an elevation of 700 m, stretched all the way to Shellharbour on the coast. Marie visited several times a year for two or three days over weekends or for two or three weeks, depending on her health. Peter picked her up at Kiama station in his old jeep and hoped he could get her up the steep and winding mountain road alive because she was so sick. In later years Rae reminisced:

> It used to do her good to come here. I think her innards were upset … Marie always had to eat very little and very often. There was something wrong with her stomach and I think also she worked too hard and she gave of herself a lot to her clients.

Only if it teemed with rain did Marie stay in the house. Instead, she camped down the hill in a clearing in the forest she called 'lyrebird glen'. Peter and Rae had done many bushwalks with Marie and were familiar with her idiosyncratic need for independence. She often camped alone outside of the group. In lyrebird glen she sat outside the tent in the early morning and late afternoon watching for those enchanting birds that would spread their impressive tails and mimic every other bird and noise in the forest. There she would meditate in the peace and solitude.

Rae noted, 'She used to declare that you had to lose yourself and she said she could, that she was entirely shut off from the rest of the world.'

Marie urged Rae to meditate with her but Rae found it too difficult to still her mind. Instead, she tried to convince Marie that, 'when I work in the garden or work outside I feel as though I have meditated because I am accepting what is coming'. But Marie disagreed with Rae, insisting she was not doing it correctly. There was only one way, the right way. As Rae observed, 'She had a great gentleness about her when she wanted to, yet she could be very, very dominant.'

They often walked together along the lush rainforest road with its dark jungle vegetation highlighted by bright green fern trees. In the rarefied air at the top of the mountain they strolled through the flat heathland with its mass of wildflowers in springtime and came to the ridge that overlooked Kiama. Below was a sudden drop into an escarpment of rainforest and waterfalls with spectacular views of the Illawarra coastline and surrounding countryside. Marie became enamoured of the area and its abundant bird life (an ornithologist had counted 38 different birds outside his cabin), and declared that this state-owned land should be a reserve. She invited the Minister for Lands to visit the area with her. Together, they addressed a meeting of the district's farmers about its value as a reserve.*

The peace and serenity of Jamberoo was so restorative that, when an adjoining property of 80 hectares came up for sale in 1947, Marie conceived the idea of buying the land and creating a Buddhist community there. Having a place to meditate with others would give her the support she needed and refuge from the 'greedy business world and the heavy burden of other people's problems that a family lawyer must always shoulder.'

After lengthy negotiations the owners of the land at Jamberoo refused to sell, perhaps because Marie tried to bargain them down too aggressively.

This was her second attempt to create a Buddhist community. According to Paul Croucher in *A History of Buddhism in Australia*, her first attempt the year before, was ill fated.

> As early as 1946 Marie Byles had plans to develop a Buddhist Retreat Centre with a Dr Chalmers, a Mount Stromlo astronomer, and his wife, who owned 900 acres [364 ha] of land on a 3000 ft [914 m] mountain plateau near Shelley in Victoria. They advertised their intentions to this effect in the May 1946 edition of The Middle Way, and Marie tried to recruit some of her bushwalking friends, but why the plan fell through is not known. Although the Chalmers, like Marie Byles, were keen naturalists, they were basically Zen-oriented, and

---

*Eventually, Barren Grounds Nature Reserve was established in 1956 with an area of 2024 hectares.

so there may have been some friction on this count, given her Theravadin leanings. What is perhaps more likely is that the centre was conceived of only by correspondence, and when the Chalmers actually met her they were put off by her somewhat domineering personality.

While Marie knew that Buddha's teachings were beneficial to all, including Westerners, her intentions were often thwarted by her inability to maintain interpersonal relationships.

As Rae Page observed, 'She couldn't work with a group of people. She was an individual and, unless everything went her way, she would pull out and not have anything to do with it which was a great pity … but that was her way.'

Paradoxically, it was her friends who tolerated her abrasiveness, who blessed her with the human kindness that sustained her.

CHAPTER 11

No Peace to be Found

1946 –1953

LIKE RAE Page, Erika Wohlwill was a gentle, loving person attracted to Marie's active energy. Erika and her husband Max were refugees from Germany whom Marie had met through the Quakers. Max, an industrial chemist, was a close friend of Rudi Lemberg. Both men were confirmed pacifists, as were many of the European refugees, having experienced the destruction of the Great War. Marie gave employment to Erika as a registration clerk and Erika spent every spare moment she could at Ahimsa when she was not looking after her family of four children. Often borrowing books from Marie's library, she sometimes ignored her family responsibilities and spent the night there enjoying the intellectual stimulation Marie provided. Erika was a loving person whose spiritual affinity was through the heart. But Marie glorified the intellect and was adamant that heart did not come into it.

Erika noted, 'She always said, "No, no heart." She didn't want any tenderness or any of that sort of thing.'

The Buddha advocated the Noble Eightfold Path, a practical guide to ethical and mental development with the goal of freeing the individual from attachments and delusions. Attachments produce suffering and the karma that ensures constant rebirth on the wheel of life. A particular trap for Westerners following Buddhist teachings is to interpret non-attachment as meaning non-emotional. Marie interpreted the teaching this way which reinforced her inclination to emotional suppression. To her, emotions were disruptive and incompatible with spiritual growth.

When Erika returned from a meditation retreat at the Catholic convent in Rose Bay, she told Marie of the wonderful experience she'd had, kneeling down, talking to God. Marie's immediate reaction was, 'We can build our own retreat centre here!'

It was a practical solution to a practical problem. A Quaker architect friend prepared the plans for a basic three-sided sleep-out to be built on a rise twenty metres from Marie's house. Friends helped in the construction. The unlined fibro structure resembled a mountain hut with double bunks along two walls. The focus of the room was an impressive open stone fireplace that had an arch modelled over half an old corrugated-iron tank. The three wise monkeys took pride of place on the mantelpiece. The Hut of Happy Omen, as Marie named it, became well known throughout Sydney. Inspired by Buddhist notions of service to others she made it accessible to a wide range of groups and people on the spiritual path. At the time there were virtually no facilities that were not church-based available in which to meditate or use for a silent retreat. The Hut provided peace in a quiet and natural setting that nurtured and rewarded those who were drawn to it.

Although she was intensely interested in Buddhism, there was no organised group of Buddhists in Australia at the time that Marie could connect with and from whom she could gain support. By the end of World War II, Buddhism had hardly penetrated Western culture. As James William Coleman writes in *The New Buddhism*:

> A few intellectuals knew something of Buddhist philosophy, but it was often misunderstood or interpreted ... Real Buddhist practice was even more rare. There were only a handful of qualified teachers, and even those few had to water down their practice or risk driving off the students they had managed to attract. While many Westerners were drawn to the 'mysteries of the East', there was little appetite for the years of hard practice necessary to follow the Buddhist path to its fruition.

Marie relied on the Quaker weekly meetings to deepen her practice of peaceful reflection, but it was not enough for her to sit peacefully in touch with the Divine Presence. She was inspired to share what she had learnt from other spiritual paths. When she first became interested in the spiritual life, she often heard the assertion that Christianity was the only true religion. Her sense of justice rebelled, especially as she believed that Mahatma Gandhi was a towering spiritual genius and he was a Hindu. Ever since her first exposure to Buddhism in Burma, the teachings had appealed to her because it made no demands upon credulity. The Buddha said nothing was to be believed unless and until one could prove it out of one's own experience. With her discerning legal mind, Marie was drawn to the logical, rational nature of this training that had such practical application in daily life. She also found an irresistible role model in Gautama, the Buddha, as he radiated love, kindness, peace and truth. Gautama was born an ordinary man who made extraordinary efforts to transcend his human limitations.

In 1947, when she applied for membership of the Quakers, she wrote in her letter of application, that, while she desired to be a Quaker, she was a Buddhist too. The process of acceptance required the appointment of two representatives to interview her. During this meeting, she expanded on her beliefs and described her level of moral and spiritual aspiration. To the Quaker representatives, it was obvious that she was clearly not a Christian. The Quakers never vote on issues; they merely wait for guidance from the spirit. If something doesn't feel right, they use the expression, 'Not in Right Ordering'. Fearful that her dominant nature would create conflict among them, with these words, Marie's application was rejected. Her friends were convinced it was because she wore pants. This rejection caused Marie acute pain. It served, however, to 'throw me more firmly into the arms of the Buddhists. I even got known abroad as the representative in Australia of Buddhism!'

She read everything she could but remained dissatisfied with the material that communicated the essence of Buddha's teachings to Westerners. While there were many books with the legends that surrounded his birth, youth and death, there were none about his teaching life. There were learned discourses that made his teaching seem difficult and anthologies that purported to give his actual words, but did not show him as a living being teaching men and women. Accepting that Westerners, including herself, were not interested in Buddha as a legendary figure, Marie considered writing such a biography that expounded his actual teaching as given to his disciples. Her intention was confirmed by a conversation with a woman in a train who said, 'Buddhism! Oh, that's far too deep for me. I can't understand it at all.' The book she planned to write was entitled *Footprints of Gautama the Buddha*, because it would show how the lives of men and women were touched and altered by his teaching.

Through the Melbourne Public Library, Marie accessed a rare complete set of the English translations of the Pali Canon, the sacred books of the Buddhists. Immersing herself in this study, she focused on creating stories about the people whom the Buddha taught. She also corresponded with the eminent English

Buddhist scholar, F.L. Woodward, the author of an accessible introduction to Buddhism for many Westerners, *Some Sayings of the Buddha*, one of the first books Marie had read on the subject. Woodward lived like a mystic on an isolated orchard outside of Launceston, Tasmania, in order to devote himself to translating the ancient Buddhist texts written on thousands of palm-leaves that he had collected. To have this eminent scholar in close proximity was of great assistance to her.

The articles Marie wrote for international journals helped to popularise Buddhism, as she reinterpreted the teachings for a contemporary Western audience, and they made her a prominent figure. In 1948, Leo Berkeley, a prominent Sydney businessman, approached her about forming a Buddhist society. As an immigrant who had left Europe before the war, Dutch-born Berkeley (who had changed his name from Berkelouw) had prospered with the family's antiquarian bookshops. He then established a successful clothing business in Sydney. Once the war was over he took a boat trip to England to visit family. On the boat he and his wife made acquaintance with Sri Lanka's Minister of Justice, who was returning from a Commonwealth Law Conference in Australia. During the course of their conversation, Sir Lalita Rajapakse, a devout Buddhist, made reference to a verse from the Dhammapada, an anthology of verses spoken by the Buddha. It struck a chord with Leo.

> By ourselves is evil done; by ourselves we pain endure.
> By ourselves we cease from ill; by ourselves become we pure.
> No one can save us but ourselves, no one can and no one may.
> We ourselves must walk the Path; Buddhas only point the way.

A self-made millionaire, Leo always believed that each person created his or her life and destiny. He asked his new friend to tell him more about aspects of Buddha's teachings, known as the Dhamma. Sir Lalita suggested Leo and his wife come the next day when they docked in Colombo to meet a learned monk he knew. The monk turned out to be the Venerable Narada Maha Thera, a highly respected, university-educated author of numerous books and articles on Buddhist teachings who had travelled widely throughout Asia and the West. During their discussions, Venerable Narada suggested to Leo that he could establish a Buddhist society in Australia. Soon after returning to Sydney, Leo read about Marie Byles' interest in Buddhism in the *Sydney Morning Herald* and contacted her. When he brought up the idea of a society she apparently dismissed it with, 'Oh, Mr Berkeley, Australians are not yet ready for the teaching of the Buddha.'

Leo replied, 'Miss Byles, if you are ready and I am ready, we can start together an association.'

He put an advertisement in the *SMH* and twenty people responded. Each Sunday night the group gathered at his house in East Roseville on Sydney's Upper North Shore to study the Dhamma. A photograph taken of the group at this time shows most of them were middle-aged with the men dressed in suits.

Marie became close friends with Leo and his wife Lummechien. According to their son Klaas, they both had great respect for Marie, valuing her forthrightness and honesty. Their association would last many years and make a profound impact on the introduction of Buddhist teachings to Australia. During their regular meditation evenings, the group practised Anapana Sati, awareness of the breath, a technique that turns awareness inward to each moment. However, these hourly sittings were insufficient to gain the full benefits of the technique that required sustained periods of concentration. Weekend retreats were organised. The first recorded intensive meditation retreat with seven people attending was on 11–13 February 1949, at a house in the picturesque garden town of Leura in the upper Blue Mountains. A day of silent introspection was followed by an evening discussion on "The Buddha and the Great Law". At this stage, no ordained member of the Buddhist community had visited Australia, so a layperson like Marie, with specialist knowledge of Buddha's teachings was invaluable.

On 15 May 1949, the group celebrated Vesak at Ahimsa. Vesak is held according to the lunar calendar on the auspicious Full Moon Day of May, the day Gautama Buddha was born, became enlightened, and died in his eightieth year. In Asian communities, Vesak is often celebrated as a festival with a joyful atmosphere, enhanced by the sharing of food and decorative flowers for offerings. It is mixed with a strong devotional program that allows participants to express their deep gratitude towards Buddha and his legacy. Westerners in general are less inclined towards the devotional aspects of Buddhism and tend to take a more rationalist approach. The ceremonial or ritualistic expressions are considered to be a degeneration of Buddha's teachings that happened inevitably centuries after his death when they had been absorbed by the dominant religion of Hinduism. Marie strongly believed that the teachings should remain in their original, unadulterated form that emphasised meditation practice for mental purification and the study of the Dhamma through classic Buddhist texts. She was not inclined towards any practice of rites and rituals. On that occasion, the focus for the eighteen people present was on Readings and Meditation on the Life and Teaching of the Buddha. Significantly, this was the first time Vesak was celebrated by a group of non-Asians in Australia.

IN JANUARY 1949, the entire Byles family, including grandchildren, gathered at Seawards in Palm Beach to celebrate Ida and Cyril's golden wedding anniversary. Ida was 80, and, while physically healthy, her mind was tragically weak. Well past being able to remake her will as Marie had wished, by now she needed constant care and support with housekeeping. A bout of pleurisy two years earlier, which had been treated with penicillin to prevent the onset of pneumonia, had, Marie felt, precipitated her mother's mental decline. This convinced her that she needed to act to avert the same outcome. She left written directions that no drug was to be given to keep her alive, as she firmly believed that pneumonia ought to remain the old person's friend, as it used to be.

Cyril was naturally affected by his wife's decline and worried incessantly. Marie 'caught the contagion' and kept obsessing about what she would do if the housekeeper suddenly gave notice. In response to a newspaper advertisement for a new housekeeper, Mrs Lily Griffin came with her husband, a sea captain recently retired. Marie had her old shack glassed-in for them. As both her brothers were married with children and living outside Sydney, it was up to Marie to supervise her parents' wellbeing. The last years of their lives were extremely difficult for her and caused her health to suffer.

The continuous pain in her feet was also draining. Fortunately, she found an osteopath who was able to explain exactly why it hurt to walk and who 'gradually threw me back into the right position'. However, having more to do than she could possibly cope with, Marie still felt chronically rundown and overextended with her community work. Citing ill health, headaches and sore feet as her reasons, but with what would now be diagnosed as burnout, Marie resigned as vice-president of the NSW Federation of Bushwalking Clubs in 1950, and as honorary secretary of the Bush Club in 1951. On one of her solitary annual retreats in the Snowy Mountains in 1952, she contemplated resigning from the Bouddi Trust, as she was no longer mobile enough to supervise the maintenance work at the park.

> The tent was beside the glorious swift flowing river near Adaminaby, the fertile valley that would soon be flooded by the Snowy River Hydro Electric Scheme which would leave only the barren soil, eroded slopes and the forests of ringbarked trees bleaching under the blue sky. Perhaps it was a scene suitable to learn the lesson that we can keep nothing of the world. I could no longer walk well, no longer inspire the work for Bouddi Natural Park which had been 'my baby'. I must give up the trusteeship. No-one else would love my parkland as I did. No-one knows what it cost me to give it up.

Temperamentally, Marie was not one to participate from the sidelines giving support and advice; it was all or nothing. Her decision to resign from the Bouddi Trust effectively ended her active involvement with the conservation movement.

AS OUTDOOR activities decreased, Marie's involvement in Buddhism increased. She frequently hosted visiting Buddhists from overseas. With her ecumenical inclination, she invited friends from various religious backgrounds to come and hear them speak at Ahimsa. In September 1951, David Maurice, an Australian-born Buddhist of international regard whom Marie had been corresponding with, visited from his home in Burma. His visit contributed to coalescing the small groups of people in Sydney and Melbourne interested in furthering their knowledge and practice of Dhamma. Maurice was a unique and distinctive figure in Western Buddhism, having immersed himself in it from the age of twelve. After university he travelled to Burma and stayed for 34 years, working for a variety of companies and becoming a high-ranking government public servant. He chose to live simply like the Burmese in a thatched bamboo hut; Marie's home and the Hut of Happy Omen would have been admirable to him.

While Maurice had acquired a thorough knowledge of the Pali Canon (Pali being the language of many of the earliest Buddhist scriptures) and the fundamentals of Theravadin Buddhism, it was his knowledge of meditation that made him of interest to Marie. He had studied meditation with many teachers in Burma, in particular Mahasi Sayadaw, a renowned teacher of Vipassana meditation, the practical method of Buddha's path of mindfulness. Present to meet him at Ahimsa on 9 September 1951 were a few of the group who met at Leo Berkeley's. A month later, on 18 November, David Maurice was again present at Ahimsa to lead a retreat on "Calming the Heart Within". On 17 December, he led a retreat entitled "Meditation as in a Burmese Monastery".

Although Marie gained invaluable support from meditation, it was not enough to prevent the decline in her health. She later reflected on this time as 'floundering in the Slough of Despond':

> Life seemed to consist mainly of worry, struggle and depression, straining after the right way and endless failure. Often it seemed like groping without a path through an endless forest on a dark night, with only an occasional break between the trees and clouds to show that a star of peace did exist.

A lot of Marie's problems though, were self-made. Her inability to suffer fools gladly meant that she did not have as much patience with her clients as she might have. Marie was explicitly forthright in her dealings with people, often brutally so and liked to have the last word. When clients came into the office, they would ask Ruth, 'Is Miss Byles in?' When she replied affirmatively, the client would often say, 'Oh, I don't really want to see her. Can I see you?' They preferred to deal with Ruth, because she was more patient and considerate , but lacked the necessary legal qualifications.

As the business grew throughout the 1940s and '50s, so did the size of the staff and the bonuses, which regularly reached £100 a quarter. But the money was no compensation for Ruth who, besides doing the books, was also responsible for much of the conveyancing and probate work. She later commented, 'I was working far too hard and she expected far too much of me ... I almost had a couple of nervous breakdowns in the office because the pace was really more than I could cope with.' At one point Ruth took extended sick leave. Marie fretted about not having a bookkeeper at this time, but was fortunate to find a highly trained replacement, Peg Willis, who became a permanent member of staff. Peg was a single mother from England who had taught shorthand at Pitman's Business College in London and brought a new level of professionalism to the office. She was earthy and practical and could withstand the pressure Marie placed on her.

By 1952, the extra staff made the small two-roomed office space they occupied in Eastwood feel like a 'mousetrap'. In winter when the sun was shining, Marie organised a desk onto the front doorstop and worked from there. One day, Ruth pointed to the vacant block next door and suggested to Marie that she build her own office building. 'By Jove, you've got it!' said Marie, who set about organising the financing. Floating a private company, Berangie Pty Ltd. ("berangie" being an Aboriginal word meaning "friend"), Marie cajoled a few friends and relatives to join the staff in taking up shares. Having achieved this, there was the difficulty of getting a permit to build; 1952 was still considered to be post-war and building materials were restricted. As she did with Ahimsa, Marie involved herself in every aspect of the design and had a bushwalker architect friend put it into proper shape. Her main criterion for the new building was that it caught every possible ray of sunshine.

The building project was totally absorbing and, on top of this, the post-war housing boom saw her legal workload increase rapidly. At an age when Marie would have been undergoing menopause, the strain weakened her health to the point where she practically collapsed at lunchtime. Ruth Milton verified Marie's condition:

… She certainly was very depressed and each day at lunchtime she would go out of the office for at least an hour, sometimes longer and she would go and lie in the backyard of Mrs Haber who lived not far away. Or if the weather was not good, there was a couch we had upstairs and she would go and lie there to meditate, but I feel some of it was depression and great disappointment because the operation on her foot had not been successful. And in the office she would get very tired and we were always making her cups of tea or quite often she would say, 'I've got a bad head, I'll have to lie down'.

Maria Haber was a Jewish refugee from Germany who Marie employed to clean the office. A distant relative of Albert Einstein, Maria had managed to escape from Germany before the war with her parents' blessing, never to hear from them again. Trained as a dressmaker in Berlin and Paris, Marie trusted her to help choose her office clothes. Twice a year they travelled into the city to find clothes that suited Marie's style – plain but of good quality. Often at lunchtime, Marie entered Maria's backyard by the side gate, took off her shoes and walked barefoot on the grass to relax her feet. Then she sat and meditated on the grass or if it rained, went into the workshop. Then she lay down to rest.

IN SEPTEMBER 1952 there was what Marie termed, a 'semi-comic, semi-tragic interlude', when Sister Dhammadina, an American-born Buddhist nun, arrived for a visit. Sister Dhammadina, who had been living in Sri Lanka for nearly thirty years, contacted Marie as the only person in Sydney she had heard of interested in Buddhism. Marie offered to put her up at Ahimsa. Because Baldur had just been transferred to Sydney and was staying in the guest room, she was offered the Hut of Happy Omen to sleep in. Peg Willis collected Sister Dhammadina from the airline office in the city and brought her to Eastwood where Marie accompanied her home. In the taxi she impressed the elderly nun with her knowledge of the Buddhist scriptures by comparing Sister Dhammadina to Punna, the missionary of the Buddha's time, who was prepared to meet anger and even death. Marie, who was a literalist in her interpretation of the Buddhist rules for monks and nuns, assumed Sister Dhammadina would conform to her idealised image of a renunciate. Instead, she was horrified by the amount of luggage the taxi driver unloaded and carried up to the Hut.

There was suitcase after suitcase, and not just the needle and thread and other personal effects that one of Buddha's Order was allowed. I had read the Buddhist scriptures fairly extensively by now and was familiar with the four requisites – rags for robes, scraps for food, tree roots for lodgings, and a common village remedy for medicine. The Hut of Happy Omen was luxurious compared with tree roots, and Baldur had made it comfortable by hanging heavy curtains for privacy…and making a track to the sentry box latrine, while I had provided an excellent commode and all conveniences.

The 71-year-old took one look at the "beautiful Hut" and threw up her hands in horror.

'Oh, I couldn't stay here; it's got no windows or doors!'

'But you lived in caves in Ceylon,' I protested.

'But they have windows and doors. I couldn't possibly stay here, and all my things would get stolen.'

Sister Dhammadina had lived in the Forest Hermitage above Kandy, in the centre of Sri Lanka, built by a wealthy benefactress, Lady de Silva. Although basic, the Hermitage would not have conformed to Marie's concept of a lifestyle in existence at the time of the Buddha, 2500 years before. Marie took Sister Dhammadina down to the cottage and hastily fixed up the living room for her while she gathered up her own bedding and took it to the Hut. Leo Berkeley arranged alternative accommodation for her in an apartment with two other women who were not as staunchly vegetarian as she was. One night she smelled meat cooking and demanded to know, 'Is there a corpse incinerating in here?'

On Sunday evenings at the Berkeleys' house in Roseville, Sister Dhammadina conducted Dhamma talks and meditation sessions for between fifteen and twenty people. A charismatic and articulate speaker, she was the first member of a Buddhist order to teach in Australia and soon attracted a growing number of interested people.

Graeme Lyall was a young man eager to learn to meditate. He made several fruitless phone calls to find out if there were any Buddhist organisations in Sydney. He then contacted the Theosophical Society who informed him that an elderly American Buddhist nun had just arrived in Australia. He rang her at the home of Leo Berkeley and asked if he could attend her next talk. Sister Dhammadina replied, 'Yes you can attend my group.'

Graeme sat in a chair at the back of Leo Berkeley's living room while others sat on the floor. He was taken aback when a strange apparition entered, a woman with no hair wearing a yellow robe. Sister Dhammadina immediately demanded, 'Which one is Mr Lyall?'

'That's me, Sister,' Graeme responded.

'Well, if you can't sit properly, get out of the room!'

The others were horrified by her antagonism, but Graeme didn't object. After the session Sister Dhammadina came over to him and said, 'You passed my test. If you'd been insulted you would make no progress in Buddhism.'

Graeme found her to be a very good speaker and teacher. He remembers, 'There were all kinds of stories circulating about her origins, that she had been married to a general of the Russian czar, had been educated at the Sorbonne, and was reputedly a member of the family that owned Standard Oil. I can well believe that she came from a well-to-do background. She was very well educated and had a cultured American accent.'

Marie reflected on her own impressions of this enigmatic personality:

Whatever Sr. Dhammadina's faults, she was brave and fearless... She was seventy-two years of age and had suffered a severe injury so that she had to wear a metal support for her back. It had been hard to bear the excruciating pain and hard to accept the remedy, but one day she took up the metal support and kissed it. All life is suffering, and she would thenceforth bear it.

I do not know what impression she made on Sydney audiences, but the fact was that when she left, a little Buddhist society had been started in Sydney.

On Saturday 25 October 1952, the Buddhist Society of New South Wales came into being, a historic event for Buddhism in Australia. A committee was formed, with Leo Berkeley, as its principal benefactor and instigator, elected president. It was agreed that the Pali Canon should be the basis of the society's studies and publications and it was decided to publish a quarterly journal entitled *Buddhist News*. The society thrived and paved the way for many future visits by members of the Sangha who adhered more strictly to the Buddha's guidelines for monks and nuns.

Soon after the Buddhist Society was formed they had a visit from the police Special Squad wanting to know if Buddhism was connected with communism. This was during the McCarthy era when, as the threat of the Cold War increased, those with progressive tendencies were accused of being communists or communist sympathisers. Graeme Lyall recalls, 'They thought we were part of the dominoes that were going to fall in Asia and this was Communism getting in by the back door by calling itself Buddhism.'

IN NOVEMBER of 1952, Marie wrote, 'When the azaleas were in flower and the streets and gardens were a mass of spring blooms and sweet scents, Father passed into a coma and then into death.' By this stage Ida had forgotten her husband. A Unitarian minister conducted a service at the crematorium.

As Cyril had especially requested, there was no public announcement and no flowers. Marie honoured this request and his only other one, that his ashes be scattered under the signal box at Redfern Railway Station close to Eveleigh headquarters.

By 1953, Ida needed a 24-hour carer. Marie shouldered all the burden of her mother's care, but unlike most women of her generation, she was a busy professional woman. The additional strain tested her dwindling personal resources. After months of searching she found a nursing home in Eastwood that would accept Ida. Bicycling over every day, it became increasingly difficult to force her body to struggle up the hills, but an enormous responsibility had been taken from her mind: 'Mother had forgotten her husband even before he died. Next she forgot her sons, but she remembered her first baby until about September. Then she forgot me too.'

This was the final straw. Having lost respect for Ida long ago, Marie could not restrain herself from getting cranky with her mother for behaving 'like a silly old woman'. Unable to take the strain any longer, Marie employed a partner to take care of the office and booked ship's passage for a year's holiday in India.

Before the boat left in October, Ida passed peacefully away 'with that same smile on her face she had always worn'. Her timely death was her final act of accommodation; it allowed Marie to attend her funeral before she left. There was no Unitarian minister now and Baldur, who made the cremation arrangements, engaged the local Presbyterian minister to take the funeral. When the minister spoke about being saved by the blood of the Lamb, Marie could see her mother's ghost arising in horror at what she would have regarded as blasphemy. Marie wrote, 'I was hysterical with misery.'

It would be a long time before she could remember her mother in a kindly light and reflect on 'what a very wonderful woman my mother was in her earlier years'. Of Ida's early life, she recalled 'the vigorous, heretical young woman who refused to wear skirts trailing in the mud' before she became the 'self-effacing servant of us all'. Ida's inability to assert her own individuality in the face of Cyril's opposition was, Marie felt, 'an indication of her one great weakness which was to lead to greater tragedy [senility]. She was not able to distinguish between "turning the other cheek" and being a doormat, and there is a very great difference indeed.'

CHAPTER 12

Lead Kindly Light

1953–1954

'IN OCTOBER 1953 ten years of strain and suffering, physical and mental, lay behind me, and the sea voyage brought no improvement,' Marie reflected. Due to the war and her parents' infirmity it had been fourteen years since her last overseas trip, but she was not as enthusiastic as she had been on previous expeditions. On board the SS *Carpentaria* she spent most of her time looking at the sea and meditating. The only book she brought for the journey was the *Tao Te Ching*, hoping to find guidance and inspiration in its ancient wisdom. A text attributed to the venerable Chinese philosopher Lao Tzu, the *Tao Te Ching* attempts to capture the dynamic cosmic forces at work in the world. Being in harmony with those forces brings peace and profound learning, whereas being in opposition, trying to bend things to individual will, brings pain. This was the sense of harmony that Marie was hoping to discover on her visit to the East.

Apart from regaining her health, she had three objectives for the journey. The first was a pilgrimage to the sacred places where Buddha had lived and taught in northern India to absorb the atmosphere for the book she was writing, *Footprints of Gautama the Buddha*. The second objective was a visit to Gandhi's ashram in the centre of India to see how much of the Mahatma's influence remained. The third was to find a teacher of meditation and a meditation ashram. The first two objectives she would accomplish successfully; the third would elude her.

Sceptical as to the value of a guru insisted upon by Indian religious traditions, Marie was more interested in Burmese Buddhist meditation because of its scientific approach. Although her first two objectives lay in India, when the ship stopped at Rangoon, she hoped she would find an appropriate Burmese meditation centre to learn to meditate. She met up with David Maurice, who took her through alleys to the little bamboo monastery where he had learnt meditation. They discovered that the instructor under whom he had studied was now dead. Marie first visited Shwe Dagon Pagoda in 1938, but then she knew nothing of Buddha or his teachings and had not the slightest interest in them. Then, apart from legal work, there was only one dominant objective – the climbing of mountain peaks. This time she came as a believer. While sitting at the foot of a Buddha statue she watched as the faithful came to take refuge in the Buddha, the Dhamma, and the Sangha, much as Catholics might say their Hail Marys, noting, 'The troubled heart seeks refuge under different names, but it is the same refuge it finds.'

The next day she met with the eminent Buddhist scholar, Francis Story, an Englishman who had lived mostly in the East since the end of World War II and had become a monk in 1948. Marie invited him to lunch on the boat and afterwards he took her to visit a nunnery. Qualified to comment, Story observed that there was much more genuine devotion among the nuns than the monks. However, Marie reflected,

> No special respect is paid to them as it is to monks, and they are not members of the Sangha or Order as they were in the Buddha's day. They are humble, ordinary folk. Perhaps for this very reason, those we met were altogether charming … The head nun, who was fifty-nine, had a look of great sweetness and inner peace seemed to shine from her eyes. 'Yes, nuns were sometimes arahats in the Buddha's day', she said sadly, 'but not now.'

Looking at her, Marie felt the nun might be near to being an enlightened person herself.

On her last day in port, Marie visited the Sulay Pagoda where she sat in one of the shrines and meditated while watching people come in and out. Around the top of the walls was a frieze illustrating the stories from the Buddha's life. Its central theme was his calm serene figure amid the troubles of the world. She was left with the impression of Buddha's radiant joy, tranquillity and purity. If the way to study meditation in Burma had opened up she would have returned there, but it did not. She proceeded to mystic India. For those interested in the spiritual search, India holds an eternal attraction. There is an unparalleled diversity of customs, thought and ways of life in a country where every religion of the world is represented, many having originated there, and flourishes in comparative harmony.

For anyone, a first encounter with India, especially in a big overcrowded city like Calcutta where there is so much poverty, can be overwhelming. Travelling alone makes India harder, especially for a woman. It is made harder still when coping with depression, as low energy, negative thoughts and lack of motivation multiply the naturally occurring difficulties of this challenging country. After five days, 'an intolerable feeling of loneliness' that had been with her since landing, persisted. Marie resorted to reciting Christian hymns, 'but such meditation did not dispel the gloom'.

At the first ashram she visited, Marie met two American women, novice nuns who studied under a swami. According to their description, his practice of the spiritual way was accompanied by much ritual and ceremony. Marie knew that it was obviously not the place for her. She was conscious of the American women travelling through India safe in the arms of their church with everything arranged for them. In contrast, she 'would not know from day to day what would happen, and there would never be anyone to take care of me. The body was still far from well and the disintegrating power of self-pity made it worse.'

Through a chance connection, she was taken to meet a guru passing through Calcutta. The air was filled with the ceaseless beating of drums as she was ushered into a huge, colourful Shamiana tent. Led through the crowd of devotees to a seat next to His Holiness dressed in a loincloth, a rosary of huge wooden beads and two white markings on his forehead. 'Intense longing and devotion shone from the faces of all … It was the darshan of a saint. They were gathering a tiny spark of the grace that he had accumulated during many myriad lives of goodness…' Afterwards, Marie spoke with the guru's personal assistant and asked him whether a guru was necessary for a spiritual aspirant. He replied that a guru was not essential but that progress was speedier with one. Marie thought this was probably correct.

After a week in Calcutta, witnessing the most beautiful religious ceremonies she had ever seen but that affected her not at all, and managing to avoid the mass psychology of crowds pressing towards their Holy Ones for blessings, she remained in accord with Gandhi's dictum, 'There is no Guru but God.'

On 30 November 1953, Marie set forth by train for northern India, the land the Buddha trod. Falling in love with Varanasi, she stayed for two weeks and then took the train north to Rajgiri in Bihar state. Rajgiri is situated on what was the site of the ancient city of Rajagaha where King Bimbisara noticed

Siddhartha Gautama walking by soon after giving up his royal status to go forth into homelessness on his quest for enlightenment. The king was so struck by his regal appearance, physical beauty and grace, that he made an offer to Siddhartha to remain in Rajagaha and be his heir. Siddhartha explained that he had given up his own royal inheritance to achieve Final Deliverance from suffering. He would pursue this quest on behalf of all beings until it was attained. The king wished him well and invited him to return once he had succeeded in order to hear the truths he would reveal.

Six years later, Siddhartha, the fully enlightened Buddha, entered the city to fulfil that promise. King Bimbisara gratefully offered him the site of a bamboo grove to use as a retreat for his monks. Wandering through the same dense grove, Marie pictured the robed monks sitting among the giant bamboos, per-haps in thatched shelters where they sat in meditation during the heat of the day, with the multitudes listening in rapt attention as Buddha unfolded the Eightfold Way 'which brings peace and happiness to them that follow it'.

From Rajgiri she made the 100 km bus trip to the location of Buddha's enlightenment under the Bodhi tree at Bodh Gaya. Arriving late at night and unable to arouse attention, she parked her sleeping bag on the verandah of the Burmese pilgrim guesthouse and went to sleep hungry. The next day, after managing to arrange some breakfast, she made her way to the main temple next to the Bodhi tree that Siddhartha had sat under on the night of the full moon of May. Tibetan pilgrims prostrated themselves full length around the temple complex, but the hubbub faded away as she was back with Siddhartha. Taking a position under the great tree he had declared, 'My bones and sinews may rot away, but I will not leave this seat until I have seen the light.'

Throughout the long night of intense meditation, Siddharta resisted the enticing visions of pleasure and comforts that Mara, the personification of human desire and human failings, conjured for him to distract him from his efforts. As he sat resolved and unmoving, his mind became calm and still. From the depths of this silent stillness came the insights that transformed him. Existing in a state of bliss that had arisen since his full realisation, Siddhartha sat meditating under the tree for weeks before he struggled with the question of whether it would be possible to communicate the truths he had discovered to others or whether attachment to sense pleasures excluded them from appre-ciating deeper reality. Eventually, he accepted there were some who had only a thin layer of ignorance that prevented their understanding. Compassion for all suffering people overwhelmed him and he went forth to teach all who would listen. Taking up his alms bowl he travelled to Sarnath, an outlying suburb of Varanasi, where his five disciples had gathered at Isipathana Deer Park. His disciples had followed him through the six years of his austerities when, in an attempt to force a breakthrough of spiritual insight, he had starved his body to a skeleton without success. When Siddhartha realised this method was not the way to liberation and began eating to recover his strength, they left him for Sarnath, believing he could no longer take them to the final goal.

Marie's journey from Bodh Gaya to Varanasi by train was in a typically over-crowded carriage stacked with luggage and bodies asleep over them. Arriving exhausted, she gave up on the idea of going straight out to nearby Sarnath. She took a rickshaw to a hotel in the city, succumbing to the reality that is India, where confusion reigns and the fatigue of travelling demands that allowances be made. Feeling revived the next morning she took a taxi to Sarnath where, in the Isipathana Deer Park, the five disciples saw Gautama after his enlightenment walking towards them with an aura they could not ignore. After listening to his discourse on the Middle Way, they became the core of a legion of monks that built up around the Buddha and went out into the world to teach the Dhamma.

Not all of Buddha's followers who could appreciate the truth of his teachings had a direct path to full enlightenment. Marie's book, *Footprints of Gautama Buddha,* is told from the perspective of one of Buddha's early disciples, Yasa, the son of a wealthy Benares merchant, who became his first lay convert. At one point, Yasa regretted having given up the privileged life he had led, as his enjoyment of music was a great loss to him. Buddha based his Four Noble Truths on the craving that is at the core of human suffering, and Yasa's dilemma runs throughout the book. Marie used this device to describe the human condition and the inherent unsatisfactoriness of existence. Yasa's narration allowed Marie to expound the Buddha's teachings in a light, readable and personal way that engaged her readers and ensured its success, remaining in print for thirty years.

Immersing herself in the atmosphere of the sacred sites she visited, Marie wandered through the ruins of dwellings used by monks over the centuries since Buddha's death. In some places, tall, magnificently constructed and carved stupas (temples) stood in commemoration of the events that took place there. Excavated by the Archaeological Survey of India, the remains of these structures had been protected by Lord Curzon's *Ancient Monuments Act 1903*. So impressed was she with their preservation within large well-maintained parks that Marie declared, 'Lord Curzon's care of India's historical sites must have expiated a great many of Britain's sins against India!'

In the mist of early winter mornings she stood where Buddha gave his sermons. Reading between the lines of the formal accounts written down by monks a hundred years after his death, she attempted to see him as his disciples saw him hoping to find the magic – the magnetic influence – that radiated from him and drew people to him. She attempted to get as close as she could to that magic in her own search for answers.

Her next stop was Kushinagar, where Buddha breathed his last and passed into Final Nibbana (Sanskrit: nirvana). From there she visited Lumbini, Buddha's birthplace over the border in Nepal. Marie stayed at a pilgrim guest-house and slept on the stone floor of the verandah. When the sun rose, the white snows of distant peaks 7500 m high gleamed above the dark foothills. Marie declared, 'Never before have I seen mountains so remote and so ethereal as this, my first glimpse of the Himalayas.' As she gazed across at them, beyond where Siddhartha Gautama's mother gave birth to him in the fields, she wondered what parts of the legends surrounding the Buddha were historically true, sure only that the symbolic truth behind those legends was far more important.

MARIE THEN travelled by train to Sevagram, Gandhi's ashram, the training ground for his Satyagraha (non-violence) disciples. The ashram is positioned in the heart of India where the east-west and north-south railway lines intersect. Arriving at the village by pony cart on January 15, 1954, she was given a sparsely furnished room that had only a plank bed. Through the moonlit night she could see Gandhi's own kuti, a cottage made of mud, in the distance. But that is as close as she got to it for a fortnight. After breakfast on the morning of her arrival, 'ripening karma of a lifetime of worry and worship of efficiency now took effect'. Her body collapsed on the bed with every imaginable ache and pain. Tossing helplessly on the hard plank bed, Marie missed even the thin mattress usual in India. The children delegated to look after her were not capable of the level of nursing she required. She acknowledged that, while the mental agony of spending weeks in pain lying on her bed for most of the day gave her an excellent opportunity to meditate on the nature of suffering, excruciating headaches meant that her desire to get well completely overwhelmed her.

January 30 was the anniversary of Gandhi's death. In 1948, when she first heard the devastating news of his assassination, it felt to her like a personal loss. At the time she wrote, 'It is not often that I weep ... but the tears flowed copiously ... the news seemed completely to unhinge me.' At six o'clock in the morning twilight, a procession of chanting disciples walked past her bed on the verandah to his cottage where a sacred light was lit and incense burned. For the next twelve days, the disciples met every evening in the square behind his house. They spent their time spinning cotton then placed it in a box beside his empty bed. Their symbolic act affected Marie deeply: 'Surely no one could see that gesture without tears!'

Part of her reason for visiting Gandhi's ashram was to discover how, as a social activist, she could find the balance between making effort to change the world for the better and maintaining peace of mind. In *The Lotus and the Spinning Wheel,* the second book she wrote from her research on this Indian journey, Marie explored the differing philosophies of Buddha and Gandhi and the questions that were at the heart of her personal dilemma. While both Buddha and Gandhi wished for personal liberation, she explained that the Mahatma's path was through ceaseless service to humanity. He worked through the world as a lawyer and social activist, to solve the problems of the present reality – political freedom for India, the amelioration of the conditions of India's destitute and downtrodden poor, and to help find peace between Hindus and Moslems. He struggled with detachment, becoming overwhelmed by the misery caused by Partition. Buddha took the opposite approach and, through meditation, gained insight into the deeper causes of suffering. Although Buddha was the All-Compassionate One, understanding human nature both in its joy and suffering, he was yet detached from it. He knew that man's wants would remain unsatisfied. If he could convince mankind of the source of those wants, then all problems would solve themselves.

Training in loving-kindness was, Marie concluded, essential before attempting to reform the outer world. Ahimsa was Gandhi's guiding truth that ensured relations between Indians and English after independence were harmonious. After witnessing the carnage of Hindu-Moslem riots, Gandhi questioned what had been wrong with the weapons of truth, love and non-violence that he practised. He realised more and more the hopelessness of expecting non-violence unless there was peace within the heart of the individual.

As the hot weather rolled inexorably in, Marie got weaker, not stronger.

Cleaning rice, she kept repeating over and over Gandhi's favourite hymn *Lead Kindly Light!* (amid the encircling doom, lead thou me on! The night is dark, and I am far from home; lead thou me on!). With a flash of determination, she decided that in nine days she would leave Sevagram for her destination in the Himalayas, whether well or not. Her health seemed to improve perceptibly after that. The night before she left, there was a sudden cool change that meant she could leave without difficulty in the pony cart that took her to the railway station.

THE HIMALAYAN hill-town of Almora lies between two sacred pilgrim routes, one to the source of the Ganges River and the other to Mount Kailash in Tibet, 'the holiest mountain in the world,' where, Marie said, 'The vibrations there were very good, I was told, and ashrams abounded.' The Himalayan hills rose straight from the plains, and the road to Almora wound corkscrew fashion through forests, and little villages of stone-roofed houses clung to the steep hillsides. The air grew cooler as the train carriage conveyed Marie up into the mountains she loved. On arrival, she experienced a sense of having been in this place before, a feeling that never left her.

At the beginning of March 1954, she arrived at a whitewashed guesthouse with dark deodars framing the white Himalayas beyond. It would be her home for a month, as the miracle of spring unfolded and apricot, peach and plum trees opened their delicate flowers. Everywhere she walked, she was greeted jubilantly with 'Namaste' in the Indian style with hands together. Declaring her love for Almora and the people, she was incredulous that only six years after the long campaign against 200 years of colonial rule, Indians expressed no resentment or animosity towards the British. All the while she continued to seek out those who could potentially help her, having 'the usual Westerner's expectation of something wonderful to be obtained from yogis and swamis in the way of an open sesame to relaxation and inward peace'. But although there was an array of ashrams, entry for Westerners, especially single women, was forbidden. Westerners, like Indian untouchables, were outcastes. Although Marie met many expatriates who lived in Almora, and students of gurus who told her about their teachers and ashrams, she never saw 'that all-compelling yellow robe disappearing round the corner, nor felt the least inclination to drop the money and the bus-ticket and follow after'.

With summer approaching, she convinced the guesthouse owner, Mr Shah, to open one of his bungalows at Binsar, 1000 m higher up. She could take a cook of her choice, allowing her to live like a hermit for five months during the heat and following monsoon. On 8 April, her fifty-fourth birthday, Marie sat in the bus looking down the fearful slopes as the crowded, rickety old vehicle negotiated the narrow mountain roads. 'I had the comfortable feeling that one slip of the driver's hand would mean a sudden flash of light and sudden death.' They arrived safely and Marie, Mr Shah and his family party left the bus to walk the remaining five kilometres to Binsar, a collection of bungalows that allowed tourists to enjoy the forest reserve atop the Jhandi Dhar hills. Once the ancient capital of the Chand Raj kings who ruled in the seventh and eighth centuries, Binsar, set among spectacular natural beauty, was the epitome of the quiet and solitude Marie desired. At 2400 m the bungalow faced the long line of white peaks that stretched almost 135 degrees. The weather was perfect, and crimson rhododendrons blazed against blue skies and white snows. Whether she had exhausted herself on the walk or there was something in the spring water she had drunk along the road, the first night there she awoke with a bilious attack and had to rush outside to vomit. It was the beginning of stomach trouble that was to plague her until her return to Australia.

With four months ahead in which to do nothing, Marie felt that was the best thing she could do. At night she took her sleeping bag to sleep under a giant crimson rhododendron and woke in the morning to see the mountains gleaming in the sunlight. By the end of April, clouds warning of the monsoon season obscured the mountain view, but after a thunderstorm the sky cleared to reveal a new range of snow peaks. By the end of May, the heat meant she did not venture out on her daily stroll until 4 pm. When the rains finally came in July, it was too wet to sleep out under the rhododendron tree any longer. Between rainstorms there were brilliant bursts of sunshine that lit up the valleys and hills. However, the beauty of the landscape was rudely interrupted by news from the office; her stomach literally turned over at the thought of returning to staff-shortage, 'and re-entering the torture chamber of terrible headaches and ghastly weariness'. Marie still experienced the depression that had accompanied her for the entire trip and felt incapable of returning home to resume her responsibilities. Her cook, Ahmed, got almost angry at her inability to eat food. 'I throw away!' he said, in unutterable disgust. Instead, she read light novels that had the ability to distract her from feelings of hopelessness.

By August she began to find food almost attractive again and as her strength improved, so did her desire to do some climbing. Although the rains had not completely disappeared, she planned a trek to the Pindari Glacier where she could camp alone and feel her feet on ice once more. Mr Shah's brother insisted she take a bearer by the name of Uttam Singh with her party of cook and two coolies. Eight kilometres down the valley they picked up a pony and pony-wallah, but the pony 'turned out to be as decrepit as his rider'. The scenery became wilder and grander as the pony stumbled up to where a bungalow overlooked a magnificent range of snow-covered peaks. The higher they went and the more spectacular the scenery, the more her aches and pains disappeared. The last bungalow was at 3800 m She discarded most of her support team and set off for a lonely camp amid the alpine lands at the foot of the glacier. There she found some yogis caves and a small temple, all half underground. She pitched her tent in view of the snowy mountains that at night were bathed in silver moonlight. Uttam Singh brought up firewood for her each day for a campfire and assisted her across a rushing stream that separated her from the ice. It was not the lonely camp she had planned but she was very grateful for his ministrations. In her weakened vulnerable state, Uttam Singh's loving care was exactly what Marie needed.

> He had come very inadequately provided with warm garments … and a striped cotton pyjama suit is hardly suitable for icy rain at over 12,000 feet. He never complained … He was the most self-effacing person I have ever met.

As the days passed, the misty mornings changed to rainy ones and making fires or washing became more difficult. Snug in the tent at night with eiderdown sleeping bag, hot water bottle and kerosene lamp, it seemed all the more snug when a sadhu arrived clad only in a white cotton gown to occupy one of the underground caves. He carried two small deerskins, some sacred books, and a large tin by way of a begging bowl. Marie's stomach had again rebelled against food and she was glad to fill his begging bowl with what she had cooked for herself. As she conversed with him, Marie felt disappointment that he was not an advanced rishi who passed the winter snows in meditation, probably without food or sleep. But, 'I have to admit that this man had risen above cold and bodily discomfort and that I had not.'

The rain continued and the mountains were sprinkled with new snow. With one day remaining before she was scheduled to return, she reflected that the experience had not brought her the joy it would have twenty years before when in good health. Back in Almora, Marie had Uttam Singh fitted for a new suit and then said goodbye.

> It was hard to think that I would see his gentle smile no more. Until the very last I could find no fault with him. He had taught me by his example the meaning of kind and selfless service. He would be incredulous had anyone told him that such a humble person as himself could be a memsahib's guru, but such was in fact the case; for he showed both the meaning of humble service and also the meaning and constant awareness of the reality of Ishwara [Godliness].

Three days before her departure for Calcutta, a thief stole her handbag containing her passport. She was furious for having left it unguarded. At least he had not touched her camera next to the handbag in the drawer. In Delhi, when confessing her sin of losing the taxation clearance to an official, he asked her why she had stayed longer than the three months allowed to the ordinary tourist. 'Because I love India!' Marie declared. Solemnly the official wrote on the form, 'She loves India.'

While walking in a pine forest outside of Almora, Marie was affected in a way she could not understand by a shrine to the goddess Kali. Known as the Dark Mother, Kali has a black face, holds a sword in one hand, and a freshly severed head in another and wears a necklace of skulls. She is depicted standing on her consort Siva, the Destroyer, but to Marie's untutored eye it looked as if she were trampling mankind underfoot. In the pantheon of Hindu gods and goddesses, Kali, the goddess of enlightenment or liberation, is the most misunderstood, commonly associated with death. In fact, Kali brings death of the ego as the illusory self-centred view of reality. Despite her fearful appearance, the goddess represents on the one hand the compassionate, nurturing energy, and on the other the punisher who confronts negative, demonic forces, bringing light.

In Calcutta, Marie wanted to purchase a statue of Kali. She mentioned the apparent contradiction in Kali's character to a woman she met while staying at the YWCA. This woman, always dressed in yellow saris, took no part in the social life and ate her meals alone. Intrigued, Marie discovered that she was the head of a large government laboratory and asked about her choice of sari. 'Do you always wear yellow saris because you would like to be a sadhu [an ascetic]?'

The woman replied, 'I am a sadhu, that is, I have simplified my life. Apart from religion, my only interest is my science.' The sadhu woman spoke to Marie of Kali.

> In our religion we worship the terrible as well as the compassionate aspect
> of Reality. Perhaps if we recognised and accepted the terrible aspect of God,
> there would be fewer inmates of mental homes because we should not struggle
> against the pain and suffering life brings.

Unconsciously, this Hindu goddess spoke directly to Marie's own need to integrate the disowned feminine aspect of her own character.

Despite ill health, she achieved an astonishing amount on her twelve-month sabbatical in India. She gathered enough material for the two books she would write on Buddha and Gandhi, *Footprints of Gautama Buddha* and *The Lotus and the Spinning Wheel*. But she came no closer to achieving her third objective – finding relief from psycho-spiritual distress. Arriving back home in January 1955, she reflected, 'I felt no better than when I had left.'

CHAPTER 13

Pioneering Buddhism in the West

1955–1957

AFTER HER twelve-month sojourn, Eastwood's housing boom alone provided sufficient income, so Marie gave up the city office. In time she bought out the other shareholders of Berangie Chambers and took over the ground floor of the building when her tenants vacated. As the staff increased, she built another spacious room at the rear. With an all-female staff there was a positive, cheerful and communal feeling in the office. Every morning at 11 o'clock Marie rang a bell declaring, 'Ladies, morning tea.' Work stopped and the switchboard turned off as every member of staff came into her front office to have tea, and cake if it was someone's birthday. Having delegated so much of the work, it was an opportune time for Marie to be brought up to date.

Treated as if they were needed and respected, the women staff members felt honoured to work for Marie. And she believed that many of them were just as good as any qualified solicitor: they were keen, interested in their work, able to look up the law, and handle clients. Marie recognised initiative and encouraged staff members to take on levels of responsibility they otherwise could not have imagined. Enid Ronalds, for example, began working for M.B. Byles & Co. with no legal training at all. Initially, she was trained to attend to property settlements, do property and probate searches and a range of associated work in the city. Within a few years, Marie could see she had greater capacity and trained Enid to be a law clerk in the areas of family law and personal injury law.

Every afternoon, Enid's eleven-year-old daughter Chris came by after school to collect her mother and walk home together. Chris was in her first year at Cheltenham Girls High School. On occasion, Marie called her in for a chat, as she took particular interest in her academic progress. To the young girl, it felt more like an interrogation. Chris was not confident or outgoing and was terrified of the woman in the front office. Although Marie was slight of build she had a powerful, even intimidating, presence and her steely gaze was quite severe. In one afternoon chat, when Chris was about 14, she reported to Marie that her school's career adviser told her that she should consider leaving school at the end of the School Certificate (Year 10) and become a secretary, as she thought it would suit her abilities. Marie sat for a moment and then leapt from her seat, frightening the young girl as she exclaimed, 'Ridiculous! I have never heard anything so silly. You are going to finish school, get a scholarship, go to university and study law.' Marie called Enid in and repeated her views. Enid, who also believed girls should be economically independent, was in full agreement.

'So that was it, really', recalled Chris. 'The women in the office never argued with her and as a fourteen-year-old, I certainly was not able to!'

It all went according to plan. After winning a Commonwealth Scholarship, Chris gained entry into the University of Sydney's law school. Without Marie's early encouragement, she believes that she would have become a teacher, 'as was more usual for girls then', as the fees charged by the law school were prohibitive. In 1969, when Chris entered university, females made up only 8 per cent of the first-year law students. Marie was surprised to hear that it was still such a low number. In her final year, Chris requested her mentor to move her admission as a solicitor. However, by July 1973, Marie was physically unable to do so. Instead, her law partner, Helen Larcombe, stood in for her.

Later, Chris reflected, 'To anyone who has attended an admission ceremony in recent years, it would be remarkable to note that Helen was the only woman moving an admission, and I was the only woman being admitted.'

The level of general and sexual harassment Chris suffered at law school, and later in her first job as a lawyer meant that, while working in Canberra drafting the *Sex Discrimination Act 1984*, she insisted there be a specific provision making sexual harassment unlawful. She explained,

> This was the first legislation in the world to use the term "sexual harassment". It was entirely reflective of my experience as a law student and a new law graduate. I suppose, in a perverse sort of way, that my learning environment at law school influenced my later career choices and fed my determination that no other young woman would suffer as I had.

Chris became a leading Sydney barrister specialising in discrimination law, employment law and administrative law. In 1994, Chris Ronalds SC was appointed a Member of the Order of Australia (AM) for her services to women and, in particular, anti-discrimination and affirmative action legislation.

WITH THE practice booming and the office running smoothly, Marie continued researching and writing *Footprints of Gautama Buddha*. The Theosophical Society's library attached to their bookshop Adyar, in their city headquarters, was a great resource. The Theosophical Society was the hub of alternative spiritual beliefs in Australia and Adyar was the only bookshop in Sydney for literature on related subjects. The 1950s and early '60s were an exciting time in Sydney as alternative belief systems gained greater acceptance. The few alternative health practitioners, naturopaths and chiropractors gave talks there as well as visiting teachers from overseas, Krishnamurti, the renowned Indian spiritual master, among them. Through the society, Marie came into contact with people a world away from the bourgeois legal fraternity who, although espousing leftist political beliefs, were happily materialistic and not remotely interested in anything spiritual.

In a bid to restore her physical health, Marie taught herself yoga postures from a book *Yoga and Health*, a classic text, but fell frequently into the fireplace when trying to stand on her head. When she met Michael Volin, who taught classes at the Theosophical Society, she began taking lessons from him. Volin had travelled widely in Asia and had learnt yoga in India. Considered one of the foremost practitioners in Sydney, he struggled to become established while introducing a technique of physical training that seemed exotic and strange to most Australians. Marie mustered all the friends and relatives she could and convinced Volin to come to Cheltenham to teach a class in a local church hall. Her young nephew, Peter de Beuzeville, was very impressed with the teacher and his physical prowess as he demonstrated postures with his shirt off:

> He would have been in his 40s. At the time, as an adolescent boy, I was mainly impressed with the athletic side of this. And I remember being really impressed by what this man could do with his abdominal muscles, by pulling in one side at the top or bottom.

The Buddhist Society of New South Wales had thrived during Marie's absence in India. They gladly admitted her, even though she emphatically told them she belonged to *all* religions. Its headquarters was in the top floor above Leo Berkeley's clothing shop in Oxford Street, Darlinghurst. Interest in Sister Dhammadina's public talks at the Berkeley's house had grown to the point where the society needed to find a larger and more central location. The Centre Club in George Street became the regular venue for Marie's talks.

In *The History of Buddhism in Australia,* Paul Croucher writes, 'The years 1954–56 were halcyon for Australian Buddhism, with eminent visitors lecturing to packed auditoriums and receiving wide media attention ...'

This auspicious time for Buddhism's growth coincided with the Buddha Jayanti, the 2500-year anniversary of Buddha's parinibbana, his passing into Final Nibbana. This date was propitious as it forecast the new sasana (world era) of awareness of Buddha's teachings. There was great positive energy as Buddhists from around the world attended the Sixth Buddhist Council in Burma. As the country that maintained the last real vestiges of the original Theravadin tradition intact, Burma was the obvious choice to hold this auspicious event. It had held the previous council meeting in 1875, the fifth since Buddha's death. This event also had social and political significance, as Burma and Sri Lanka, countries that had helped keep Buddha's teachings in their purest state, were newly independent after centuries of colonial rule. With their emerging sense of identity, Buddhists from these two countries met with representatives from Nepal, Thailand, Laos and Cambodia, countries with uninterrupted Buddhist traditions and rulers who were protectors of Buddhism. India was represented, although Buddhism had essentially died out in the land of its birth.

Burma's Prime Minister, U Nu, supported the establishment of meditation centres, appreciating that trained minds and higher morality, inherent in Buddha's teachings, were an asset to the newly independent country. His government willingly financed overseas lecture tours to countries like Australia that were open to hearing about this non-sectarian, universal method of upliftment. Through this program, close ties were forged between Australia and Burma, two countries with a shared British Empire heritage. Burmese monks had good English language skills, which made their mission that much easier.

The next few years saw a growing interest in, and popularity of, Buddhism in Australia as eminent monks lectured to full auditoriums, attracting wide media attention. April 1954 heralded the arrival of the Burmese monk Venerable Sayadaw U Thittila, a lecturer at the University of Rangoon, the most qualified meditation master to teach in Australia. His visit was organised by David Maurice and sponsored by Leo Berkeley, in whose Sydney house the venerable monk stayed. U Thittila enjoyed an international reputation; his personal qualities of humility and scholarly erudition drew people to Dhamma and exemplified its wisdom. He had lived in England for eighteen years, driving an ambulance in London during the blitz, and had written many articles on Buddhism for English magazines. While in Sydney he lectured on "Buddhism for the West" and "The Fruits of Meditation". He gave instruction to smaller groups at Leo's house during intensive weeklong Vipassana meditation retreats.

The object of Vipassana is to gain insight through moment-to-moment mindfulness into the nature of physical and mental phenomena as they arise and disappear. Intellectual knowledge cannot help one discover that dukkha (unsatisfactoriness), anicca (transience), and anatta (no self-inherent entity) are inherent in all things. As awareness deepens, there develops greater equanimity and peace in the face of challenges, and wisdom and compassion increasingly become the meditator's guiding principles.

During U Thittila's month-long visit, the membership of both the Victorian and New South Wales Buddhist societies doubled to about forty in Melbourne and a hundred in Sydney. While Marie got on well personally with U Thittila and respected his level of spiritual attainments, she openly expressed her strong opinions and criticism of monks, as she resented their privileged position within a traditional, patriarchal society. Although she did concede that without such a strong organisational structure, Buddha's teachings would not have remained in their pure state and been handed down intact over the millennia. Her opinions did not endear her to her fellow Buddhists, mostly men, but she was more concerned with telling the truth than in gaining favour.

In February 1955, the Sri Lankan monk, Venerable Narada Maha Thera, who had originally suggested the formation of a Buddhist society to Leo Berkeley, arrived in Sydney to a fanfare of publicity. A photograph of him holding an umbrella raised above his head featured in the newspapers under the caption "Cool Customer". 'I am here to explain Buddha's teachings to those interested,' said the smiling monk in orange robes whose appearance so captivated the press.

The media found more than just the venerable monk's appearance newsworthy. They reported enthusiastically on his captivating public talks to 500 people at a time. Misconceptions abounded about Buddha's teachings – many people came to the Berkeleys' Sunday night meditation group in expectation of gaining magical powers or to contact the dead through psychic means. Many more were attracted to Buddhism as a philosophy they could adopt as an interesting and exotic pastime, as it had more modern appeal than Christianity. The public talks were designed to dispel some of the misconceptions and tried to explain the serious nature and genuine benefits of meditation. While the upsurge of interest in Buddhism attracted well-educated Australians, serious members of the society felt they were transient converts, 'lovers of the exotic – the lunatic fringe of society', only interested in the mystical aspects.

Venerable Narada had a more optimistic view and was enthusiastic about the establishment in Sydney of a Buddhist vihara (a meeting place to meditate and practise the teachings, unlike a temple that is primarily for worship). He announced a £25 contribution to start a Vihara Fund. Two members of the Buddhist Society promised £250 each. Venerable Narada had brought sacred relics and seedlings of the Bodhi tree for this purpose and offered his best wishes for the success of this 'noble endeavour' declaring,

> For the development of a nation, both worldly progress and spiritual progress are essential. One should not be divorced from the other.
>
> Australia is a prosperous continent and is bound to reach the zenith of material progress. As every other nation in the world, she too needs spiritual advancement to ensure substantial Peace and Happiness. Buddhism offers its modest contribution to this Southern Continent to achieve this end.

According to the Vinaya rules, a monk cannot stay for an extended period in the home of a lay-follower. As the society was serious about attracting a resident teacher who could maintain and strengthen the Dhamma in Australia, the establishment of a vihara to house a monk was one of the society's highest priorities. While the venerable bikkhu offered thoughts of peace and happiness that he hoped would spread through the establishment of a Buddhist vihara, the actuality would be far different. Ideally, the plan would lead to the first Buddhist meditation centre being established in Australia. For Marie Byles, the purchase of land was the beginning of the end of her involvement with the society.

Once the money to buy the land had been raised by public appeal, mostly funded by Leo Berkeley, Marie wasted no time in looking for property. She found a suitable allotment of two hectares of natural bushland on top of a plateau and surrounded by parklands of the Pennant Hills Recreation Reserve. Within easy walking distance from Ahimsa, it was ideal. Marie urged the society to secure it, offering to do the legal work gratis. A trust was formed to purchase the land in January 1956 and two monks from Thailand came for its formal dedication. The possibility of an Australian monk being in residence there when the building was complete was seriously discussed.

In May 1956, U Thittila made a return visit to Sydney. The highlight was a three-week meditation retreat he conducted for 35 participants at the Berkeleys' new home in Belrose, in the northern suburbs of Sydney. The Sayadaw then inspected the land that had been acquired for the vihara site and was full of enthusiasm for it. This was to be the last visit to Australia by an eminent bhikkhu for some years to come; as Buddhism's popularity grew the demand on their time to visit other Western countries increased. This lack of a stabilising influence meant that ideological differences came to dominate because various people had their own attitudes to the teachings, how they should be practised, and what agenda the society should have.

Within the Buddhist Society of NSW, Natasha Jackson emerged as the dominant voice through her role as editor of its newsletter *The Buddhist News*, renamed *Metta* by the Ven. Narada. Born in Moscow, Jackson was brought to Australia at the age of six and joined the communist party in the 1930s. She was a firebrand who did not suffer fools lightly. After having heard Sr Dhammadina speak, she became interested in Buddhism and joined the society. Described as an "armchair philosopher" with a strongly intellectual-ised approach to Buddhism, Jackson had not the slightest interest in medi-tation. With her partner, Charles Knight, an ex-trade unionist, together they brought their own radical, almost Marxist, interpretation of Buddhism that emphasised humanism and social reform.

Soon, two different camps formed. Committed to maintaining the purity of the teachings, Marie and Leo placed emphasis on practising mindfulness med-itation. They believed this was the key to helping others actualise the teachings, the primary purpose of a Buddhist society. Throughout this era, Marie main-tained well-defined boundaries around the purity of the technique. At times people thought she was too tough, but she felt this was more important than seeking popularity. She went to great pains to eliminate the miracles and the accretions that had been added over the centuries that portrayed Buddha as a god, one among India's pantheon. Some people brought their Christian ideas of ritual and worship but Marie, with her dissenting Christian background, reviled that attitude.

Natasha Jackson interpreted the teachings to suit her own beliefs and domi-nated the discussion group with her views. She thought people needed to have a strong theoretical knowledge before gaining insight through meditation. With her communist background, Jackson resented the millionaire Berkeley who, when talking to the media, emphasised the number of the society's members from the upper echelons of society – university professors, doctors, architects and politicians. Jackson had a horror of monks: she said they were parasites, and argued against the establishment of a meditation centre. She felt that the society, with a membership of only a hundred people, was in no way able to embark on such an ambitious plan. Leo Berekely had put up most of the money for the land, but his generosity made Jackson uncomfortable. It was an indication of his success as a 'capitalist ogre'. It got to the point in the society where friction caused a major rift, which resulted in Leo Berkeley's pioneering leadership being replaced by that of Natasha Jackson and Charles Knight. There were now two groups functioning in Sydney – the Buddhist Society under the new leadership, and what was referred to as the Buddhist Group, which consisted of Marie, Leo and others who had studied under Sister Dhammadina.

In his account of the history of the Buddhist Society of NSW, Graeme Lyall wrote:

> Hearing of the schism, Venerable Narada returned to Australia to plead with the two groups to sort out their differences and to re-unite. A meeting of both groups was called by him at the home of the Berkeleys. He warned that, as Buddhism was relatively new to Australia and had, as yet, few adherents, we could not afford the luxury of schisms. His pleas, however, fell on deaf ears – neither group would give way.

The changing orientation of the Buddhist Society, and Marie's conviction that it only had value if it trained people in experiential methods of learning, prompted her to step up the number of devotional full moon services and meditation days at the Hut of Happy Omen.

While these differences dominated the agenda, the building plans for the vihara stalled. Leo's interest in the society began to wane as did Marie's and many others affected by the unconstructive atmosphere. Obviously something needed to change. At a specially convened meeting on the 23 July 1959, Charles Knight and Natasha Jackson gained complete control of the society. This threatened the land bought for the vihara. Five years of bitter legal wrangling ensued while Marie, the honorary solicitor of the society, did her best to delay proceedings through whatever means possible.

IN 1957, *Footprints of Gautama Buddha, the Story of His Life and Teaching,* was published by Rider and Company in London. It was received with great acclaim throughout the Buddhist world. Marie not only humanised a god-like figure and made his teachings understandable to ordinary readers, she acknowledged the part women had played in the development of the Dhamma, and proclaimed their level of spiritual attainment equal to men's. Women's historical neglect, she felt, was an oversight brought about through the recording of Buddha's words by celibate monks.

Since the publication in 1930 of *Women under Primitive Buddhism,* a work that presented the position of lay and ordained women in historical focus by the distinguished Pali scholar Mrs I.B. Horner, nothing much had been written examining Theravadin Buddhist teachings concerning women. This subject was of intense interest to Marie and one she promoted through her efforts to bring Buddhism to the West. She acknowledged that the strictly formal patriarchal structure of Buddhism had brought an enduring legacy, but decried the affronts women had to suffer. Her great achievement was that this feminist approach did not undermine the fundamental truths of the teachings in her account of Buddha's life and mission.

After his enlightenment, Buddha made a vow, out of compassion for all suffering beings, that he would 'never cease from his labours in the world until there were ordained men and ordained women and devout lay men and lay women able to show forth the Dhamma'. But for women, it was his cousin Ananda, for many years Buddha's devoted personal assistant, who championed their cause and advocated on their behalf to gain equal access to the teachings and join the order. Buddha's hesitation in ordaining women might have related to the common fear that traditional society would collapse as women abandoned their household duties to take refuge from the relentless toil that was their lives. In the India of that time, the ruling Brahmin's Code of Laws was extreme in its treatment of women, depriving them of all religious rights. A woman could not attain heaven through any merit of her own but could do so only through implicit obedience to her husband. Acknowledging women's equal potential would upset Brahmin dogma and diminish the exclusive supremacy of men. Buddha might also have been concerned for the women's safety. Being a nomadic community, monks and nuns needed to travel the country to spread the Dhamma, but how could women be protected while they travelled? Perhaps he also believed, like many men, that women's physical capacity was limited due to their menstrual cycle.

Out of compassion for the many exceptional women who deeply desired to have access to Dhamma, Ananda persisted in his attempts to advocate on their behalf. Through logical argument he forced Buddha to admit that, as he had taught that salvation was through individual effort, there was no reason why women who followed the teachings could not also achieve the highest goal. Reluctantly, but also understanding it was inevitable, Buddha made the decision to allow a group of sincere women (including his aunt who had raised him after his mother died), who had renounced the luxuries of household life, cut their hair, dressed in yellow robes and lived on scraps of food, to join the order. For them, an additional 84 rules were added on top of the monks' 227 that made up the Vinaya, the principles of monastic discipline.

While presumably done with the best intentions, this ensured that only women of sincere commitment joined, and it meant their complete subjugation to the monks' dominance. On no account may a nun criticise a monk or admonish him. Although a monk bows only to another monk ordained before him, all nuns, even those of long seniority, needed to bow down to every monk, even the youngest and the newest. Through these rules, nuns would always be, despite their level of wisdom, on the footing of pupils, never the teacher, even when the nun was the monk's own mother as happened in the early years. One of the newly ordained nuns, Pajapati, had run a large household and turned her talents to the task of organising the Sisterhood as separate from the Brotherhood. Once their comparative status was established, the Buddha ensured that women had the ideal conditions to receive the teachings from monks, but the arrangement was paternalistic at best. At the time of Buddha it was taken for granted that the bikkhunis, as fully ordained nuns are called, would look to the more experienced Brotherhood with respect. Marie's view, however, was that once the Dhamma had been comprehended, all consciousness of gender departs. She asserted that, 'Insight into the Dhamma wipes away all distinctions of sex, and some of the Master's ablest and wisest disciples … were women.'

From the time their order died out, devout women in Theravadin Buddhist countries, such as Sri Lanka, Thailand, Tibet and Burma, existed in the monastic order to serve men. Most importantly, they do not enjoy the same privilege as monks of being supported by the community through alms, so are socially constrained in making the decision to ordain. Grounded in the belief of women's equal potential, feminism is a framework to understand the power dynamics in any system. It was these historical facts that fuelled Marie's antipathy to the patriarchal Buddhist Order. If women could be as wise and as committed to spiritual liberation as men, then surely their status should be equal to men's.

Marie's estimation of Buddha, the Dhamma and the benefits that could be obtained through practising meditation were held high until the end of her life, but the iniquitous social disadvantage women suffered never ceased to inflame her sense of justice. It was this burning issue that she would be personally confronted with on the next step of her spiritual journey. For someone as committed to personal liberation as Marie, it was not sufficient to have a well-received book that educated readers about Buddha's life and mission and to be considered an expert; she knew that she was not where she needed to be in herself.

Buddha taught that suffering is the common human experience and that there is a way out of suffering through personal effort. The Way of Mindfulness, Buddha stated, makes for the overcoming of sorrow and misery, for the destruction of pain and grief. He described the three steps that need to be walked on the path to liberation: hearing the teachings on the universal laws of nature that educate and inspire; understanding these truths at a deep level through mastery of the mind so that every action is wholesome; then penetrating our own reality and experiencing the great stock of accumulated impurities within. Even with awareness, it is difficult to control our physical and vocal actions because they can easily overwhelm at times when emotion runs high. A strong practice of samadhi, mastery of mind, is essential in being able to personally experience truths at a deeper level. Marie understood that she had achieved only the level of intellectual awareness. In order to achieve her goal of Nibbana, full liberation from suffering, she needed to practise more intensively.

Through meeting Burmese monks in Australia, Marie learnt about monasteries where Vipassana meditation was taught, but her preference was to study under a lay teacher. After one Saturday meditation group meeting in the Hut, she was introduced to Daw Toke Gale, a Burmese woman studying welfare work in Sydney, and told her of her aspiration. Daw Toke Gale reassured Marie that if she came to Mandalay, the spiritual centre of Burma, she would help her find a centre where she could learn Vipassana meditation under the guidance of a lay teacher.

Although her health had improved sufficiently to contemplate another overseas trip, it seemed impossible that she could forsake her steadily expanding legal practice. A Western spiritual mentor that she had met in India responded to her plea for advice with, 'You will be guided. You are already being guided.' One by one the doors opened. She acquired an articled clerk who qualified in time for her to leave him in charge by the end of 1957, less than three years since returning from India.

At each stage of her journey through life, Marie dived headlong into the next adventure: a cargo boat voyage around the world, extreme mountaineering expeditions, or a lonely quest to find inner peace. In Burma, she would be confronted by her strong reactions to patriarchal Buddhism, but Marie's thirst for spiritual awakening was greater than any other force.

CHAPTER 14

Journey Into Burmese Silence

1957–1960

FATE, OR KARMA, Marie believed, determined that she would, for the third time, be visiting Burma, the country where Buddha's teachings had been kept in its purest state among all the Asian countries. Yet it was her own adventurous spirit that gave her the courage to do what in 1957 very few Westerners had done at this time – participate in an intensive month-long retreat in an Asian meditation centre.

From Mandalay airport Marie was driven to the Maha Bodhi Meditation Centre near the city. It had formerly been a prince's pleasure garden and the car came to a stop just inside the gate beside an ornamental pool full of fish and tortoises. Beyond was a moat and ornamental trees for shade, and further off were rice fields. Immediately, she felt surrounded by an atmosphere of peace. Near the gate was a symbol of the three limbs of a perfected life – Sila (morality), Samadhi (mindfulness and concentration) and Paññā (supreme wisdom). 'I do not think anyone will quarrel with these three ingredients,' she noted. Beside a noticeboard was the daily timetable. To her satisfaction, it indicated a regime that stood middle way between asceticism and luxury. Knowing that monks and nuns may eat only before midday, Marie had gone without the evening meal for six months before her departure in preparation for the life of renunciation, another indicator of her willingness to commit fully to everything she did.

There to meet Marie was Daw Saranawati, a Burmese Buddhist nun in apricot robes, 'who spoke excellent English and was to become my dear friend'. Daw Saranawati had only a few months previously decided to become a nun.

As no one else at the other centres spoke English, the decision as to which centre Marie would study at was, indeed, made through fate. Her accommodation was a one-roomed wooden hut with a verandah built over a moat for coolness, reached by a walkway. Daw Saranawati (Marie soon shortened her name to Sarana) had furnished it with a brick on which to stand a candle, a bamboo mat on which to lie, and a chamber pot. This modest abode was perfectly suitable to her needs with the setting restfully picturesque.

When Marie first met with the instructor, U Thein, with Sarana as translator, he asked questions concerning her history and background. Although she was suspicious of gurus, she understood the need for a teacher. In the true spiritual sense, a guru is simply the conduit for the teachings. In reality, U Thein would act as her guide through the intensive journey into the unconscious and play a critical role in helping her open to her inner self.

That evening, after she had settled in, Marie went to the Dhamma Hall to undertake the initiation ritual and begin her silent retreat. U Thein began by explaining the technique that would help her gain concentration, by focusing on the breath coming in and out of the nostrils. He then began the initiation ceremony of taking refuge in Buddha, in the Dhamma (Buddha's teachings) and the Sangha (the community of spiritual beings). Not one for rituals, Marie nevertheless relaxed into an attitude of surrender; she relinquished control and placed her trust in a power not herself. This process, she later noted, creates the right conditions for healing the mind.

The atmosphere at the centre was most conducive to meditation, but in the early days she struggled. Throughout the retreat she wrote copious notes in her journal and asked questions incessantly. This allowed her relentless intellect to engage with the process. Later, she wrote a detailed description of her experiences in the book *Journey Into Burmese Silence*. Inspired by the knowledge that the suffering she experienced, the anxiety and depression, was not only hers but a universal condition, she felt compelled to discover solutions she could pass on to others. That task was the easy part. The real purpose of her journey, being present to whatever arose, proved harder than anything she had ever done. In this process of delving into the subconscious mind, resistance is a natural reaction, because the conscious mind does not want to lose control.

It was acceptable to change positions during meditation and change to walking, as long as the students were mindful when doing so. Sometimes, during the long afternoon sessions Marie left her hut to walk mindfully around the lake, but returned only to find the brain as bright and lively as ever, jumping about like a monkey instead of lying quiet as it was being trained to do. It was not until the fifth day that it began to quiet down and become absorbed in the breath, 'where life forever comes and goes, creation and destruction, ceaselessly coming into existence and passing out of existence'. With longer periods of absorption in the breath, Marie's striving mind could rest. At last she could tap into her true nature, her natural loving self. Appreciation surfaced for the extraordinary kindness of her Burmese friends who were becoming like brothers and sisters to her. 'I had never before been in such surroundings of boundless love and blissful peace,' she wrote. 'The very garden seemed to lie in an atmosphere of love, serenity and self-giving.'

On the fifth day, instructions were given for the next stage of the meditation training. At 1 pm, Marie went to the Dhamma Hall with Sarana where U Thein placed a white scarf over her shoulders telling her that she was now a yogi. He then gave instructions on the technique of mindfulness meditation they were to adopt. While the focus had been on the breath, he turned their attention to the physical sensations of the body to experience the constantly changing phenomena. Marie entered into the essence of the meditation experience, the intense feeling state where, if absorbed completely in awareness, the thoughts, body, emotions, fade away. One of the assistants kept checking on Marie, asking if she could feel anything.

> I was sorry I could not oblige by feeling anything at all except a blessed relief that all within the body and mind were ceaselessly changing. I had never realised before the blessedness of ceaseless creation and destruction – ideas always coming-to-be – body's troubles, coming, going – how wonderful that things never stayed the same. The mind was marvellously at peace and there was not the slightest difficulty in concentrating.

With this step Marie moved from the intellectual, to the felt experience of deeper reality.

Each morning, life assumed a harmonious daily routine. At 4 am, U Thein rang the huge triangular gong sending waves of loving-kindness across the eighty huts and cottages of the meditation compound and the mist-covered rice fields beyond. Crawling out from under the mosquito net and the eiderdown sleeping bag spread on the bamboo mat over the floor of the hut, Marie did a few yoga exercises to loosen up. She then sat down to meditate as the Great Bear hung like a blazing kite in the northern sky. The mundane sound of the kitchen gong called the students to rice-gruel and black tea at 6 am. The first faint rays of dawn were stealing through the shadowed garden as the meditators stumbled along the cobbled paths to the dining room. Eating in silence they mindfully consumed each mouthful, aware of the food's transient nature. This was the good life to Marie and completely satisfying. She only wished it were possible to live such a life for a month every year. After experiencing the bliss of deep absorption she gained insight into how the path to happiness lies, not in avoiding suffering, but by embracing it with conscious awareness.

At the end of a Vipassana meditation course the practice of loving-kindness acts as a healing balm after the deep operation of the mind. Marie described this practice,

> You now suffuse everything with loving thoughts beginning with your own silly stupid self, admitting its mistakes and failures and not pretending any longer that it is superior to other people and forgiving yourself for being the imperfect being you are.

The thoughts of love then widen to embrace those near and dear, and then strangers and those who are difficult to love, forgiving them for their failures and imperfections. 'Having extended love to all, you now very humbly ask the love and forgiveness of all whom you yourself have injured. May they forgive you and be drawn into one great circle.'

Mandalay is surrounded by the ancient cities of Sagaing, Amarapura and Mingun, all former royal capitals, and then religious centres. There monks and nuns had, since ancient times, devoted themselves to Buddhist practice. With Sarana as her guide Marie travelled north to the sacred Sagaing Hills to visit various meditation centres, monasteries and convents. Her travels took her back into another time and in this traditional society, into situations that were bound to offend her sense of justice. As she observed:

> The vast majority of nuns were merely servants of monks, cooking for them, fetching and carrying and scrubbing floors for them, and generally waiting upon them. At one meditation centre the monks occupied clean, airy, well-paved quarters, while the nuns' dwellings and unpaved paths were the equivalent of slums.

As Marie and Sarana approached Sagaing village, the monks were on alms round, carrying their large black bowls for collecting food from the villagers. Among the orange-robed monks were two nuns dressed in their paler, apricot-pink robes carrying huge bundles of foodstuff on their heads. They were returning with supplies from their home villages, as they were not eligible for the same support as the monks from the local villagers. The way in which her gender was regarded as unclean was disheartening to Marie, but the nuns did not feel aggrieved. They were humble and alive with love and kindness. 'Their faces were beautiful with inner peace and love for all, and there was an atmosphere of happiness and joy you would travel far to find in the West.'

The differences between Asian women Buddhists, conditioned by an ingrained patriarchal social system, and Western women Buddhists who had fought for the expansion of women's rights and had an expectation of equality, were vast. Adopting a submissive attitude seemed like defeat to Marie. On the other hand, she reflected, 'The very object of meditation is to rise above the pairs of opposites – the congenial and the uncongenial, the pleasant and the unpleasant. So in a sense perhaps [it] might be the very best of places for such a one.'

Nevertheless, it was a relief to arrive back at the Maha Bodhi Meditation Centre, 'where sex did not seem to matter so much, and where monks and nuns and lay men and women were considered equally capable of realising the truth of anatta, that there is in reality, no permanent individual self, either male or female, ordained or non-ordained.

Before leaving Burma Marie attempted to have a discussion with U Thein about the need for Westerners to learn to relax before they sat for meditation. He disagreed but she insisted on making her point. She clenched her fists and put on a frown to show the tense, strained state of mind of many Westerners but,

> … he had obviously not the faintest idea what I was talking about. Burmese people were always relaxed; the trouble was that they did not strive earnestly enough, and inner conflict was apparently something he had never come across in all the thousands of meditators whom he had known.

As she was leaving, U Thein told Marie, 'The Dhamma brought you here, and the Dhamma will be your Teacher when you leave.' He was certain that in Australia she would be able to show others how to meditate. He gave her the same advice that his teacher had given him, emphasising the need to teach purely from the motivation of loving-kindness, not for money or personal gain; not for her own benefit, power or fame nor for renown or praise. It was not necessary, he said, for Australians to become Buddhists, nor even understand the basic principles of Buddhism. Through Vipassana meditation they could learn, 'there is only one Dhamma, one Law which holds all'.

Marie herself did not identify as Buddhist. She once wrote, 'I'm labelled a Buddhist, of course. I don't mind, although I am not one. But I do know that the practice of meditation that I learned in Burma has brought me increasingly an experience of inner peace and calm.'

ON HER return to Sydney in February 1958, Marie settled back into normal life. Relishing the opportunity to share the experiences she had had in Burma, she broadcast regularly on Sunday evenings on 2GB, the Theosophical Society's radio station. In one armchair chat she spoke about "Living the life of a Burmese Buddhist nun".

> I went to Burma to learn the art of meditation, how to still the thoughts and find inner peace. Obviously we should not see so many unhappy people or so many suffering from nervous strain if we learned this art.

Continuing her participation in the Sunday night meditation meetings at Leo Berkeley's house, Marie acted as a guide to others. After an hour's silent meditation practice she led a discussion on a theme, usually the Four Noble Truths – suffering, the cause of suffering, the end of suffering, and how to achieve that through the Noble Eightfold Path. It was not a theoretical discussion; Marie spoke on life and how it was lived in actual experience.

One night, a young woman listening attentively felt drawn in. Later, Elva Mniksevicus told Marie, 'I felt you were speaking directly to me tonight.'

Marie, in her straightforward way, looked at Elva and said, 'Well, that means that you're on the path.'

Elva almost staggered back to her seat and thought, 'What does that mean exactly?' Marie never wasted words, she expressed herself succinctly and what she said jolted the young woman. Elva admired her devotion and clarity about the Buddhist teachings. When interviewed many years later, Elva described Marie as,

> … one of the very early pioneers of a pure Theravadin teaching … a great purist. She would never approve of me studying, reading Mahayana – being terribly fond of the Dalai Lama! Marie was like a very strict protestant. Very strict … but oh she had so much to give. She was a wonderful person. She was one of the few people who was able to inspire people. She was able to convey it, certainly to me, much better than just reading it. She wasn't a meditation teacher. She was an excellent lecturer. Of course she was a solicitor so she was able to express herself very well. She was really able to get through to people in an undramatic fashion.

Elva's Lithuanian husband, Jurvis, was equally impressed with Marie's authority and grasp of her subject. She was not just talking about ideas but spoke about actual things she had done and experienced in meditation. Jurvis considered himself a Buddhist since first reading about it in Germany after the war. Originally from Lithuania, his whole world collapsed when the Soviets invaded; and then came five years of war. He arrived in Australia as a displaced person in 1948, and when he sought out a library with books on Buddhism, he was directed to the Theosophical Society in Sydney. Through that he discovered Leo and Marie's Sunday night group. After one talk he approached Marie to ask about her views on Buddhism and if she could help him with the difficulties he had. Marie pointed out that what he knew about Buddhism was only on the intellectual level. While the philosophy of Buddhism might appeal to him, Buddhism is not a philosophy. It had a philosophy but that is not its vital part. She recommended a book, which was not available in Australia in the 1950s but became standard reading to those interested in Buddhism, *The Heart of Buddhist Meditation* by Ven. Nyanaponika, a German monk resident in Ceylon. Jurvis benefited from having a teacher who could address his specific problems with meditation. To him, Marie was not just an ordinary person: 'She was one of those exceptionally rare beings – one in a million, or even more.'

BETWEEN VISITS to Burma, Marie maintained her annual retreats in a cave in the Blue Mountains about two kilometres from her brother David's house at Clarence. To reach the cave, David drove her to the closest point on the road, and then she walked down a steep hill between the giant stone formations, paradoxically called pagodas, to an overhang that gave her protection from the weather. Inspired by the accounts of early Buddhist monks and nuns who dwelt in mountain caves that gave them the privacy they needed, the setting appealed both to Marie's nature-loving sensibility and her need to cut herself off completely from the world in order to disengage from it. David and his wife Babette worried about Marie's safety alone in the cave. Once, when they drove to pick her up on the designated day, there was a flock of crows circling the area in which she camped. They feared the worst, but she paid them and their concerns no heed.

The private diaries Marie kept at this time reveal her struggles to rise above doubt and overcome the pain she suffered both mentally, from depression and anxiety, and from the related physical symptoms. Her stomach problems were often exacerbated by her diet of raw vegetables and dried fruit, giving her painful wind and making it difficult to sleep at night:

> About 3 hours of fair absorption this morning. Tummy better. Bright clear summer day, cool breeze, cave is cool. Very depressed this afternoon, lay by the stream below Malley's Cave and wondered was it all futile. Mathew Arnold:

'weary of myself, sick of asking what I am' etc. Is there no way out of the unutterable futility of life …

Perfect day but inner pain. I seem to get nowhere. How terrible to be a hermit forever, not to be able to lose oneself in doing and helping others – helping? What for? For the same futility of living.

Typically, over the ten days her moods would swing between utter despair and the pain of loneliness to contentment when, after a week, meditation went well and it seemed she was making progress:

It will probably be many, many years before these blissful experiences become habitual. Practice and trust. The hermit's life has been worthwhile and I have now grown accustomed to it and would willingly continue. I almost forget the misery of it at the beginning.

Depressive episodes had become habitual, increasing in intensity with each reoccurrence. Mindfulness meditation gave Marie relief at a profound level. Aware of the universality of suffering, she felt moved to connect with others also in the grip of grief, fear and despair, and to share the benefits she had found. In November 1960, she put a notice in the Buddhist Society's newsletter, offering the Hut of Happy Omen on Saturday afternoons to anyone interested in relaxation, meditation and inner peace. She took the dozen or so participants through a relaxation process before they started meditation. Afterwards, she guided the participants to empty their minds using meditation on the breath. At the end of an hour's silence, a session of loving-kindness meditation followed. Afterwards, Marie facilitated a discussion that focused on the participants' experiences, not on intellectual subjects. Subtly guiding the conversation, she encouraged each person to discover their own truth.

One of the participants who appreciated this tangible opportunity to develop self-compassion was Bart Brown. Then in his 30s, Bart had been on the edge of suicide after walking out on his wife and children:

I was in a shocking state – mentally, physically, spiritually – totally dead. A neighbour said: 'Why don't you come to meditation on Saturday afternoons at somebody's house?' I said 'Yes, OK.' So, I came to Ahimsa. That was the start. I went for quite a number of years.

Never having meditated in his life, these sessions gave Bart a mental calm that he had not experienced before. Marie showed him the path of freedom. Bart reminisced,

For me, it was the most wonderful experience because I've never had a guru. Never met anyone like her. She gave me peace in my heart that I'd never known before. I needed peace in my heart and she helped me get in touch with it.

Bart and Marie became good friends. He often met up with her at the Eastwood office after work and accompanied her home on the train. For dinner she served him steamed frangipani leaves with polenta or rice, but he was oblivious to the unusual fare as their discussions satisfied his spirit. He could talk to her about his anger and distrust; she was a good listener, empathetic and not afraid of the intensity of his emotions. This was Marie at her best. When her heart was engaged with her mind, she could support others on their journey. Although she worked hard at being detached from outcomes, occasionally her doing self broke through in the meditation group. Bart did not mind that aspect of her, though, as he needed her strength, her "spirit conviction" as he called it. He repaid her support by working in the garden at Ahimsa, something she always appreciated.

There was an increasingly peaceful atmosphere in the office as Marie became ever more content to leave things to the Dhamma, but the goddess of efficiency remained her ruling deity. She was prey to anxiety and continued to worry that the business might fail. Suffering from stomach troubles, bouts of breathlessness and chest pains, she was learning, though, to take time out. Whenever there was an interval, she would leave the office and go to the park nearby.

Some of the staff thought that Marie genuinely lived the teachings, while others viewed her as a weekend Buddhist. Her attempts to introduce meditation practices into the workplace received mixed reactions. It was difficult for her staff to be receptive to techniques of relaxation while feeling under pressure to perform to her high standards. When the bookkeeper, Edrie, was over-stressed, Marie urged her to lie down for twenty minutes at lunchtime and meditate on a lotus flower. Edrie could not quite see how this could assist with her struggles to balance the books.

It was not easy for Marie to be the person she strived to be. She was making progress – just not as quickly as she hoped. After a crisis in the office had upset her equilibrium, she awoke in the middle of the night hearing U Thein say, 'Some get the Dhamma easily; others do not'. Marie conceded she was 'one of the others!' As she reflected,

> What is success and what is failure can never be judged at the time. It is only by looking back over many years that we can see increasing serenity, loving-kindness and compassion.

CHAPTER 15

Paths to Inner Calm

1960–1963

MARIE RETURNED to Burma in December 1960, to continue her research for *Journey into Burmese Silence*. In Mandalay she was driven straight to the Maha Bodhi Meditation Centre where U Thein and thirty other meditators gave her a surprisingly warm welcome. It felt heartless to immediately inform her mentor that she wanted to set off in two days for another meditation centre, but Marie had a strange urge to visit the "loving-kindness" centre in Mohnyin, six hours journey away. U Thein showed not the slightest disappointment saying only, 'It was the leading of the Dhamma.'

Buddha taught that the indications of progress on the path to enlightenment are not the attainment of high spiritual states, which only show that the student is practising correctly. The real indications are the feelings of gratitude and loving-kindness. Gratitude comes from an appreciation for this human existence and for the teachings that show the way out of self-created suffering. Loving-kindness, or metta, as it is called in the Pali language, is the ability to have compassion for ourselves and empathise with others in their suffering, seeing the goodness within each person.

Loving-kindness is the first of four qualities Buddha termed the Divine Abidings. The other three are compassion, sympathetic joy (happiness in another's success), and equanimity, the ability to maintain a balanced mind. They are called the Divine Abidings because these qualities allow a person to experience ultimate peace. Even if experienced only fleetingly, these feelings can bring profound changes in attitude, healing the sense of separation

147

from our true selves and all beings. The practice of metta was having a marked effect on Marie's life, not only proving beneficial in helping stave off depression but also in improving her interpersonal relationships, even in business. The first time she experienced this feeling, she recalled,

> I was interviewing an officer of one of the trustee companies on some business or other; suddenly out of nothingness an extraordinary sense of friendship swept over everything including the officer being interviewed, and when I left the building I seemed to be walking on air. When one has experienced it, one understands why the Buddha said that all ways of emancipation that could be devised were not worth one-sixteenth part of the emancipation of the heart through love.

While Marie thought she understood why she was going to the loving-kindness centre, she soon discovered the reason was far different.

Some distance from their destination in Mohnyin she and Sarana caught sight of the golden spire of the Mohnyin Pagoda. It turned out to be a fantastic fairyland of gilded and coloured cement work, the spire covered with gold flakes. Started with a donation of ten pounds, it was now worth millions. Turning into the meditation centre, the car drove between two enormous white concrete elephants and down a laneway with the turreted walls of the women's meditation compound on one side and rest houses for pilgrims on the other. Shady trees overhung the bamboo cottages with a few fragrant frangipani trees scattered among them. Alighting from the car Marie felt enfolded by a wave of peace. After meeting the head nun she chose for her accommodation a suitably remote hut, but the noise of yelping dogs, crying babies and loudspeakers still intruded.

Accompanied by Sarana, Marie went to pay respects to the old monk in charge by bowing three times, 'with frogwise body and head on the hands on the floor', a process she referred to as 'grovelling'. Sarana explained Marie's desire to learn the loving-kindness method of meditation, but the monk said he was old and never gave instruction nowadays. However, since she had come from such a great distance and was the first Westerner to come to their centre, he would make an exception. He then outlined the method, but Sarana's translation did not bring much clarity. Marie realised U Thein had been right – 'to start a new method would be like returning to kindergarten after having got as far as high school'.

Twilight was falling when they walked outside. Sarana led her on a tour of the pagoda of half a million Buddhas. Most were tiny, seated on miniature

Bodhi leaves, and some were larger lining the labyrinthine aisles of the central pagoda. The nuns had just started the evening's meditation session as Marie gazed at the beautiful spiral stairway that led up to the top of a cylindrical tower, just the place from which to photograph the fairyland of spires. 'But women may not climb it,' Sarana told her, 'for women are unclean.' She was shocked and initially wanted to leave as quickly as possible. Then U Thein's words rose to mind: 'Never run away from pain; it will only return. Face it, become detached and it will not return.' It was clear to her that the least feeling of righteous indignation or ill-will prevented right meditation and liberation from suffering. There was only one thing to do, stay and face the issue and learn to find loving-kindness even towards monks who were worshipped as gods and who treated nuns as servants, and root out the asavas, the conditioned attachments to ideals and ideas.

For three weeks as she meditated, Marie was dependent on the selfless service of the nuns who devoted themselves to helping others become liberated through meditation. Twice a day they brought meals to her room, refusing to allow her to carry the tray back to the kitchen. Apart from learning tolerance of other ways of being and relating, Marie knew that, at a deeper level, the real nature of her struggle was to learn to disidentify with all aspects of the self, including her ideals and ideas about how the world should be.

After three weeks the air cleared and her animosity disappeared as she surrendered her self-imposed ideal for the Burmese nuns:

> I saw that this monk-worship is essential to the pattern of Burmese life, and that to end it would be to destroy the morale of the people and end their happiness and contentment. The little village monastery, with its three or four monks, is the centre of village life. To worship the monks and serve them is the greatest blessing of all; "to look on the yellow robe is to feel cool" so that evil-doing is restrained. Take the yellow robe away and people would have nothing to look up to, nothing to remind them that there is something more than growing rice and cotton. And the real Burma is not in Rangoon or even Mandalay, it is in those thousands of little villages.
>
> Suppose too, that a well-meaning reformer were to insist that some of the huge donations to the pagoda were given to the nuns to purchase food, soap or candles and so save them from having to go long distances to their villages twice a year to procure such things. The nuns would be the first to complain, for they would be deprived of the merit of serving the monks. To give is the greatest joy of the Burmese and to give to monks is the best giving of all.

It is all most illogical. But it works. And men and women are not governed by logic.

Marie also realised that the monks' status made it difficult for them to be humble and lowly of heart, to dissolve their ego and therefore to succeed in reaching the peace that passes understanding, the peace of Nibbana. A 'strange peace' brought complete contentment. Her purpose of coming to Mohnyin had been fulfilled.

Returning to the centre in Mandalay, U Thein offered Marie the lonely hermitage on the outskirts of the compound in which to meditate for the five weeks she had left. She soon settled into a routine, rising about 2 am when the Great Bear flamed through the window, through to going to bed at about 9 pm. During her meditation course, Marie continued to interview monks and teachers who visited the centre in order to discover how they came to Dhamma and how they lived it. However, a humble old man who worked in the vegetable garden challenged her intellectual efforts. Marie often passed the old man watering and hoeing the parched soil in his attempt to grow small cauliflowers, onions and Chinese cabbages for the centre's kitchen. Working mindfully, his face was usually impassive but when she caught his eye and smiled, his face lit up and he returned her smile. With Sarana's assistance as translator, she discovered that he had been a coolie in the village. Since his wife had died, he was spending his last days in a Dhamma environment practising meditation and giving service. Marie asked him, 'Is there anything at all you now desire?'

'Nothing at all,' he replied. 'The Instructor provides me with food and clothing. What more could a man want?'

When Marie next spoke with U Thein, she recounted his words. She said, 'You see, that old man proves that the simple-minded find the secret of meditation far more easily than clever intellectuals.'

U Thein smiled and observed, 'The peasant from the jungle village usually finds the Dhamma easily. The learned monk sometimes never finds it.'

Reflecting on Christ's words, 'except ye become as little children, ye shall in nowise enter the Kingdom of Heaven', it was with a pang of envy that Marie settled down to meditate again telling Mara, the personification of ego, that he was very clever but that she was not going to play with him anymore. 'I had discovered that cleverness is the worst enemy of meditation.'

ON HER return to Australia, Marie made plans to create a community of like-minded people. Inspired by the Gandhian ideal of bringing about social and economic reforms through land redistribution, she subdivided her own property, her precious bush reserve, and offered a portion of it to friends, John and Vreni Fallding. She had met John and Vreni through the Quakers youth group, the Young Friends, who regularly met at the Hut to discuss how to resolve social conflict and attain world peace. John was an idealistic young man, a committed pacifist who had been a conscientious objector during the war. After standing trial, he and sixteen other conscientious objectors were sent to do compulsory community service for two years in a remote Forestry Commission camp west of Lake Macquarie on the Central Coast of New South Wales. Unlike similar groups, these men all agreed to live as a community, although it took them a year before friendly fellowship was achieved. John believed that the peaceful and beautiful forest surroundings had been very helpful. While labouring on road construction in the forests, he gained an appreciation for the natural environment and brought this to the Ahimsa community.

During the war Marie had taken an active interest in the pacifist cause and often spoke at meetings in the Quaker Meeting House on topics such as "Gandhi and recent developments in India", and "Non-Violence and Social Change". John shared her devotion to Gandhi. In 1949, he had attended a World Pacifist meeting held at Sevagram, Gandhi's ashram, where he met the future prime minister, Pandit Nehru. This trip radicalised him. He took to wearing handspun cotton clothing and open sandals. Marie, too, adopted her version of the satyagrahi's (peaceworkers) uniform of loose cotton shirts and trousers, usually dyed green that she wore when not at the office.

John's wife Vreni was German-born and had worked for the Red Cross in Germany during the war. On her arrival in Sydney in 1952 she joined the Quakers and through them met John. When Marie travelled through India the next year, the couple minded her house. Like John, Vreni had a strong desire for a healthy and simple lifestyle and shared his concern about the state of the environment and social justice issues. Her first given name, Erdmuthe, was an old German name meaning 'Earth Mother'. Vreni embodied those qualities. By the time the Falldings built their home in the Ahimsa compound they had two children, Heidi and Martin. Taking a close interest in the children, Marie encouraged their bushwalking, giving them each a little backpack.

Marie offered another portion of land to her bushwalking friend Dorothy Hasluck who had been of great support in caring for Ida. Dorothy was a Theosophist, a cultured intellectual who published art books and gave Marie invaluable help in writing her books. Dorothy embodied all the spiritual qualities to which Marie aspired; she was a gentle person with a warm sunny personality, always helping someone.

The gift of land was not entirely altruistic as it created a family for Marie, a community of philosophically harmonious people who socialised together and participated in various activities held at the Hut. Apart from their common vision of a simpler, semi-communal lifestyle, they also shared her deep appreciation for the natural environment. Their support would be vital in her struggle to maintain the integrity of the local bushland.

Although the Buddhist Society of NSW owned the vihara land near Ahimsa in Pennant Hills, the certificate of title was made out to the trustees, Leo Berkeley and Eric Penrose. Leo Berkeley held the Deed of Trust. Marie supported Leo with advice that he was on sure legal footing, but he finally handed over the deed after threats of court action. He did not want to tarnish the name of Buddhism in the courts. The land was still classified as green belt but there were plans afoot in council to have this changed to interim development. The battle raged over whether the society should sell it. Charles Knight's economic arguments swayed some of the members. He said the society could not afford to pay the rates or develop the land.

Marie threw herself into saving the area. She organised a committee comprised of herself and Baldur – who had built a house in Welham St at the front of their parents' property – John and Vreni Fallding, Dorothy Hasluck and another local resident, Enid Bell. The Provisional Committee met at Ahimsa on the 6 August 1961. They drafted a proposal to the Minister for Local Government for the Hills Community Bushland Area. In it they eloquently stated their beliefs on why the area should be protected:

> Around Sydney we have primeval forest, sandstone caves, sub-tropical jungle in deep gorges, mountain crags and waterfalls, possums, lyre birds and koala bears – all of these within fifteen miles of the General Post Office, Sydney. Surely no other two million-population city in the world has such assets within its own boundaries. Yet Australians are all too modest about their heritage. It has been rightly said that if Sydney were owned by America, the fame of these things would be known the whole world over.

The nearby Pennant Hills Recreation Reserve was vast. It catered for organised sporting groups with football and hockey fields, basketball and tennis courts, and even a rifle range. The committee's proposal made the case for maintaining the area as a passive recreational area, 'where open-air community activities of the less boisterous kind can be followed with freedom, yet with sufficient privacy and in a natural bushland setting'.

The submission was a desperate bid to resist the inevitable subdivision of the seven allotments that L.J. Hooker, the real estate agency, wanted to develop into a housing estate. It maintained the possibility of building a meditation retreat centre while sharing the area with other groups who would conform to the passive recreational guidelines. The committee's suggested plan for development of the area was that it be added to Lane Cove National Park, a strip of natural bushland that runs upriver from Sydney Harbour. That way it would be dedicated under the National Parks Administration Act and revocable only by Act of Parliament.

The committee's next move was to draw up a flyer outlining the proposal and to distribute it around the local area, asking people to write a letter of support to the Minister for Local Government and Hornsby Shire Council. Their attempts to ensure the land would be resumed were brought to the Buddhist Society's attention by one of the landowners, Mr Stephens. Stephens, a developer, was negotiating with Hookers. A Special General Meeting of the society was called. After linking the flyer to Marie Byles, it was decided that her membership should be terminated for being 'primarily responsible for the troubles connected with the land'.

Marie noted wryly, 'So neither the Buddhists nor the Quakers would have me. When my heretic grandfather was forced to leave his church I think he passed his inheritance to his grand-daughter!'

About this period, Paul Croucher commented in *The History of Buddhism in Australia*,

> Although a considerable intellectual force … Natasha Jackson was not the sort of person to be in charge of a society, least of all a Buddhist society. There were a number of other instances of her having ousted members who happened to disagree. Even though she gave twenty years of her life to the society, it is hard not to conclude … that in many ways she also sabotaged it.

The threat of subdivision of an area of parkland mobilised the community. Applications for the subdivisions of land for development were made to Hornsby Shire Council but refused on account of local objections. There was a two-year deadlock before the developers appealed to the Minister for Local Government. He appointed a commissioner to hear the case. Community members took it in turns to attend the hearing at Hornsby Council Chambers. They listened to the environmentalists and the Hooker lawyer arguing about the significance of the blackbutt trees on the ridge, among other things. Having studied geology, Marie helped formulate the case that the area was significant because it was an ecotone, a zone of transition between two different ecosystems, where the shale country and the sandstone country met and two distinct types of vegetation occurred. The evidence given at the inquiry was overwhelmingly against any subdivision and in favour of the retention of the land as a natural bushland area. Impressed with the evidence presented before it, the council voted to grant £25,000 for the acquisition of the land, but was unwilling to resume it, because the amount of compensation was an unknown quantity.

Compensation would have been far less than what the Buddhist Society could get for it if they had sold it to Hookers. At the time of purchase, in 1956, the land had been valued at £450. By1963, when the inquiry was conducted, the value, if in Green Belt, had risen to £24,000. Its value, if zoned as residential, was £105,000. In 1963, the land was sold to Hookers for £10,000, realising more than 2000 per cent profit on the original investment. The developers now held all the titles to the estate, making development possible. Marie was outraged that the society had chosen to sell land that had been dedicated by the Sangha for a vihara, for money!

When the Minister for Local Government ordered them to pass plans for subdivision, the council, after initial resistance, drew up plans for housing blocks with landscaping 'after the style of Canberra'. In what resulted in Cheltenham Heights Estate, the committee members were incensed when, during subdivision, 'a noble Blackbutt, perfect in form and of classic beauty, over a hundred feet high and estimated to have been between 150 and 200 years old' was axed by developers when it could easily have been preserved as a landmark with minimal realignment of road works. At the committee's request, one of the streets in the new estate was named after the tall magnificent trees that had dominated the ridge for unknown millennia.

The committee's campaign was not successful in halting the development, but it was successful in raising awareness. Education was a chief objective, to mobilise the community to act when necessary. The committee Marie and her neighbours had convened was the beginning of a movement that led to the formation of the Beecroft-Cheltenham Civic Trust in 1964, the first community civic trust in Australia. The trust was formed to fight all who attempted to spoil the beauty of their local area – the developers and elected government officials who, 'too frequently are either apathetic, contemptuous or misguided in their appraisal of losses suffered, or about to be suffered, by their constituents in the "sacred" name of "Progress and Development".'

There were a great number of matters on which the trust was compelled to act immediately. The district was under threat: from the Electricity Commission that planned to put huge pylons through the pristine native bushland beyond Marie's property, and by paper roads that could at some future stage be put through. Marie was one of the district's most significant residents and as vice-president her voice is clear in the trust's constitution:

> Sydney was once set in a natural forest of some of the most beautiful bushland in the whole of Australia. But this has been almost systematically destroyed till there are now but scattered remnants in the metropolitan area; and if some developers, public utilities, and organisations had their way, even these few remnants would disappear and be replaced by bricks and concrete.

Since its inception the trust has continued to monitor and influence many developments in Beecroft and Cheltenham. Just as it was unsuccessful in stopping the M2 motorway being built at the end of Wellham Street where Chilworth and Chilworth Reserve are situated, the trust could not stop other major incursions. However, its hard work and persistent efforts have impacted on smaller developments and modified many larger proposals. The trust helped retain to a greater degree the village character, its heritage values, and the natural beauty of the Beecroft and Cheltenham district.

CHAPTER 16

Cleaning Honourable Toilets

1961–1965

W HEN *Journey Into Burmese Silence* was published in 1961, it coincided with the unexpected upsurge of interest in Buddhism in the
West. A vivid account of Marie's deep immersion experience of
Buddhist meditation, it was also a technical manual on the various aspects of
the Vipassana technique, possibly the first such written by a Westerner. This
book helped bring forward the shift in consciousness Marie was hoping for;
it inspired many young people to travel to Asian countries in search of their
own spiritual awakening. Among them were some who later became respected
teachers in the West, such as the American Joseph Goldstein.

While the tone of *Journey Into Burmese Silence* was suitable for Westerners,
her criticisms of the 'autocracy of the orange robe' inevitably upset some orthodox Buddhists. Despite her attempts to practise tolerance of the patriarchal
hierarchy, its inherent social inequalities profoundly affected her relationship
with Burmese Buddhism.

Marie's antipathy to monks resurfaced on her next visit to the Maha Bodhi
Meditation Centre in 1962, when Sarana came to visit her. Usually, when this
self-effacing young nun passed by the monks, she removed her sandals and knelt
down with her face on the ground. But once, when she thought she was far
enough away from a group of them to not have to perform this ritual, one of
the monks turned to another and said loudly, 'That's a rude nun. Don't take any
notice of her.'

Marie made no attempt to pay respect when she passed by them as she
noted wryly, 'I was always deep in meditation when I walked to my hut.' The

adverse reaction to her book in Burma and the death of U Thein, her revered spiritual guide who embodied the Dhamma with such humility, meant this visit to the Mandalay meditation centre was her last.

On her return to the office, she was confronted with the shock of her law partner's desertion. While the female staff members were more than satisfied with their conditions, the lone male in the office was not. Robert Moin had joined M.B. Byles & Co. after his final law exams. He qualified as a solicitor in 1957, just before Marie left on her first visit to the Maha Bodhi centre. Employing a male, instead of a female, solicitor was a given considering the prejudice against women professionals at that time. It was a smart business decision, as many men preferred talking with another man when confiding their private affairs. Moin was a young man working among an all-female staff of mostly older women. Although he related well to each of them, other male solicitors used to make fun of him working in an all-female office. When he started with Marie, he was 25 and she was in her late 50s. He had assumed that she would, in the not-too-distant-future, be winding down her involvement in the business and handing the over the reins to him. However, after Marie reached the usual retiring age for women of 60, it was obvious she had different plans, and Moin decided to move on. When Marie returned from Burma in 1962, he left to set up his own practice taking with him the clients he had cultivated as well as at least one of Marie's, the Building Society upstairs.

Hurt by the thought that the deception had been there a long time, Marie was resigned to the situation and told him to just 'take it'. The women on her staff were disgusted with Moin, but even more disgusted with Marie. They did not understand how she could react so passively. While, from the moral point of view, Moin did the wrong thing, because he was not breaking the law there was nothing she could do. In that situation, her choice was either to get upset or remain calm. She was not going to sacrifice her hard-won equanimity just because the staff did not understand her 'Buddhist' approach. As she explained in her next book, *Paths to Inner Calm*

> To solve the small and large problems of everyday life we must learn to live our religion, whatever that religion may be. The daily problems of everyday life are themselves the training course. The training is the practice of selflessness, truthfulness, loving-kindness and equanimity. Enlightenment lies beyond all these higher states of mind ... the irony is that the hardest part of this training is learning how to let go, relax, do nothing, and leave everything to the Law of Being, or God.

The strain of running a business that employed 13 staff gave Marie considerable opportunity to practise this teaching. However, the setback with her business did not curtail her travel plans. In the process of researching *Paths to Inner Calm,* she planned to visit Japan to immerse herself in Zen practice. Zen Buddhism was all the rage in the West thanks to the books of Dr D.T. Suzuki, a Japanese scholar who had lived and studied in America. Having had success with her previous two books on Eastern philosophies, published at a time when the counter-culture movement was arising in the West, Marie was able to interest her uncle Sir Stanley Unwin in publishing another book on a similar theme. She planned a visit to Japan in April 1963, but adamantly refused to leave the practice in the hands of a man. She was delighted to find a suitable female locum, Judith King. King recalled how impressed she was with how efficiently the office ran:

> Marie was the best lawyer in this part of the world for miles around. She was a very good lawyer. But her reputation with me lies with her work practices. I haven't ever struck any other office that was as good on delegation ... And what impressed me was that all these ladies were so keen on their jobs because Marie accommodated their personal circumstances, so they all worked hard when they were there. Believe you me they worked very, very hard when they were there. There was none of this jazzing on the phone and doing their nails talking to their boyfriend for hours.

The practice was growing considerably, mainly due to the increase in Eastwood's population; the suburb had become a thriving business centre. A senior member of staff, Wyn Fensom, told King that even though Robert Moin had taken many of the easier cases, because of his inexperience, anything complicated still came to M.B. Byles & Co.

IN JAPAN, Marie's destination was the headquarters of the Rinsai Sect in Kyoto, formerly the Imperial capital. Abounding in temples and monasteries, Kyoto is a sacred pilgrimage site for Buddhists in Japan. Buddha Dhamma was absorbed into the cultures of the countries it travelled to, and over the centuries developed different doctrines. Though different in method, aim and basic philosophical conception to Theravadin Buddhism (the original teachings), there are certain commonalities of approach in Zen. Nonetheless, Marie was unprepared for the culture shock. Japanese culture and Zen Buddhism were completely different from anything she had experienced in Burma.

An American woman Zen priest, Mrs Ruth Fuller Sasaki, made arrangements for Marie to live at a temple within the main compound of the Rinsai Sect. Each temple within the compound was walled. Found within were exquisite Japanese gardens. Mrs Sasaki had built a *zendo* (meditation hall) specifically for Westerners. It was the only zendo in Japan where the presiding priest did not use Manjushri's sword, the stick used to hit meditators' backs to improve concentration. Attending the zendo for two hours every evening, Marie took her place on a platform that ran down the side of the zendo covered with tatami matting. She had a hard low cushion to sit on.

> The priest, striding silently round, did not whack <u>us</u>, but we could hear the monks in the training school being wacked – especially frequently during Sesshin, the week of intensive training. I also once attended Zazen in the shrine room attached to the monastery and saw the monks being beaten to force them into the daily interview with the Roshi, or Teacher.

The sound of people being whacked made it impossible for Marie to concentrate. After weeks of serious but fruitless attempts to penetrate its mysteries, she realised that the austerity of Zen was not for her. 'It was not relaxing for me, the spirit of the soldier still runs through the training.'

From visitors, she heard about a spiritual community nearby that sounded exactly what she was looking for. Convincing two other visitors at the zendo to accompany her, she crossed the mountains outside Kyoto to arrive at the village of Ittoen. There, about 300 men, women and children lived practising the highest spiritual principles, performing social service as an integral part of their practice. Driving into the village, the visitors passed embankments of flowering azalea bushes and crossed a swiftly rushing river overhung with cherry trees. At the unpretentious office, the inter-community telephone summonsed a young woman dressed in a short black kimono and black pants. Ayako Isakawa was the teacher of English in Ittoen who could act as their interpreter.

Ittoen's name means Garden of the One Light, so-called because its members were drawn from all religions and found the same Light at the heart of each. Ayako led Marie and the other visitors on a tour through the picturesque village of stone bridges and summer pavilions. Inside the new lecture hall was a plaque of Mahatma Gandhi. After visiting the printing and knitting works, agricultural bureau, vegetable gardens and forestry plantation that fed the community's need for fuel, they were taken to meet the founder, Tenko Nishida. Over ninety years of age, he was frail and deaf, but still very alert in practical affairs. As they drank tea together, he told them his story of having left his life as a businessman to lead an exemplary spiritual existence. As Marie recounted:

> Ittoen was founded by Tenko San quite unconsciously at the beginning of the century when he gave away his property and found that in having nothing there is inexhaustible wealth. He has been called the St. Francis of Japan, depending on Light (or God) alone for everything. Like him, the members of Ittoen have no individual property.

Tenko San's face glowed, Marie wrote, with 'that indescribable universal love seen only on the faces of the aged who have lived a long time within its radiance'. The extraordinary atmosphere of peace and harmony at Ittoen impressed Marie. It occurred to her that perhaps she had not come to Japan to investigate Zen, but to find 'a virile new religion with a message for the modern world.'

After sightseeing and visiting a range of Buddhist and Shinto temples, Marie returned to Ittoen at the end of May for a longer visit before departure. After settling in, she wanted to render whatever service she could. Ayako arranged for her to help teach English to the children who, she discovered, were bright, interested and full of humour. After a tiring day, she indulged in the rituals of communal bathing and soaked away the tiredness. At five o'clock the next morning, the big Buddhist drum called the community to *sutra* chanting in the Hall of the Spirits. The radiant serenity of the old Shinshu priest who led the worship was deeply moving for her as she repeated the five prayers of penitence and the vows of service. Still chanting, the community members filed out of the hall, arriving at the dining room where they sat down on the hard boards. Hands held prayer-wise, the chanting continued for another five minutes as the food was served.

At 7.30 am everyone was called to work. The entire compound was cleaned from top to bottom. 'Every window, ledge, basin, floor, tile, o-benjo [squat toilet] and board was despoiled of its dust and dirt.' Then Marie was summoned by Ayako to join the monthly o-benjo cleaning expedition to the nearby town of Yamashina. About seventy people, including all the guests, lined up on the school playing field. They recited the poem of service that elaborated on Tenko San's belief that 'the source of all evil lay within ourselves, so that we can never blame another, but find it a privilege to help expiate evil by selfless service'.

Each person picked up a bucket, a thick rag and a small bamboo brush. The long file started down the road. Ayako and Marie brought up the rear, dressed in black pants and a short black kimono tied around her waist. It was a long walk under the hot sun. Eventually, Ayako stopped opposite a temple and told Marie their assignment started there. The rest of the line continued on as they knocked on the door. A genial priest of the Jodo sect came out and Ayako said: 'We are from Ittoen; we have come to clean your honourable toilet for the sake of the peace of the world and our own renunciation of selfhood.' The priest thanked her and showed them to what was already a very clean o-benjo. They made it a little cleaner by washing down the walls and door.

The same process was repeated at every house. Many women said they had already cleaned the toilet that morning. At some houses no one was home. At others, their services were very much needed. One mother washing clothes in her tiny backyard with the help of her baby was genuinely grateful. She gave them soap and water to wash their hands afterwards. At another house there was no tap so they had to dip water out of the stream that ran through the township. Afterwards, Marie noted disapprovingly, they emptied the dirty water and washed the rag and brush in the same stream.

Ittoen was the most inspiring organisation she had come across. Its philosophy of gaining world peace through self-renunciation was the pinnacle of all the spiritual paths she had studied. Tenko San was, she believed, the living embodiment of spiritual attainment. Before she left she met again with him for tea and cakes and asked the question that most engaged her when visiting spiritual communities: 'Are there ever any quarrels in Ittoen?'

Tenko San replied, 'No quarrels, but sometimes there may be a difference of opinion. Then each one asks himself wherein lay his fault. If only one asks himself this question, the differences will be resolved and ill-will will die.'

The loving-kindness that shone from his face when he shook hands to say goodbye was, to Marie, the greatest illustration of his virtuous life of selfless service. At Ittoen she found a glimpse of heaven on earth, demonstrating how people could live together in peace and harmony, 'and in this world of strife this is no mean thing'.

After this visit Marie felt the basis of her life was somehow reoriented. She felt less critical, happier within herself and suffused with loving thoughts. In particular, Ayako's spirit of complete self-surrender to the Light made a deep impression. Enlightenment was Marie's aim but she realised that the great stumbling block was the ego that 'forever prevents or tries to prevent our realising our oneness with the Universal'. Ittoen's training in humility, Marie believed, could give her something that other philosophies had not: the state of selflessness that leads to enlightenment.

SOON AFTER returning to Sydney in August 1963, Marie wrote to Makoto Ohashi, an English-speaker, and asked for more information. In response, he translated part of a book that Tenko San had written *Life of Sange* (translated as *Life of Penitence*). The book spoke directly to her heart and Marie believed it could also speak to the hearts of others. She wrote to the Ittoen Elders, suggesting that Makoto San translate the book into English, and then she would revise it in a way that communicated to Westerners. The book, *A New Road to Ancient Truth*, would eventually be published in 1969 by George Allen & Unwin UK after what would be a complicated and frustrating process.

Although Marie's workload was constantly increasing, trusting in the Light allowed her to manage the workload. She wrote glowing articles about Ittoen in a range of Buddhist and Gandhian publications. On occasion, when she was asked to be a guest speaker by a charity or community group, she spoke on "Ittoen: The Garden of the One Light". Audience members sometimes came up to her afterwards to express how the talk changed their lives. To her disappointment, however, most Westerners interpreted the Ittoen approach (especially cleaning toilets) as taking pride in being humble. Marie's staff could not understand why she felt the need to perform these sorts of duties.

Writing to Ayako, she explained part of her motivation in getting the book published.

> It sometimes makes me weep when people come into money unexpectedly (usually through making a huge profit on the sale of land) and become hard and embittered and grasping almost overnight. I want to write an introduction to the book to show how a man can be wealthy and yet non-attached to wealth (and a woman of course!).

Over the next twelve months, Ayako acted as intermediary between Marie and the Elders. She answered Marie's specific requests for information, checked the English translations, handled all the financial transactions necessary to complete the project and complied with Marie's written requests regarding the illustrations for the book's cover. To Marie, Ayako's ability to remain at peace within, while undertaking these tasks, exemplified her ability to die to self. Acknowledging her own inability to do so, Marie wrote, 'In theory I know that dying to self is all that is necessary, but it takes many years of training. And I am far from having done so.'

By July 1965, problems with the Elders were starting to emerge. They were becoming suspicious of the tone of the translations. They believed that

Marie was reinterpreting Tenko San's philosophy to make it more appealing to Westerners and wanted some things changed. Wondering whether she should continue, she had 'a wonderful dream in which Tenko San seemed very close to me, and told me to go ahead with the work.' After that she felt at peace and 'utterly certain that whatever happened, all was as the Light designed'. She explained to Ayako, 'Whether the book is published or not, doing the work with Makoto has altered my life.'

Before Marie returned to Japan for more research and to continue negotiations with the Elders, she found another female locum, Helen Larcombe, to mind the office while she was away. On boarding the plane, Marie felt like 'one of those pious Buddhist pilgrims from China who went to India to get the Scriptures' to take back to their own people. On arrival, however, matters immediately became complicated. Her publisher's agent in Tokyo informed her that Tenko San had deliberately withdrawn his *Life of Sange* from public sale. After running into 301 editions, he was afraid that it was starting another new religion to add to the 170 other new religions in Japan that had arisen in the 1950s and '60s out of the traumatic defeat in World War II.

At Ittoen, Ayako told her that Takeshi San, the grandson of Tenko San and now the manager of the community, would take his time before seeing her about arranging for the publication in England of *A New Road to Ancient Truth*. This had been the object of her visit to Japan, but he was too busy then and would be too busy for about a week. After that, he would hear what she had to say, but it was by no means certain that he would permit the book to be published.

Finally able to meet with Takeshi San, he told Marie that no translation would be acceptable 'unless written by a person who was humble and serious and that for Ittoen Tenko San was God just as Jesus Christ was God to Christians'. They then discussed publication rights. Next day there followed a formal meeting with all nine Elders, only one a woman. They sat on cushions on the floor and asked Marie many questions concerning herself, her life history, the aspect of Tenko San's teaching that appealed to her, and what aspects of Ittoen life seemed the most important to her.

Attempting to explain equity, company and contracts law through an interpreter, Marie declared that the Elders ('some of them half my age!') seemed to have no comprehension of the legal aspects of publication. Drafting a suggested agreement with the English publishers that would protect Ittoen legally, she felt entirely misunderstood: 'The more I tried to explain English law, the more their suspicions gathered around me like threatening clouds.'

The character traits that allowed Marie to achieve so much in the West made it more difficult for her in the East. It drove her to distraction that her position, based on pedantic legal logic, did not prevail. One of her Ittoen friends warned her: 'The Western mind likes things clear as crystal and hard as concrete. The Eastern mind likes to leave them nebulous and hazy.' It was difficult for Marie to make the necessary adjustment.

Although she told the Elders that she wanted no share of the profits, they accused her of trying to make an arrangement for her own advantage. Too late she realised that she had handled the matter badly. There was no certainty she would be given permission to publish. Marie worried that all the labour of writing and expense of coming to Japan might be thrown away. When the Elders had agreed to the translations they had no idea just how difficult it would be to maintain ownership of their teacher's philosophy and negotiate with this intense Western woman with her incisive legal mind. It was an impossible collaboration. By the end she 'felt like murdering everyone'. Physically, she was a complete wreck. In a letter to an osteopath friend in Sydney to request a treatment on her return, Marie wrote,

> As long as I shoulder all the blame myself, all is well and of course the more I think on my misdeeds and misthoughts, the blacker they become, and when I try to shoulder the faults of others as Tenko San says, and rightly says one should do, well no wonder that I am passing through the worst depression of the last 11 years.

Departing Ittoen for the plane home, Marie's English students, who had given her so much pleasure, saw her off at the front gate. They sang the hymn of parting, "God be with you till we meet again". It was an unforgettable scene and one that touched her deeply. These two groups – the young, unquestioning students and the authoritarian Elders – represented the two extremes of Marie's interpersonal relationships: those she could control and those she could not. With the former, she gave unconditional love and support but with the latter, she was more often in conflict.

Two months after returning to Sydney, Marie wrote to Ayako attempting to justify her constant striving for results. Despite the mental and physical toll, she wrote, 'the quest for enlightenment is all that matters'. Rather than recognising that the path to enlightenment involves learning to be, to rest in the present moment, to Marie, enlightenment was some sort of objective – like a mountain peak – that can and will be achieved at all costs.

By November 1966, after repeated letters to the Ittoen Elders remained unanswered, Marie wrote again to Ayako despairing of any response. She compared herself with Gandhi who was 'fated to lead India to independence and I think I am the one fated to do something about this book. The one fated always has to work and suffer, for what in the long run turns out to be inevitable.' One and a half years would elapse before consent was finally given to publish *A New Road to Ancient Truth*. 'This was an excellent training for the transcriber in humility and non-attachment,' Marie noted. Many years later, after gaining insight into her behaviour and its disastrous consequences, she wrote,

> It is reported that Tagore once said to CF Andrews, Gandhi's Christian disciple, 'Charlie, Charlie, why must you always be <u>doing</u> something? Is it not enough to <u>be</u>?' ... After the usual retiring age of 65, I am now satisfied that the very law of my being, or Light, was asking me precisely this question and that I ignored it.

CHAPTER 17

The Measure of Our Gift

1966–1970

T HE NIGHT of 20 November 1966 heralded the end of a perfect spring day in Sydney. Sleeping as usual on her verandah, Marie was snug under her eiderdown beneath the starry moonlit sky. Suddenly, she was dragged off the bed. Crash! Her head held roughly in a man's strong hands was being smashed against the floorboards. Crash! Again … and … Crash! Again. So powerfully did the assailant bash her head against the hard wood that her skull fractured and her jaw broken. She was mercifully unconscious when he took further vengeance on her inert body, tearing off her pyjamas and raping her.

With the chill of the cold night air on her half-naked body Marie awoke in the darkness, unsure where she was. Slowly she realised that she, or the top half of her, was inside a wardrobe in the guest room. In excruciating pain and with great effort, she managed to prop herself up into a sitting position. Without the strength to climb up onto the bed, she dragged her body across the floor to a folded rug on the other side of the room and wrapped herself in it.

In the morning, John Fallding came by to find out why she had not collected her milk bottles. Seeing bedding strewn about the verandah, he searched inside the house. He found her in the guest room with her face, swollen and bruised, a mass of blood. Though unconscious, she was still breathing. John ran to get Vreni. While waiting for a doctor to arrive, they treated her for shock. Marie was taken to the nearby Sydney Sanitarium, a private hospital in Wahroonga known as a "home of health". As Dorothy Hasluck wrote in a letter to Marie's old friend, the writer Florence James,

> The Doctor who is a personal friend was very grave at first but now says she has rallied and although still a very sick woman he thinks with careful nursing & rest she will pull through but it will be a long business.

Marie drifted in and out of consciousness while her head was being X-rayed. When full consciousness returned and the numbness in her head wore off, she went through hell with a throbbing headache. Answering the detectives' questions, Marie felt she was not very helpful because she had no memory of anything beyond being dragged off the bed.

Dorothy gave this account to Florence:

> The worrying thing is that the detectives haven't any clues, & the fingerprints were not very satisfactory as they were on wood. Her wristlet watch was torn off & thrown on the floor & her bag with 12 dollars in it was also on the floor. All the drawers & cupboards were open but nothing was taken; as of course there was nothing else worthwhile. John [Fallding] had the camera. It is most mystifying but looks to me like someone with a bad grudge.

During the next few days as the pain increased, Marie became conscious of being something more than 'an animal-with-a-brain'. The sexual assault had been so brutal that her bladder had been damaged; fortunately, the urologist managed to affect a 'miraculous recovery' without the need for an operation, allowing her to pass water freely. Despite the sign "Visitors not permitted", one of her staff June Taylor managed to see Marie. She let her know that Helen Larcombe, the locum she had used while in Japan, had taken over the running of the office. Marie felt reassured that her clients would not be inconvenienced. She did not feel quite so reassured by June's comment that she looked like a tomcat that had been in a very bad fight.

A reluctant patient, Marie was nevertheless satisfied with "the San" as it served vegetarian food and the wards had no air conditioning; she preferred to have fresh air coming through the doors that opened onto the verandah. The doctor respected her wishes that 'there should be no sedatives, pain-killers or drugs'. The hospital was near her home so friends and neighbours could easily visit. Baldur came over most evenings to read into her 'not-so-deaf ear'.

Although she was a high-profile public figure, her friends had made sure the story of the assault stayed out of the newspapers. Many thought the perpetrator must have been a client with a grudge. For whatever reason, the police did not interview anyone at the office until two weeks after the attack and the staff had no idea who was responsible. Marie admitted how much the incident had unsettled her:

> But despite the fact that there was obviously a Providence that shapes our ends I was very frightened – I used to think I was brave – except when nearly falling into a crevasse of course! Two acquaintances who could throw themselves into a trance did so, and each got a vision of an Italian. Once when I was taken out to lie on the verandah, an Italian patient happened to walk onto the same verandah. I was terrified.

Marie struggled to stay in control of her emotions in an attempt to avoid the overwhelming fear of vulnerability. She reflected on Tenko San's teachings that 'we carry all evil within ourselves' and pondered what a retiring judge meant when he had said that everyone at one time or another has been capable of murder. The man who attacked her 'was obviously suffering from the epidemic of violence that was sweeping through the world; I was sorry for him'. She was horrified at the suggestion by a friend that she would want to see him punished: 'Inflicting a second injury does not cancel the first; it merely doubles it, just as adding a second negative to the first does not cancel it but merely doubles it.'

It was not her assailant whom she wanted to hurt, but 'the good nurses' who were attending to her. 'I told myself, or my ego insisted, that I had risen successfully in my profession, and was now being treated as a mere cypher.' Throughout her life Marie had viewed her small, weak body as something to be borne, and had a low tolerance for frailty. Always strong and independent, she now found herself an invalid, at the mercy of others.

When a young friend began to speak to her with condescension, she 'tried to have only thoughts of loving-kindness (when sometimes I would have liked to commit murder!)'. Marie came to the realisation that this was exactly how she had behaved towards others. She had imposed her opinions without consideration for their feelings: 'I was merely working through my karma ... there is no occasion for praise or blame but only for acceptance.' In her weakened state, this spiritual attitude helped her recovery. Her friends said of her during this time that she was her sweetest self. They were able to give her their love and support without brushing up against her prickliness.

Marie was determined to return home to live, hoping to be nursed by the Falldings and Dorothy Hasluck. But they feared for her safety in the isolated house and the return of her attacker. To their relief, Florence James offered an alternative. The year before, Florence had been a guest of Marie's and lived in the Hut for three months while helping her with *New Road to Ancient Truths*. Friends since university, it was during this time of meditating and working closely together that a deep bond had been forged. Immediately after Marie regained consciousness, she requested that if the okay from the Ittoen Elders came through, Florence, who had worked as an editor with Constables, a publishing house in London, would take on the project. Florence immediately replied, 'Of course I will gladly do this so don't have it on your mind at all.'

Writing to Dorothy Hasluck, Florence described the peace and beauty of a friend's house in which she was staying in the Blue Mountains. Lumeah was positioned in a secluded bushland setting with a sunny verandah and a view over the ranges. Florence generously offered the loving care and solitude Marie needed for healing. But in another letter she expressed the fears of a mutual friend that Marie 'may not recover … from the spiritual damage'. Responding to her kind invitation, Marie wrote to Florence describing her pitiable condition. She expressed the feeling that it may have been a mistake not to let her die and save all the trouble.

In mid-January, six weeks after the attack, Marie left hospital in an ambulance to reside temporarily in Thornleigh with Bertel Wernitzky, a Theosophist friend. Looking outwardly better, she felt 'positively ghastly' with her 'defective head and hearing'. Waking up on the first morning in Bertel's house, the whole atmosphere breathed 'peace'. Bertel, a trained nurse, had run a rest home in Holland. Her clinical approach and strong boundaries regarding the house made it easier for Marie, an intensely private person, to tolerate her state of dependence. The next two months were spent in painful but comfortable recovery from her 'mixed-up vision, deafness, dizziness, headaches, separated head and body'. The doctors had warned her that head injuries cannot be hurried but she remained optimistic: 'I cannot think the Law of Life has brought me this far from death without completing the cure.'

An unexpected pleasure came when the American Theosophical Society offered to publish *Footprints of Gautama Buddha* in paperback. The alterations Marie wanted to make to the manuscript and the complicated legal requirements of the contract were a distraction from her physical woes. Florence willingly offered to act on her behalf in corresponding with the publishers. In response to one of Marie's letters regarding the reprinting of *Footprints*, Florence wrote, 'Your writing is so much better and your spirit so full of courage I can feel your improvement. Linda and I both look forward to helping you further on the way back to health.' She described Linda MacIntosh, the owner of Lumeah, as 'the most healing person in herself that I know, gentle, loving and sensitive, and deeply Christian, but bound by no dogmas.'

At the height of Sydney's steamy summer, Marie was conveyed into the cooler air of the mountains and into Florence's care. Not wanting to be an imposition or beholden in any way, she insisted on paying $25 per week. She was aware that Linda took in paying guests and, as her jaw still could not chew solid food, she wanted to drink a lot of fruit and vegetable juices 'which are expensive'. She arrived with the Vitamizer juicer that she had especially imported. She had made good progress at Bertel's and was confident that in another six months she would be well again. Lumeah's wide verandah looked over a big green lawn, and through wooded hills the distant lights of Sydney could be seen. At Florence's suggestion, Marie had brought her sleeping bag and was soon sleeping out of doors on the verandah. Though still too dizzy to walk unaided, it lifted her spirits being able to lie on a settee and hear the birds and at night see the stars.

Considering her needs in every respect, Florence had taken great pains to prepare for Marie's visit and wanted to share the peace and serenity she found in this tranquil place. In contrast to Bertel's detached clinical approach, Florence and Linda attempted to heal with the power of their love. Unused to emotional intimacy and heavily defended against it, Marie felt smothered. The closer the two women came to her, the more threatened she felt. The feelings of rage she had attempted to bypass built up inside her. Marie berated herself for the 'intolerable burden of sin' that was at the root of all her bad karma. While she rationalised that the violence was her fault and had nothing to do with external reasons, Florence and Linda did not share that view.

Marie had brought with her the manuscript of her own book on Ittoen, "Hidden Light from Japan", hoping to get Florence's help with completing it. Having read of an incident recounted in the preface, both Florence and Linda were concerned that the attack on Marie *was* personal. The episode describes how a young man of Marie's acquaintance, attempting to live as a Buddhist monk, had come to Ahimsa to beg for food. He took it for granted that Marie, having lived in Asia and being familiar with Buddhist customs, would cook some rice for him, add some other tasty food, and hand it to him with due reverence. Indignant at his pose, and harbouring an intense feeling of ill will towards young men who expected females to act subserviently, Marie dismissed him. Giving him a packet of rice and a box of matches, she told him to go up to the Hut and boil it himself. So incensed was the young man by this insulting act of rejection he knocked the rice out of her hand, screamed abuse at her for behaving so disrespectfully, and stormed off.

Concerned about this behaviour, Marie immediately rang a psychiatrist friend for advice on how to handle the situation. Later, she received a 'horrible letter' from the young man's mother. Apparently his father was in a mental hospital and his behaviour indicated that he too had serious mental problems. The young man never forgave her. Florence wrote to Baldur, '... we wondered whether, with this man's history of family instability and his own and his mother's resentment against Marie, there should be an investigation.'

Marie desperately wanted to return home. Ahimsa, to which she was deeply attached, nurtured and protected her sense of self. Despite the haunting threat of another attack, she was determined to reclaim her refuge. Realising they could no longer be of help to her, neither Florence nor Linda attempted to dissuade her from leaving. Florence wrote to Baldur, describing how critical was Marie's unbalanced emotional state. While Marie had been deeply depressed throughout her stay these periods had become less frequent. However, as the time of her intended return approached, she had had three hysterical outbursts in the previous two days.

> When she is in this condition, she is full of confusion, except in one respect: whatever she says, she demands that we accept it without question, from trifling opinions to sharing her belief in a pre-ordained fate which has had violence in store for her from the beginning, and at the same time we must agree that she carries an intolerable burden of sin that lies at the root of her bad karma. When she beat her breast with anguish for the evil that is in her, we felt she was near to breaking point.

Florence was most concerned for Marie returning alone to her isolated house, as her worst outburst had been in the loneliness of night after she had gone to bed. Florence and Linda feared more for her being left alone in the house than if the attacker returned. Florence believed that Marie should see her psychiatrist friend, as hysteria was close to the surface at all times. However, she feared they could upset her delicate mental state further by disagreeing with her intention to leave on 15 June, a date she had carefully worked out. Baldur, who had known Marie over a lifetime, merely noted that she was her father's daughter, and Cyril had always demanded to have his own way.

By the time friends brought Marie home, the double vision had gone, but 'the dark cloud of depression' remained. Although it was good to be back among the familiar wooded hills and wildflowers, she was now afraid as well as depressed. Her first night at home was spent alone. Baldur, who had intended to give her company, had come down with bronchitis. The pain of a cracked rib, incurred during one of her hysterical episodes, forced Marie to sleep sitting upright inside the guest bedroom. This discomfort served to intensify her state of hyper-vigilance:

> At night when the rain dripped down the chimney, or the wind blew the leaves against the window, I would wake in terror. It could not go on like this. Furiously I started repeating thousands of times:
> No coward soul is mine,
> No trembler in the world's storm-troubled sphere;
> I see heaven's glory shine,
> And faith shines equal arming me from fear.

Defiantly Marie beat out this affirmation, refusing to allow her spirit to be crushed. Rain flooded the house and prevented water from flowing through the taps, causing more difficulties. Ultimately, though, being brought into contact with practical matters proved beneficial. Slowly, Marie took inventory of her neglected property. In the six months she had been away, the possums had eaten through the vegetable patch but the tree tomatoes had grown, as had three electricity pylons across the gully, despite the community protests she had led.

Attempting to apologise to Florence for the state she had been in during her stay, Marie wrote a letter of thanks acknowledging the difficulties she and Linda had endured: 'I am terribly sorry I was so irritating. I truly did my best, but it was a poor best.'

Florence, though, was not so easily mollified. She now understood Marie better than Marie appeared to understand herself. In a letter to Baldur she noted,

> ... the gulf that divided Marie's belief in her attainment of self-forgetfulness from her unremitting self-concern & self-will, and her repudiation of the need for human affection when she craves love with her whole being, although she would never acknowledge it ...

Florence felt that it was just one aspect of a 'multi-faceted self-deception' that held potential danger for such a passionate nature kept 'precariously in check by heady theory'. While sharing Marie's spiritual aspirations, Florence expressed frustration that if she had come to these insights earlier she could have helped Marie, but her patience and tolerance were exhausted by Marie's need to dominate with her extreme views. Nevertheless, Florence continued to give her support with her literary affairs and correspondence with the Ittoen Elders, who had finally given their approval for the publication of the translations.

Against all advice, Marie started sleeping out on the verandah again, battling fear each night until she overcame it. Her friends wanted her to have a dog, or a live-in companion, and one even gave her a burglar alarm, but she held close Gandhi's advice to 'shed fear' and rise above it, though she did agree to have lights installed outside the house. One night she awoke in fright to a possum nibbling her nose, mistaking it for an apple.

> That kind of fear did eventually depart but did not touch the far greater fear that comes from misery and depression, making me feel that the world was on top of me instead of I on top of it. Broken skulls do not mend as easily as broken limbs, and I was physically perennially exhausted and giddy, even though I could laugh and joke outwardly when friends called.

Despite her attempts, Marie could not keep up appearances with everyone. On his first visit since the attack, Jurvis Mniksevicus felt Marie was suspicious of him:

> All her life Marie was battling men. With me she talked as a fellow meditator. But that last time, she looked at me as a man, and a man had attacked her. That last attack was a culmination of her whole life's relationship with men. They all attacked her, so she probably expected me to attack her too.

One man who Marie did feel safe with was her brother Baldur, the family member she felt closest to and with whom she had most in common. They both had an affinity with nature and were committed to conservation. They also shared their father's temperament and drive while David, though closer in age to Marie, was the calm quiet one, perhaps taking after their mother more. As a father of six, and with a position as Chief Electrical Engineer for Hartley County Council based in Lithgow, David rarely had the chance to visit his sister.

As a single woman living alone, Marie prevailed upon any visiting male to help with manual labour and odd jobs around the place. Baldur was indispensable as he lived in nearby Beecroft and visited regularly. Now that she was completely infirm, Marie decided to employ a Girl Saturday, Margaret Ravizza, the thirteen-year-old daughter of a local builder. When Margaret first started working in 1967, Marie was extremely fragile and suffered from terrible headaches. On some days she could just manage to raise her head up from her bed to give instructions. Other days, when Margaret arrived, she would find Marie well enough to sit up and meditate. As Margaret recalled,

> I was quite amazed the way she could put her legs up in lotus position. She'd meditate like that on her bed while I was doing the gardening.
>
> She always seemed to be on that balcony area. She fed the little lizards with cheese.

Helen Larcombe often visited for lunch on Fridays, keeping Marie up to date on office affairs and answering her queries on the progress of each of the staff and their welfare. When Larcombe stepped in to run Marie's practice in response to the emergency, it was a big responsibility for the young mother of two children. As she recalled: 'We had 13 women [on staff]. I had to feed 13 women. It was huge. But you see that's what she liked because that was her support structure.' Larcombe soon became Marie's partner in M.B. Byles & Larcombe. Under their business agreement, Marie took one-third of the profits. This arrangement allowed her to maintain an association with the company she had established 37 years earlier.

Without her neighbours' assistance, Marie could not have remained at home. They nursed her through the three years that passed before any physical improvement occurred. Vreni Fallding made vegetable juices and Dorothy Hasluck provided dinner. Always the strong, dominant one of the group and very much the lady of the manor, Marie now needed their support, thus fulfilling the prophecy of her mother's family motto, "Sooner or later, near or far, the strong have need of the weak", just as her father had. Dependent on others, Marie accepted that her will could not rule. Though insight can come in a flash, patterns of a lifetime do not change overnight.

> Three springtimes came and went with the glory of golden wattle along the creeks and the air laden with perfume of pittosporum; and I was very little better. But this very depression, exhaustion, fear and helplessness then began to bring one lesson after another in quick succession and each took me a little further on. Life always brings exactly what is required, the result on the one hand of past karma, for one reaps what one has sown, but on the other of the ceaseless pull towards liberation from the bondage of this world and with it inner peace and joy. All that one need do is to accept what comes, but often this is not easy.

Weakness and depression make one very sensitive to any unkindness and also very susceptible to that disintegrating force of self-pity. I found that I must learn to live to myself and make no demands upon others for 'love, amusement, sympathy', as Mathew Arnold said.

I was probably fortunate in having this lesson forced upon me. At the same time I was forced to learn as a fact what hitherto I had known only intellectually that what is hurt is only the ego, which is always changing, pride of self, desire to stand well in the opinion of others and of oneself. Again, I was fortunate in being forced to be a little more humble, and not to mind what others said or thought. I confess that I have not yet fulfilled Gandhi's insistence that one must reduce self to zero. But I do know that it is only by leaving the burden of self behind that one is able to climb the mountain heights from which one can look down unperturbed at the really non-existent problems which seem so ridiculously real when down among them.

Spiritually, this was the summit of her ambition, humble compared to her other achievements, but deceptively difficult to achieve.

CHAPTER 18

The Greatest Lesson Learnt

1970 – 1974

*Another vital lesson that life brought was the need to live
in the present and not waste time on thoughts of the past or
hopes for the future, or on trying to do more than one thing
at a time. It is only through the present moment that one
can pierce through to eternity and peace …*

BY HER 70th birthday, Marie's health had recovered sufficiently to visit
her brother, David, in Clarence. There she reflected on two major decisions she was about to make. The first was to sever all connection with
legal work and hand over the practice to Helen Larcombe. While Marie had
filled in at the office for brief periods, she was no longer interested in returning
to work as a lawyer. She was ready to let go of that aspect of her life. Also, she
made the momentous decision to gift her property Ahimsa to the state branch
of the National Trust of Australia. This visionary gesture meant there could be
no future development of the semi-natural bushland. As she wrote in a letter
to the Deputy Director, Landscape Conservation:

> The object of Ahimsa is to provide a beauty spot of natural unspoilt bushland
> close to Sydney and a place where people can go to find peace and quietness
> from the hectic life in Sydney and its suburbs, and especially, I hope through
> the practice of meditation.

Once the newspapers got hold of the story, fame again found her at this
late stage of her life.

> There followed the most ridiculous newspaper publicity, not merely in
> Sydney, but also in other states and even America. Friends suggested that this

… betokened a 'protest' against making money for its own sake, a fool's game if only people knew it. I hope the friends were right, for no advantage would have come to me had I subdivided the land and made what the newspapers called 'a small fortune'.

Under her agreement with the National Trust, Marie could live in Ahimsa indefinitely as the honorary curator. Roslyn Muston, the trust's Environment Director, responsible for the management of the property, spoke with Marie on the phone. On her first visit to Ahimsa, the 25-year-old expected to be intimidated by such a strong-willed person. As Roslyn walked up the bush path below the house she could see Marie waiting for her on the verandah, 'a little bird of a woman'. They discussed her preferences, needs and aspirations for the property. Roslyn found her awe-inspiring: 'Very alert, very determined, but not aggressive at all and not at all frightening.'

During her semi-regular visits, they developed a mutual respect. Roslyn had a PhD in hydrology, and she had worked alone in remote bushland researching what happened when a fire went through an area: how the plant and animal community recovered and how the flow of water was affected. It was a subject Marie knew well having written authoritatively about the complex issue of fire ecology in the *Bushwalker* journal since the 1940s. During their discussions she never made the young graduate aware of the level of her own expertise. Instead, Marie reminisced about bushwalking and mountaineering, and spoke of how she never let what anybody else thought stop her from achieving her goals. Roslyn admired her tremendously, 'Her strength was absolutely amazing. Her wisdom seemed to be something that I couldn't really fully understand at that early age, but … when I sat with her I felt wiser when I left.'

When, after a couple of years in the job, Roslyn announced that she was leaving to get married, Marie was deeply disappointed. She tried to impress on the young woman that marrying was unnecessary, if she only thought about it rationally. The lecture Roslyn received 'Was on how I didn't need to do this because I could actually make this journey on my own. This is something I would find the inner strength for and it would be quite satisfactorily interesting, full and rich.' After that, Roslyn felt that Marie no longer saw her as 'interesting'. Some time later, having had two children, Roslyn returned to university to complete a second PhD and lecture. For inspiration, she kept a photograph of Marie on her desk.

> … And every time I felt like buckling at the knees I'd just look at that beady-eye and think, 'I can't, I'd better keep going. I've got to prove her wrong.' It's

hilarious. Now I'm self-employed [as a leading consultant in environmental sustainability]. I don't think Marie would be disappointed in me.

THOUGH STILL a semi-invalid, Marie was able to direct her intellectual energies into writing for international Buddhist journals, such as *Metta* (Sydney), *World Buddhism* (Colombo), *The Middle Way* (London) and *Gandhi Marg* (New Delhi). In this way she continued her commitment to the deeper understanding and popularisation of Buddhism. Buddhist visitors from around the world, including monks, came to visit when they were in Sydney.

Life became more difficult for her close neighbours with Marie at home constantly. She left copious notes reminding them to do various tasks. Having made them a gift of the land, she expected to have everything her way. Vreni learned to stand up to Marie, quietly telling her, 'No, we're doing it our way.' Perhaps Dorothy Hasluck, not having the support of a partner, was unable to be that assertive. Marie's fixation with the native bushland eventually led to a falling-out that became notorious within their circle of acquaintances. Against the terms of the agreement that Marie had drawn up with both sets of tenants, Dorothy had planted Wandering Willie, an aggressive scrambling creeper that Marie believed would destroy their lovely piece of natural bushland. While Dorothy was away and without consulting her, she gathered voluntary help to eliminate it. From then on, their relationship was strained.

WHILE MARIE'S injured head continued to slowly improve, any strain caused shocking headaches that kept her in bed for most of the afternoon. Through Aldous Huxley she learnt of the Alexander Technique, a postural therapy that sounded promising. Practise of this technique would eventually return a significant level of mobility.

Marie contacted Alan Murray, the only teacher of the Alexander Technique in Sydney. Convincing him to come to Ahimsa, Marie had her first lesson in September 1970. Each week, Alan made the train journey out to Cheltenham. While the treatment only lasted fifteen minutes, Marie found it so challenging that she often needed to sleep all afternoon. Despite the 'agony and exhaustion', much to her surprise she found that within a few months it became 'almost natural to walk and sit far straighter with head, neck and back in one line'. Keeping a diary of her progress, she wrote that although she had no miracle to record, her body ultimately benefited from the months of individualised treatment. Her health slowly returned and even her feet improved: 'I feel delightfully straight after standing against the wall and rising on the toes.'

Alexander practitioners work from the basic premise that body and mind are inextricably linked. The unnatural postures the body adopts in response to physical stress and strain influences the psyche. It was a philosophy that Marie appreciated and proved profoundly therapeutic as Alexander treated the mind, body and spirit as one functional unit. This holistic approach allowed gradual but definite improvement in her physical health and vitality. It also impacted on her attitudes and emotional wellbeing; she recognised that her physical progress was in parallel with 'my own moral and spiritual progress'.

Although never regaining robust health, Marie was able to live a reasonably active and self-sufficient life, with independence being her main priority. She could now walk over a kilometre before tiring. Reading and pottering about the garden also kept her busy. When Margaret Ravizza arrived on Saturday mornings she had a list of jobs ready for them to do together. Margaret recalled,

> She'd say: 'Right, we'll be doing dyeing today.' She would put clothes, curtains and pillowcases together and it would always be this olivey-green colour. Everything would go in. She couldn't see the point of making things a different colour. They all needed to be spruced up. Her personal things were a bit faded, so we gave them a new lease of life.

Margaret learnt practical skills that would set her up for life, including how to build a rock wall, make a fishpond and waterproof it and, most importantly, how to look after tools, oiling them after use. With her mentor directing her to this branch and then that, she climbed up trees to saw off dead branches, cleaned out gutters around the house before bushfire season, and kept the weeds down. After a hard morning's work, Marie made up a drink of lemon and lime-juice. Sitting together on the verandah, she told stories of her extraordinary life, not to impress Margaret so much as to inspire the young girl.

> China came into it a lot. She was proud of it, talked about it a lot. She seemed to think: If you want anything, you can do it if you want it enough. There were no barriers.

By the winter of 1973, Alan Murray was feeling the cold during the return train journeys from the city to Cheltenham. Marie agreed that she only needed a refresher lesson every few months. So impressed was she with the Alexander Technique that she convinced Murray to collaborate on a book outlining the practical Alexander exercises. The only books then available were theoretical explanations of the foundational principles by Alexander himself. Called the four gospels by his adherents, they were written in a demanding 19th century style, impenetrable to the layperson. Since Alexander's death, the technique had gone into a hiatus. Marie felt compelled to prevent this valuable knowledge from disappearing. They began their work but Murray gave up on it fairly early, either because of Marie's attempts to dictate the style and content, or perhaps because of criticism from other teachers about oversimplifying the fundamental principles into mere exercises.

Undeterred, Marie felt that she was justified in producing her own account of what she believed was a valuable method of rehabilitation for use by nurses, osteopaths, physiotherapists and other health practitioners. Adept at mastering every subject she studied, she also had a gift for communicating in a straightforward style that made even arcane practices accessible to a general audience. Her old bushwalking friend Dot Butler gave assistance by correcting any errors of terminology in physiology and anatomy. She also drew diagrams and compiled the glossary of terms. While Marie and Dorothy Hasluck (both in their 70s) posed for the photographs that illustrated each exercise, for the cover, Marie enlisted Griselda Brown, a younger woman who regularly meditated in the Hut.

Marie sent the manuscript to George Allen & Unwin, but Sir Stanley had died and her cousin, Philip Unwin, had retired. Because it was not the style of book the company published, it was rejected. The good news was that the reprint of *Footprints of Gautama Buddha* had sold out when it was released in Sydney. However, *A New Road to Ancient Truths* was not selling as well in Japan as Marie had hoped. It failed to connect with Japan's youth who were uninterested in Eastern philosophies, unlike in the West. Marie refused to give up on the Alexander project – this was one book she was determined to see in print before she died.

Resilience was her defining quality. When a rejection letter from one publisher specified that the presentation style would need to be modernised and rewritten, she seized upon the chance and set about reworking the entire manuscript. As each chapter was finished she forwarded it to Griselda who did each exercise, testing the instructions. If Griselda felt she was not getting it right, she discussed it with Marie and together they collaborated on the rewording. Rewritten three times, the manuscript was finally accepted by an English publisher, Fowler & Co., and published in 1978. The Alexander Technique eventually became established throughout the world. With her visionary gift, Marie had, once again, promoted a technique that was beneficial to many, bringing awareness of the mind-body-spirit connection to the fore.

FROM 1970 until the end of her life, Marie worked on an autobiography enti-tled "Many Lives In One". It was an immense task to compile the various themes of her long and eventful life, and the necessary objectivity for self-portrayal ultimately proved beyond her. Throughout her life, she had used writing as a way of processing and expressing her thoughts and emotions, and this project gave her the opportunity to reflect:

> I was given a good but not a brilliant brain, along with a very flimsy body, although not one subject to popular diseases. I often look back on all the auda-cious things I have done and wonder how on earth I did them and why, for I have no outstanding talent and all is transient – a laugh or a sob in the mist of time.

Pondering the significant world events she had witnessed over her lifetime, Marie wrote, 'but it is not external events that mark the life of the individual: there is something more important that takes place inwardly'.

All the while, she continued with her main passion, maintenance of the Ahimsa property and conservation of native bushlands. In the Garden Club of Australia's quarterly magazine of May 1974, Marie exhorted its members to do their best for the natural environment:

> The bush is necessary, not only for us who reside near it but for all; it is a breathing place away from the smog of the city, a rare place of peace and quietness necessary for our health. It is essential for the preservation of our unique flora and fauna for present and future generations; but above all it is necessary for nature itself; man cannot live without nature ...
>
> Let us keep our bush and value it higher than gold or anything we can mine from the soil. Yes! Even oil. Roads and homes are also 'worthy causes' but can be put elsewhere; bush cannot. Therefore let us jealously guard our bush and please do not steal from it.

That same year her plea corresponded with the formation of a small group of local Beecroft-Cheltenham residents committed to eliminating the thick infestation of privet beside the creek that ran next to Ahimsa. Privet had been introduced into Australia to provide hedging but soon invaded wilderness areas, displacing native species.

The group met once a month on a Saturday morning with the aim of removing the weeds and replanting with natives. They met for several months before getting disheartened about how little they were achieving and went into recess. When they discovered the Bradley Method, a new approach to bush regeneration, they decided to make a new start. Joan Bradley and her sister, both Sydney residents, had devised a method of weed elimination starting in less disturbed areas so the gradual re-inhabitation of native plants occurs naturally. Wanting to learn from the expert, Marie invited Joan to visit Ahimsa hoping she would provide direction and move the work along. Joan was similar to Marie, strong-willed and direct and readily gave advice. The bush regeneration group recommended work below Ahimsa along the then unnamed creek, a tributary of Devlin's Creek. Pat Fleet reflected on Marie's leadership:

> There was a group of us every third Saturday. She'd have us all down there digging away. We used to get down there with our weeding things. The men, when they heard what we were going to do, all came down with their axes … Of course, she didn't want that. She sent them on their way. 'That's not what we want at all.' It was mostly women who went down there.

On their walks, locals saw the group at work and many became involved, getting to know their local area, to appreciate nature and the environment. Marie remained a regular and keen member for many years. When the group suggested that a suitable name for the creek would be Byles Creek she demurred, attempting to convince them that Ahimsa Creek was preferable. They insisted that Byles Creek was short and easy to say and began using what became the official name.

IT WAS eight years after the assault that Marie thought she could manage her first bushwalk. She asked Griselda Brown to accompany her through Pennant Hills Reserve to see her sister-in-law in the nearby Sanatorium. Insisting on doing the long hike properly, there was a lot of talk about needing a leader. 'I can see you'll be a very good leader,' she told Griselda, whose heart immediately sank into her boots.

> I can't remember what happened, but needless to say, I blotted my copybook in some way and she had to take over. Whether we got lost or what it was. By the time we arrived, I felt like we were explorers from a distant country coming in our rough old clothes.

Baldur's wife Janet, not a bushwalker, was sitting up in bed all made up and her hair done. Marie and Griselda sat on either side of the bed looking complete wrecks. After lunch, they took a taxi back home. One way was far enough and Marie had the satisfaction of doing one more bushwalk.

CHAPTER 19

Adventurous Spirit

1972–1979

B Y THE 1970s, the world had caught up with Marie Byles. Many of the movements she helped lay the foundations for became mainstream: women's rights, environmental conservation, and interest in the health and wellbeing of body, mind and spirit. A radical transformation of society had begun in the 1960s as mass movements for civil rights inspired protests in the streets. Women waving placards demonstrating for equal opportunity in employment and repeal of abortion laws that refused them control of their own bodies.

No longer female eunuchs cut off from their capacity for action by social mores that required their submission, women were free to explore their options. As old conventions were swept away, so too was the morality that upheld community values. Concerned about the massive rise in sexually transmitted diseases, Marie educated herself on the subject. She wrote to political parties, contributing her practical ideas for ways to combat the spread of venereal diseases, suggesting that services be provided at all public hospitals, and even mobile clinics to educate and examine those at risk.

The national campaign coordinator of one political party wrote back saying that he had 'much greater responsibilities in the party than discussing human sexuality and its related problems'. It would take another decade, with the devastating spread of HIV, for governments to realise that sexual health issues would need to be addressed. Since then, hundreds of millions of dollars are spent annually on public health campaigns along the lines that Marie had suggested. Then, as always, she was ahead of her time.

TIME, THOUGH, was catching up with her in another way. In 1974, Marie's world was shaken when Baldur suffered a series of major health crises: blood clots in the lung and brain, a heart seizure and pneumonia. The next thirteen months consisted of 'intense mental anguish and utter helplessness with many, many ups and downs' as she visited her brother twice a week in the Lottie Stewart Hospital in nearby Dundas. As his health deteriorated, Baldur passionately wished to die. When he at last yielded and was prepared to accept even a life of helplessness, 'if God so required', he found inner peace. Marie wrote in a letter to Ayako at Ittoen that, 'having given up his wish, it was fulfilled'. After living with Baldur's continuing anguish, she could not help but feel relieved when it was all over. Nevertheless, his death on 16 August 1975 came as a great shock. Suffering from delayed strain, she collapsed for two months.

While the realisation of her own mortality was brought closer with her brother's death, Marie had begun making preparations for her own inevitable demise some years before. Wanting to depart this life in as natural a way as possible, she had taken the precaution of putting up signs over her bed stipulating that, if she was no longer capable of determining her own treatment, no drug therapy should be given and her life was not to be extended artificially. It was a dictum she repeated to everyone who might have influence over the outcome.

Discovering the only female medical practitioner in the area, Dr N. Hardwicke, Marie set about cultivating her, ensuring that her wishes for a natural death at home would be respected. Palliative care – medical services for terminally ill people delivered in the environment of their own choosing – was then unknown. Dr Hardwicke lived nearby and Marie often visited her at home, walking through the bush with a bag of fresh fruit and vegetables from her garden to leave at her door. Dr Hardwicke thought she was a generous spirit, little realising her hidden agenda – to maintain control to the last. Writing to Griselda, Marie revealed that she had an annual medical check-up, 'so that I have a tame doctor to protect me from her own profession'.

THAT SAME year, the Women Lawyers Association wished to celebrate the 50th anniversary of Marie's admittance as the first female solicitor of New South Wales. The president contacted her and offered to hold a celebration but Marie, still recovering from Baldur's death, declined. Instead she invited the committee to afternoon tea at Ahimsa.

On that day in October 1974, a distinguished group of women walked up the garden path carrying a cake. Elizabeth Evatt had been educated at PLC

Pymble, as was her mother, who, inspired by Marie's trailblazing example encouraged Elizabeth to enter the profession in which both her father and uncle were prominent. At the time, Evatt was chairing the Royal Commission on Human Relationships that had lasting influence. The Commission's final report brought taboo topics related to abortion, rape, domestic violence and child abuse into public discussion. In 1976, Evatt would be appointed the inaugural Chief Judge of the Family Court and achieve outstanding social reform.

Mary Gaudron first encountered Marie when a law student at Sydney University in the mid-1960s. Representing the female law students in her year, Gaudron approached the Women Lawyer's Association for advice on surmounting the difficulties they had encountered gaining articles with city law firms. Their applications were being tersely rejected as even then law firms had a policy not to employ women as articled clerks. Marie gave them the benefit of her experience, suggesting methods to overcome their limiting beliefs and increase their chances of success. Gaudron was encouraged, noting that, 'the hurdles they had to jump had been much higher than those we were ever likely to confront'. Gaudron was admitted to the Bar in 1968. In 1974, she was appointed a federal court judge and later became the first female Solicitor-General of NSW, the first female Solicitor-General of any Australian jurisdiction.

Among her eminent visitors that day, the person Marie was most interested in speaking with was Margaret Crawley who had been articled to her in 1947. Crawley, who had an avid interest in horseracing, was in the process of taking the Australian Jockey Club of NSW to court over its refusal to admit women as members. Marie was impressed that her unassuming young clerk had turned into a tiger fighting against discrimination, responsible for a significant win against the previously all-male club.

Despite failing health, Marie maintained a reasonably active schedule. Saturday mornings were spent down by the creek with the bush regeneration team attempting to win the battle with privet. On Sunday mornings she joined with a small meditation group at the Hut of Happy Omen. It remained a popular venue for various groups to meet or conduct activities, such as meditation, fasting or bushwalking. Marie made it available free of charge in exchange for some manual labour in the garden. After they had fulfilled their obligation to Marie, they were often too tired to continue with their own activity.

In one of Griselda's letters she asked Marie if the quiet atmosphere of Ahimsa was helping her meditation. Marie responded, 'No, the quiet of the country does not banish thoughts. I more and more find that the ceaseless repetition of a mantra is the only escape to the Beyond.' In Japan, she had learnt a mantra designed to help those who found meditation too difficult: 'Buddha Amida Butsu' meaning, 'Adoration to the Buddha of Boundless Light and Love'. During 'the troublous years' of incapacity and ill health at the end of her life, Marie used this mantra to ease herself through each crisis as it arose.

Early in 1979 she noticed some alarming symptoms, bleeding from the bowel and persistent diarrhoea. When she finally consulted Dr Hardwicke, she was given the diagnosis of bowel cancer. She refused to believe it at first, exclaiming, 'That's impossible. I'm a vegetarian!'

Once she accepted the diagnosis, Marie refused to have an operation, demonstrating unconditional acceptance of her condition and imminent demise. She chose to stay at home until the end. This was very hard on Vreni Fallding especially, Dorothy Hasluck having died the year before. However, John and Vreni always knew that Marie expected them to be indebted to her for the gift of the land.

Ever the pragmatist, whenever she received a letter, Marie used the same envelope returned with a message scrawled on the back saying, 'I'm dying.' She lay on her bed on the verandah quite relaxed and at peace with the world in as close proximity to nature as she could, as family, old staff members and acquaintances came to say goodbye. Having had a mild stroke, her brother David was unable to visit from the Blue Mountains, and his voice was weak on the phone. Marie was resolved to never meeting him again.

Everyone was surprised at how accepting she was of her imminent demise. On her deathbed Marie was not plagued with questions about the point of her life. After all, she had taken every opportunity to understand its purpose and seek out truth. She took a path that most fear to tread. Jung called it 'the risk of inner experience, the adventure of the spirit', on which most people are overcome by fright and run away. Marie was not the type to run from a new adventure:

> I should like to think that I will join George Eliot's 'Choir Invisible of those immortal dead who live again in minds made better by their presence, live in pulses stirred to generosity … beget the smiles that have no cruelty' and so forth. But at the same time I confess to a more mundane longing for Peter Pan's faith. You will remember that Peter had given his wings away and standing on a lonely rock in the lagoon whose tide was steadily rising, with a smile on his lips and a drum beating in his heart, he said: 'To die would be an awfully big adventure!'

Death was no tragedy for Marie – senility, or a long lingering death in hospital, was tragedy. Through sheer determination she managed to avoid both of those outcomes. For Buddhists, death is transformation, and Marie, whose entire life was one of metamorphosis, was excited by the prospect of what would happen after all the surmising. There was no fear, just intense interest.

A frequent visitor was Nell Cusack who came with her husband Norman. Having long ago patched up their friendship, Marie had acted as Nell's solicitor until the assault. Their ongoing relationship meant so much to her. A book that Nell helped inspire and had edited had recently been made into a feature film. *Caddie*, written by Nell's cleaning lady, was an emotionally powerful memoir of life as an economically disadvantaged single mother between the wars. It became a highlight of Australia's 1970s film renaissance and was just the sort of thing that Marie admired Nell for, sharing as they did a strong sense of social justice and commitment to women's rights.

When Ruth Milton visited, Marie was still mentally alert, announcing, 'Oh well, I haven't got very long.'

Ruth responded, 'How lovely the trees are, you must be enjoying those.'

Marie said, 'Oh yes, it's just what I wanted.'

She asked Ruth to read aloud a long letter from Ayako and reply to it for her. Ruth had recently visited the Ittoen community on Marie's request while touring Japan and had met Ayako. She learnt that *A New Road to Ancient Truth* had finally sold out and Ittoen had received letters from many people around the world saying how much Tenko San's philosophy had changed their lives.

At the end of her unpublished memoirs "Many Lives In One", Marie had reflected:

> The greatest lesson learned in old age came of itself. I learned that there is something more important than bodily health and strength. It would be delightful to have a head which the body did not want removing and feet which liked walking, and health is certainly the greatest of life's blessings. But these are small matters compared with a growing consciousness that all rests in this life force which is love, light and strength far beyond anything of this world that ordinary people consider desirable.

As her condition deteriorated, a geriatric nurse was employed. Marie made the decision to hasten death by not taking food, just drinking water – in her words 'mountain spring water', even though it was from her own tank. When Griselda heard that her old friend did not have long, she dropped everything and came down from her home in the country to spend a few days with her before she died.

> I know that she was so terribly pleased to see me. I know that she had been upset that I'd gone away. She had gotten attached to me I realised … the old attachment bit. Because that was part of it, this thing that she always said, whatever she got attached to got taken away. Coming back to visit her before she died was wonderful but, after a couple of visits I could tell that she'd had enough of me. So that was good. She could get free of that bit of attachment.

Griselda was with Marie during her last days and recalled,

> There was a terrific struggle at the end because Marie didn't want to take any drugs, but the pain got so bad that the nurse and doctor persuaded her. They were using a lot of blackmail on her saying 'It's not fair for the other nurses that come in to have to put up with you being like that.'

Wanting to be fully conscious at the time of death Marie was against the use of palliative drugs because of their side-effects. Unable to resist the pressure any longer, she finally relented, 'All right. Well if the pain gets too bad, I'll have one.'

She then had a perfect night's sleep, with no medication, and died at 9 am the next morning, 21 November 1979.

MARIE'S OLD bushwalking friend, Dot Butler had visited her the week before. When she left, Dot said, 'I'll see you again next Wednesday.'

Marie responded, 'No, you won't. No, you won't. I'll be gone.'

Dot, the tough bushwalker who had suffered many tragic deaths in her immediate family replied, 'Oh you'll be around' and went off to visit family in the country. On about the sixth day there was, Dot recalled,

> … the most fearful commotion in the heavens. There was lightening and crashes of thunder and huge cumulus clouds and we just marvelled. What a sight! When I got home shortly afterwards I found out that was the night that Marie had died and everybody said, 'Well that's just what you'd expect when a dominant person like Marie seeks admittance to the heavens. Look at the reception she gets!' That was very, very typical.

A Buddhist monk who used the Hut for meditation-group retreats expressed his estimation of Marie: 'Whatever you might say about her, she was a woman of a special calibre otherwise she couldn't have achieved what she did. She had a difficult life because what she tried to achieve was difficult.'

IN THE chapel of the crematorium filled with native flowers, friends and colleagues from all of Marie's fields of interest gathered. She had stipulated that
no priest or clergyman was to be present; Dot Butler read part of a poem Marie
had chosen. By the end of her life she had come to realise that it was not success
in the material world or even spiritual development that was important, but the
awakening of that loving side of us that we can relate to others.

> So many gods, so many creeds,
> So many paths that wind and wind,
> While just the art of being kind,
> Is all the sad world needs.

Marie had informed friends that after she died she wanted everyone to have a
tea party at the Hut of Happy Omen, to enjoy themselves and have a good laugh.
And that is what they did. The sound of their laughter echoed through the bush,
just as she had wanted. No tears, no regrets – she had lived a wonderful life.

In April the following year, a ceremony was held in the grounds of Ahimsa
to scatter Marie's ashes. Ruth Milton gave a talk on Ittoen; Dot Butler spoke of
Marie's outdoor conquests as a bushwalker and mountaineer; and Pearle Pitcher
recalled Marie's office practices and influence on her staff. Then half of her ashes
were scattered. The rest were sent to Ittoen – Ayako had written to Ruth asking
if she would send something of Marie's to keep in the Spiritual House where
these memorials were kept. Ruth felt Ittoen had been so much a part of Marie's
life that she would have approved.

The Ittoen community held a special service for Marie. Tenko San's grandson attended together with 'fifteen people who had dear memories about
Marie', as Ayako later wrote to Ruth. One of them, a Buddhist priest before
he joined Ittoen, led the service chanting sutras. A special one was for Marie's
spirit. On the altar Ayako had prepared were some Buddhist statues, a small
pagoda, a candle, incense, together with different kinds of Japanese cakes and
fruits. Marie's ashes were placed on the altar underneath her photograph. After
the sutras, everyone enjoyed biscuits, cake and herbal tea.

WHEN MARIE had severed all connection with her law practice on her 70th
birthday, the staff visited as a group and presented her with a black and white
portable television set. Considering television to be her special abomination, she
exiled it to the Hut. Eventually, her attitude shifted and on Sunday afternoons
she invited her neighbours over to watch the Bolshoi Ballet or productions of
Shakespeare's plays on the ABC.

One day Marie watched a documentary on environmental pollution. It brought up issues she had felt strongly about for decades – man's deviation from the natural rhythm and the selfish need to subdue nature for economic progress and increased material comfort. She prophesied many decades ago what has now become inescapable reality:

The only pleasant thing about the [documentary] – at least to a former mountaineer – was the information that the atmosphere itself might well become so polluted that it would soon exclude the sunlight and usher in a new ice age with uncontaminated white snow mountains and the extinction or near-extinction of the species of man. If another ice age did not kill the human species there were other alternatives that would do so, all springing from this flouting of nature's rhythm. For something is never got for nothing, and the nemesis of trying to get without giving is only a matter of time. Sooner or later nature will right the balance. Nature always rights the balance and nothing that man can do can prevent it …

The destruction of nature has its origin in the mind, that is, in the thoughts, and it is only in the mind and its thoughts that the cure can be found, that is to say in the reorientation of our thoughts so that we cease asking 'Do I want it?' and instead ask, 'Do I need it?' and so that we cease destroying the least thing, unless like the wild animals in Kipling's Jungle Book, we really need to do so …

There is always a middle way. But the asking of those questions in an affluent society, is the only solution for the problem of pollution … You and I may not live to see the nemesis. But things are moving very quickly these days and the children around us may very well do so.

'Don't be an incorrigible pessimist. Man has always got over his troubles, and he always will.'

I am not a pessimist, for I think that the wonder of man's evolution is such that he will not perish like the dinosaurs, that remnants of the human species will survive, that after terrible suffering those remnants will learn to seek only what they <u>need</u> and not what they <u>want</u>, and will also learn that giving brings greater happiness than getting. And finally that they will become conscious of the unity of all life. It is a very very long-range optimism. But I have always been rather prone to long-range plans!

FEW WOMEN in the twentieth century displayed such a diverse range of interests and commitments as Marie Byles. Her versatility was staggering; she made lasting contributions as activist and publicist in many fields: as the first female lawyer of New South Wales she was an influential role model to other women in law; she fought for equal rights in an era when women had few; in nature conservation through serving as honorary solicitor to peak organisations aiding their negotiations with the Lands Department and local councils; her devotion to the bushwalking movement helped to popularise this recreational activity – the Bush Club is still in existence and thriving; as a mountaineer she drew maps of previously unexplored areas and was the first to reach the summit of peaks around the world; she was the driving force and a foundational member of the first civic trust in Australia formed to protect and value the local natural environment; as a founding member of the Buddhist Society of NSW she helped establish mindfulness meditation in Australia and make Buddha's teachings generally accessible; and through her books she brought the wisdom of the East to those grateful for the guidance they provided to understand the nature and meaning of existence.

Marie fulfilled her mother's creed by daring to have a purpose firm and daring to make it known.

Notes

Chapter 1: Dare to Have a Purpose Firm

1. My grandfather must have been': Marie Byles, unpublished autobiography "Many Lives In One" (1975) p.13. Marie Byles papers, National Trust (NSW)
2. Story of Huguenot ancestors: Beuzeville family history by Emma Mary Byles written in 1926 p.5, in possession of author
3. She was brought up 'in an atmosphere': "Many Lives In One" Preface
4. 'There was no scolding or nagging': ibid. p.17
5. 'I am not a little girl': ibid. p.1
6. 'Dare to be a Daniel': ibid. p.32
7. 'The earth is the Lord's': ibid. p.12
8. Cyril B. Byles (1910) *First Principles of Railway Signalling* Railway Gazette, London
9. 'Orange and red creepers flamed in glory': "Many Lives In One" p.25
10. Beecroft residents voted in favour of the 'no licence' option: Beecroft-Cheltenham History Group (1995) *Beecroft and Cheltenham: the Shaping of a Sydney Community to 1914* (1995) Southwood Press NSW p.273
11. 'A small quarry has been transformed': Marie Byles, *The Australian Home Beautiful* January 1, 1932 p.34 Marie Byles papers, SLNSW
12. 'At that time I did not quite see how a woman': "Many Lives In One" p.15
13. A self-admittedly 'unpleasant little girl': ibid. p.26
14. However, when the Department of Public Instruction: ibid. p.34
15. A dwelling gathers its own atmosphere': "Many Lives In One" p.33
16. 'In my third year P.L.C. Pymble': ibid. p.36

Chapter 2: The Glory of the Pioneer

1. '… both branches of the law appear as excellent an opening': High Court Justice Mary Gaudron 50th anniversary of the NSW Women Lawyer's Association 2002.
2. 'If you cannot reap all the reward': Joan O'Brien, (1986) A History of Women in the Legal Profession in New South Wales Master's thesis p.9, Fisher Library University of Sydney
3. 'brains, and compass and sun and map': "Many Lives In One" p.50
4. '… being made as I am, I am not one of the mixers': ibid. p.38
5. 'There were interesting books to read': ibid. p.40

6. She was afraid of being attractive: ibid.
7. Her two friends scrambled out of the freezing water: Dymphna Cusack to Gillian Coote. Transcriptions of taped interviews for *A Singular Woman*, a documentary by Gillian Coote on Marie Byles for ABC TV (1983), Marie Byles papers, National Trust of Australia (NSW)
8. 'Poor Father was aghast': "Many Lives In One" p.40
9. History essay "Is Christianity Obsolete?" Marie Byles papers, SLNSW
10. Many of them were 'very brainy': "Many Lives In One" p.47
11. As 'one shy little girl, afraid of young men': ibid.
12. "Byles on Bills" John Byles (1829) *A Treatise on the Law of Bills of Exchange, Promissory Notes, Bank-Notes, and Cheques*
13. 'She does wather cwamp my style'. "Many Lives In One" p.3
14. One solicitor said, 'A girl! Thank goodness': ibid. pp.2–3
15. … he impressed her 'as no speaker had ever done': ibid. p.48
16. 'some questions might be asked.': ibid p.4
17. 'You can be a solicitor's clerk but you can't practise': ibid.
18. 'I plunged into the depths of despair': ibid.
19. Marie was 'a loss to Economics': ibid. p.51
20. While gathering evidence from the local residents: ibid. pp.57-9

Chapter 3: Pioneering in Law

1. "Who Owns the House-keeping Allowance?" *The Australian Woman's Mirror* August 26, 1930. Marie Byles papers, SLNSW
2. "And They Lived Happily Ever After": ibid. January 17, 1928 Marie Byles papers, SLNSW
3. Miss Sybil Morrison, the only woman practising at the Bar: O'Brien p.30
4. 'It was rather a serious state of affairs that the mother': *The Australian Woman's Mirror* December 20, 1927 Marie Byles papers, SLNSW
5. 'In 1934 our work bore fruit': "Many Lives In One" p.89
6. When Jessie wrote to the Prime Minister urging action: Ed. Radi, H. (1990) *Jessie Street, Documents and Essays* Women's Redress Press, Sydney p.119
7. 'My mother was a great admirer of hers': Sir Laurence Street in correspondence with the author (2000)

Chapter 4: By Cargo Boat and Mountain

1. 'The train went up imperceptibly': "Many Lives In One" p.31
2. 'Each year they set out with fresh hopes': Marie Byles (1931) *By Cargo Boat and Mountain – the unconventional experiences of a woman on tramp around the world* Seeley, Service & Co. Ltd. London p.17
3. Freya Stark: 'The beckoning counts': Rebecca Seffton (1992) *Women of the World, women travellers and explorers* Oxford University Press p.11
4. 'The last bale of wool had been shipped': *By Cargo Boat and Mountain* p.31
5. Wine and whiskey flowed but Marie: ibid. p.35
6. 'Those wonderful tropic nights were more intoxicating': ibid. p.37
7. 'It was very sad, but it gave me an opportunity of killing': ibid. p.53
8. 'I am not affable by nature and the strain': ibid. p.50

9. '… there were no mountains, no water': ibid. p.56
10. 'For the first time I understood how people lose their nerve': ibid. p.83
11. The guide, pointing, said: 'If we go up that': ibid. p.140
12. He had an attitude that treated amateurs as: ibid. p.151
13. 'Now virgin peaks over ten thousand feet': ibid. p.152
14. 'California houses seemed to me': ibid. p.190
15. 'All I know is that we do these things': ibid. p.11
16. Together they set off on a venture that would: "Many Lives In One" p.65
17. 'It seemed to me to be the greatest loss: ibid. p.73
18. 'All the mountains overlooking the glacier': *By Cargo Boat and Mountain* p.272
19. It was heart-breaking work and it seemed as if: ibid. p.276
20. At 2.45 am, 25 hours and 40 minutes after they had left: ibid. p.280
21. While Arne and Marjorie slept she lay outside the hut: ibid. p.281
22. 'The serenity of Nature brooded over all things': ibid. p.283

Chapter 5: The Law of the Living World

1. New stereotypes then formed of women: O'Brien p.26
2. The result was she declared, 'that I never met it': "Many Lives In One" p.7
3. 'Next time, Miss Byles, you need not come back yourself': ibid.
4. When the Great Depression hit with full force: ibid. p.8
5. Describing herself as 'that curious entity': ibid. p.6
6. 'Sydney's winter skies reminded me most uncomfortably': ibid. p.75
7. 'To my heterodox mind': *By Cargo Boat and Mountain* p.221
8. Once, while driving with her parents to Watson's Bay: Aileen Fenwick in conversation with the author (1998)
9. Marie, who Paddy Pallin described: Paddy Pallin to Gillian Coote
10. 'There were three': Marie Byles "A Tramp in the Federal Capital Territory"
11. 'There is something in the contact': "Many Lives In One" p.50
12. 'These 'mild bushwalking adventures': ibid. p.91
13. Marie notes that her father was certainly beloved: ibid p.76
14. 'He was utterly straight and honourable': ibid. pp.78–9
15. 'As we looked down on the treetops far below': ibid. p.81
16. Baldur's environmental study: Baldur Byles (1932) "Report on Reconnaissance of the Mountainous Part of the River Murray Catchment in New South Wales" *Commonwealth Forestry Bureau Publications* Bulletin 13.
17. Although Baldur did not recommend expelling the graziers: Peter Prineas (1997) *Wild Places* Colong Foundation NSW p.140
18. Baldur's recommendations for an alpine national park: Cuneen, C. (2000) *William John McKell* UNSW Press, Sydney p.165
19. 'We cannot appreciate anything fully until we understand it': Baldur Byles *Snow Gum – the Tree*. Marie Byles papers, SLNSW

Chapter 6: Bouddi Natural Park

1. 'Esther, "the handsome he-man" carried hers ready': "Many Lives In One" p.54
2. 'Marie was a person': Myles Dunphy in conversation with Gillian Coote
3. "Maitland Park. A New Proposal" SMH 22.3.1934

4. 'They spoke disparagingly of the clear fresh': "Many Lives In One" p.89
5. Sixty people turned up armed with tools: *The Sydney Bushwalker* July 1940 p.2
6. 'The Intelligence. Stand erect with awe and respect': *The Sydney Bushwalker*, by "One of the Bees" June 1945 pp.6–7
7. "Above Bouddi Headland": NSW Federation of Bushwalking Club's annual journal *The Bushwalker* 1943 p.6
8. 'If I had my youth back again': Marie Byles *Bouddi Natural Park* Marie Byles papers, SLNSW
9. As Judge Don Stewart, head of the Coastal Zone Inquiry: Don Stewart (2007) *Recollections of an Unreasonable Man* p.253 ABC Books, Sydney

Chapter 7: Bagging Virgin Peaks

1. 'There are plenty of good solicitors': Leonard Giovanelli in conversation with the author (2001)
2. Leonard witnessed Marie's distress: ibid.
3. Marie opened up the big world: Dymphna Cusack to Gillian Coote
4. 'At the beginning of 1928 we had a large': "Many Lives In One" p.60
5. Nell had developed a keen sense of social and economic justice: Ed. D. Adelaide, (1991) *A Window in the Dark* Yarn Spinners, Sydney p.13
6. Dymphna Cusack and Florence James, *Come In Spinner* (1951) abridged edition, William Heinemann, Melbourne
7. At 33 years of age she had a bohemian streak Adelaide, D. p.5
8. She later said she found it too difficult to cope with Marie's 'very emotional attitude': Dymphna Cusack to Gillian Coote
9. 'Strong intelligent and independent women': Sally Irwin (1996) "The Fatal Passions of Freda du Faur" *HQ* magazine, Mar/April p.50
10. 'I suppose cynical people might suggest': "Many Lives In One" p.103
11. 'Being a bushwalker I merely spread': ibid. p.95
12. 'the original feminist': Pearle Giddens in conversation with the author (2001)
13. Camping in rough cattlemen's huts: "Many Lives In One" p.105
14. Back in Sydney she poured over maps: ibid. p.116
15. She met a well-travelled businessman: SMH 19 July 1938 p.13
16. '"Frankly, I don't" was his reply': Marie Byles (1939) "The Black Dragon and the White" unpublished manuscript Marie Byles papers, SLNSW
17. 'I know the whole expedition is mad': Letter from Marie Byles to Dora de Beer 15.3.1938.
18. 'Things are in a dreadful state': Letter from Marie Byles to Dora de Beer 15.4.38
19. 'Half the glamour of the expedition': "Walking Through China" SMH 19.7.38

Chapter 8: The Black Dragon

1. Shwe Dagon Pagoda: "The Black Dragon and the White" Introduction p.6.
2. There, habits and customs 'have not altered much': ibid.
3. "A Sydney Woman in the Wilds of Burma": SMH 30.8.38
4. "Through Chinese Bandit Country" SMH 7.11.38
5. *Two summers in the ice wilds of the eastern Karakoram* (1917) Fanny Bullock Workman and William Hunter Workman, E.P. Dutton & Co., London
6. 'With the mountains standing': "The Black Dragon and the White" Ch.8 p.1

7. 'Burn and bury all your rubbish': ibid. Ch.8 p.4
8. 'Now, the Black Dragon is the Deity': "Many Lives In One" p.128
9. To Marie, it was 'a superb glacier': "The Black Dragon and the White" Ch.10 p. 8
10. 'Poor Kurt Sutor sat on the top and belayed': "Many Lives In One" p.150
11. 'Alas! It was the end': "The Black Dragon and the White" Ch.10 p.10
12. 'But, oh! those peaks! Those knife edges': "Many Lives In One" p.130
13. They travelled through Kunming: ibid. p.125
14. Dora wrote in her travel diary: Dora de Beer's diary, Hocken Library, University of Otago, New Zealand
15. 'Bandits had been banished from the road': ibid. p.135

Chapter 9: Ahimsa

1. 'Eventually I found what seemed just right': "Many Lives In One" p.115
2. 'The new little cottage was a great delight': ibid. p.141
3. "I had loved old Laudate': ibid. p.156
4. 'She just told me what to do and I did it': Ruth Milton to Gillian Coote
5. 'Like other solicitors, I returned to doing': "Many Lives In One" p.8
6. 'Now let another party go': "The Black Dragon and the White" p.15
7. 'Whether this absurd suffering': *Journey Into Burmese Silence* p.18
8. 'According to Carl Jung, the great change of life': "Many Lives In One" p.137
9. 'Of all unlikely books I read *Peace with Honour*': ibid. p.137
10. 'How could such sublime wisdom': ibid. p.138
11. 'He declared that each morning he bathed his intellect': Swami Prabhupada *Bhagavad-Gita As It Is*, The Bhaktivedanta Book Trust, Sydney. Back cover
12. 'And then, oh horrors! I found myself': "Many Lives In One" p.138
13. 'There was something behind all which I had not known': ibid. p.139
14. 'This, to my mind, is what actually happens': ibid.
15. 'In our social and business life most people': ibid. p.142
16. 'Literally it means non-killing, but Gandhi said': ibid. p.139
17. 'It was the very basis on which his life's work': Marie Byles "Reduce Self to Zero" Marie Byles papers, SLNSW
18. "The Quaker Meeting": Marie Byles papers, SLNSW
19. 'The verse that sang itself on to paper shows agony': "Many Lives In One" p.149
20. 'Fate now took possession of the arena of my life': ibid. p.144
21. 'It had always been a very skinny foot': ibid.
22. Although she bore the injury with a smile: ibid.

Chapter 10: An Adventure in Loneliness

1. Used to solitary walking and even camping: "Many Lives In One" p.144
2. Though this particular book seemed appropriate: Marie Byles "An Adventure in Loneliness" *The Bushwalker* annual (1942) p.35
3. 'At the Christmas dinner table': "Many Lives In One" p.145
4. 'So here hath been dawning another blue day': ibid.
5. '… things emerged from the ground': ibid. p.146
6. 'One gets from Nature only interest': ibid. p.145

7. '... took away the things in life most treasured': Marie Byles (1965) *Paths to Inner Calm* George Allen & Unwin Ltd London p.18
8. 'Over the years I have been wonderfully blessed': "Many Lives In One" p.150
9. Male networks extended to community groups: O'Brien p.60
10. 'In those days it was very, very hard for women': Margaret Crawley in conversation with the author (1999)
11. 'It was most humiliating to accept the revelation': "Many Lives In One" p.148
12. 'The festering sore between conscious and unconscious': Marie Byles (1962) *Journey Into Burmese Silence* George Allen & Unwin Ltd. London p.184
13. 'When I was sitting there alone': "Many Lives In One" p.150
14. Myles Dunphy was at heart a recreationalist: Peter Meredith (1999) *Myles and Milo* Allen & Unwin NSW p.215
15. 'Recent discussions about the Kosciusko primitive area': Marie Byles "What is a Primitive Area?" *The Sydney Bushwalker* July 1945 p.5
16. Dunphy, devastated by the 'first and only serious setback': Meredith p.160
17. He had, Mosley believes, no comprehension that nature had rights: Dr Geoff Mosley (1999) *Battle for the Bush* Colong Foundation, NSW p.62
18. From 1946, 'the strain and tension got worse': "Many Lives In One" p.153
19. 'It used to do her good to come here': Rae Page to Gillian Coote
20. Having a place to meditate with others would give: *Paths to Inner Calm* p.12
21. 'As early as 1946 Marie Byles had plans to develop': Paul Croucher (1989) *A History of Buddhism in Australia 1848-1988*, University of New South Wales Press, Sydney p.35

Chapter 11: No Peace to be Found

1. 'She always said, "No, no heart"': Erika Wohlwill in conversation with the author (2000)
2. 'A few intellectuals knew something of Buddhist philosophy': James William Coleman (2001) *The New Buddhism, the Western Transformation of an Ancient Tradition* Oxford University Press p.60
3. Marie Byles (1957) *Footprints of Gautama Buddha* Rider and Co. London
4. 'By ourselves is evil done; by ourselves we pain endure': *Dhammapada* 165
5. 'Oh, Mr Berkeley, Australians are not yet ready': *Metta* supplement (4 May 1959), *the History of the Buddhist Society of NSW*
6. Marie became close friends with Leo and his wife: Klaas Berkeley, Leo Berkeley's son, in conversation with the author (1998)
7. The first recorded intensive meditation retreat: "Buddhism in New South Wales" Marie Byles papers, SLNSW
8. 'The tent was beside the glorious swift flowing river': Marie Byles (1964) "Dying to Self or A Week Alone" in Marie's Clarence Diary, loaned by J & V Fallding
9. 'Life seemed to consist mainly of worry, struggle': *Paths to Inner Calm* p.11
10. When clients came into the office they would ask: Ruth Milton to Gillian Coote
11. Peg was a single mother from England: David Willis, Peg's son, in conversation with the author (2000)
12. '... she certainly was very depressed': Ruth Milton to Gillian Coote
13. 'There was suitcase after suitcase': "Many Lives In One" p.157

14. Sister Dhammadina replied, 'Yes you can attend my group.' Graeme Lyall in conversation with author (2000)
15. 'Whatever Sr. Dhammadina's faults': "Many Lives In One" p.157
16. It was agreed that the Pali Canon: *Metta* supplement, 4 May 1959, the *History of the Buddhist Society of NSW*
17. In November of 1952, 'when the azaleas': "Many Lives In One" p.159
18. 'Mother had forgotten her husband even before he died': ibid. p.160
19. Having lost respect for Ida long ago: Marie Byles' letter to Florence James, Florence James papers, SLNSW
20. Before the boat left in October, Ida passed: "Many Lives In One" p.160
21. When the minister spoke about being saved: ibid.
22. 'what a very wonderful woman my mother was': Christmas letter 1970 Marie Byles papers, SLNSW
23. 'an indication of her one great weakness': "Many Lives In One" p.45

Chapter 12: Lead Kindly Light

1. 'In October 1953 ten years of strain and suffering': "Many Lives In One" p.161
2. 'The troubled heart seeks refuge': *Journey Into Burmese Silence* p.20
3. 'No special respect is paid to them as it is to monks': ibid.
4. After five days, an 'intolerable': Letter 5 to John and Vreni Falldings p.2, 27.11.53
5. In contrast, she 'would not know from day to day': *Journey Into Burmese Silence* p.24
6. Buddha unfolded the Eightfold Way: Marie Byles (1963) *The Lotus and the Spinning Wheel* George Allen & Unwin London p.18
7. 'Taking a position under the great tree: ibid. p.51
8. 'Lord Curzon's care of India's historical sites': ibid. p.18
9. 'Never before have I seen mountains': "Bushwalking in a Pilgrim Land", *The Sydney Bushwalker*, Feb. 1954
10. At the time she wrote, 'It is not often that I weep': "Many Lives In One" p.153
11. 'Surely no one could see that gesture without tears!': ibid.
12. Marie Byles (1963) *The Lotus and the Spinning Wheel* George Allen & Unwin London
13. Mount Kailash in Tibet, 'the holiest mountain': *Journey Into Burmese Silence* p.26
14. All the while she continued to seek out those: *Paths to Inner Calm* p.207
15. Although Marie met many expatriates: *Journey Into Burmese Silence* p.27
16. 'I had the comfortable feeling that one slip': "Many Lives In One" p.165
17. 'He had come very inadequately provided': ibid. p.176
18. Conversation with Sadhu woman: Letter 29 to Falldings p.5 23.11.54
19. Arriving back home in January 1955: "Many Lives In One" p.182

Chapter 13: Pioneering Buddhism in the West

1. Although Marie was slight of build: Chris Ronalds to Gillian Coote p.15
2. 'Ridiculous! I have never heard anything so silly': ibid. p.16
3. Later, Chris reflected, 'to anyone who has attended': ibid. p.17
4. 'This was the first legislation in the world to use the term': ibid. p.3
5. 'He would have been in his 40s': Peter de Beuzeville in conversation with the author (2000).
6. 'The years 1954–56 were halcyon for Australian Buddhism': Coucher p.43

7. During U Thittila's month-long visit, the membership: ibid. p.44
8. While the upsurge of interest in Buddhism: ibid. p.45
9. 'For the development of a nation, both worldly progress': ibid.
10. 'Hearing of the schism, Venerable Narada': Graeme Lyall, *History of the Buddhist Society of NSW* http://www.buddhismaustralia.org/AccBudHist.htm
11. After his enlightenment, Buddha made: *Footprints of Gautama Buddha* p.82
12. 'Insight into the Dhamma wipes away': ibid. p.84
13. 'You will be guided. You are already': "Many Lives In One" p.182

Chapter 14: Journey Into Burmese Silence

1. 'I do not think anyone will quarrel': "Many Lives In One" p.182
2. It was not until the fifth day that it began: ibid. p.42
3. 'I had never before been in such surroundings': ibid. p.45
4. 'I was sorry I could not oblige by feeling anything at all': ibid. p.47
5. 'You now suffuse everything with loving thoughts': ibid. p.195
6. 'The vast majority of nuns were merely servants': Marie Byles (1972) "The Buddha and Women" *Sirisara* journal. Marie Byles papers, SLNSW
7. 'Their faces were beautiful with inner peace': *Journey Into Burmese Silence* p.91
8. 'The very object of meditation is to rise above': ibid. p.92
9. Nevertheless, it was a relief to be back at the Maha Bodhi: ibid. p.93
10. '… he had obviously not the faintest idea': ibid. p.153
11. Through Vipassana meditation they could learn: ibid. p.179
12. 'I'm labelled a Buddhist, of course': Marie Byles article in *The Australian Women's Weekly*, Nov. 30, 1966
13. 'I went to Burma to learn the art of meditation': "Living the life of a Burmese Buddhist nun." Marie Byles papers, SLNSW
14. Marie, in her straightforward way: Elva Mniksevicus in conversation with the author (2000)
15. One of the very early pioneers of a pure Theravadin teaching: ibid.
16. To Jurvis, Marie was not just an ordinary person: Jurvis Miksevicius in conversation with author (2000)
17. 'About 3 hours of fair absorption this morning': Marie Byles' Clarence diary – lent to the author by John and Vreni Fallding
18. 'I was in a shocking state – mentally, physically, spiritually': Bart Brown in conversation with the author (1999)
19. Edrie could not quite see how: Chris Ronalds p.13
20. 'What is success and what is failure': *Paths to Inner Calm* pp.38–9

Chapter 15: The Path of Peace

1. 'It was the leading of the Dhamma': *Paths to Inner Calm* p.104
2. '… I was interviewing an officer': ibid. p. 205
3. Accompanied by Sarana, Marie went: *Journey Into Burmese Silence* p.107
4. Marie realised U Thein had been right – 'to start a new method': ibid. p.108
5. 'But women may not climb it', Sarana told her: ibid. p.109
6. 'Never run away from pain, it will only return': ibid. p.110

7. 'I saw that this monk-worship is essential to the pattern': ibid. p.127
8. Marie asked him, 'Is there anything at all you now desire?': ibid. p.164
9. 'Around Sydney we have primeval forest': "Proposal for the Hills Community Bushland Area" Marie Byles papers, SLNSW
10. After linking the flyer to Marie Byles: Minutes of Special General Meeting of Buddhist Society of NSW 7.9.1961 Marie Byles papers, SLNSW
11. 'So neither the Buddhists nor the Quakers': "Many Lives In One", 180
12. 'Although a considerable intellectual force': Croucher p.58
13. 'a noble Blackbutt, perfect in form': *The Beecroft-Cheltenham Civic-Trust Story*, published by the Beecroft-Cheltenham Civic Trust, Sydney p.9
14. 'Sydney was once set in a natural forest': ibid.

Chapter 16: Cleaning Honourable Toilets

1. 'That's a rude nun': *Paths to Inner Calm* p.20
2. Hurt by the thought: June Taylor in conversation with the author (2001)
3. 'To solve the small and large problems': *Paths to Inner Calm* p.207
4. Marie was the best lawyer in this part of the world: Judith King in conversation with the author (1999)
5. 'The priest, striding silently round did not whack': "Many Lives In One" p.188
6. 'It was not relaxing for me': *The Australian Women's Weekly*, Nov 30, 1966
7. 'Ittoen was founded by Tenko San quite unconsciously': ibid. p.189
8. Tenko San's face glowed: *Paths to Inner Calm* p.132
9. It occurred to her that perhaps she had not come to Japan: ibid. p.134
10. 'Every window, ledge, basin, floor, tile, o benjo [toilet]': ibid. p.167
11. 'Are there ever any quarrels in Ittoen?': ibid. p.187
12. At Ittoen she found a glimpse of heaven on earth: "Many Lives In One" p.190
13. Enlightenment was Marie's aim but she realised: Marie Byles "Humility and Anatta" *Sirisara Buddhist Annual*, Vesak, 1970
14. 'It sometimes makes me weep': Marie Byles letter to Ayako 16.9.64 (all correspondence between Ayako Isakawa and Marie Byles in author's possession)
15. 'In theory I know that dying to self': Marie Byles letter to Ayako 17.7.65
16. Wondering whether she should continue she had 'a wonderful dream': ibid.
17. On boarding the plane she felt like: Foreword, "Hidden Light from Japan", unpublished manuscript, Marie Byles papers SLNSW
18. Finally able to meet with Takeshi San, he told her that: ibid. Ch.4 p.7
19. 'The more I tried to explain English law, the more their suspicions': ibid.
20. 'The Western mind likes things clear as crystal': *Paths to Inner Calm* p.198
21. 'As long as I shoulder all the blame myself, all is well': Marie Byles letter to Isobel Bellamy, 8.11.1965 Marie Byles papers, SLNSW
22. Two months after returning to Sydney: Marie Byles to Ayako 25.1.66
23. She compared herself with Gandhi who was: Letter to Ayako 1.11.66
24. 'This was an excellent training': "Hidden Light from Japan" Ch.4 p.10
25. 'It is reported that Tagore once said': "Many Lives In One" p.195

Chapter 17: The Measure of Our Gift

1. He found her in the guest room, her face, swollen: Dorothy Hasluck letter to Florence James 24.11.66. Florence James papers, SLNSW
2. 'The Doctor who is a personal friend': ibid.
3. 'But despite the fact that there was obviously': "Many Lives In One" p.196
4. She reflected on Tenko San's teachings that 'we carry all evil': ibid.
5. 'Of course I will gladly do this so don't have it': Florence James to Marie Byles 26.11.66. Florence James' papers, SLNSW
6. Marie 'may not recover': Florence James to Florence Beaufoy 24.11.66. ibid.
7. The next two months were spent: Marie Byles to Florence James 25.1.67. ibid.
8. 'I cannot think the Law of Life': Marie Byles to Florence James 6.3.67. ibid.
9. She described Linda MacIntosh: Florence James to Marie Byles 15.2.1967 ibid.
10. Florence wrote to Baldur, 'we wondered': Florence James to Baldur Byles 5.6.67. ibid.
11. 'When she is in this condition': Florence James to Baldur Byles 7.6.67. ibid.
12. By the time friends brought Marie home: "Many Lives In One" p.199
13. Emily Bronte (1818-1848) "No Coward Soul"
14. 'I am terribly sorry I was so irritating': Marie Byles to Florence James, 16.6.67. Florence James' papers, SLNSW.
15. 'the gulf that divided Marie's belief: Florence James to Baldur Byles 22.6.67. ibid.
16. 'That kind of fear did eventually depart': "Many Lives In One" p. 200
17. 'All her life Marie was battling men': Jurvis Miksevicius
18. 'I was quite amazed the way she could put her legs up': Margaret Ravizza in conversation with the author (2000)
19. 'We had 13 women [on staff]. I had to feed 13 women': Helen Larcombe in conversation with the author (2000)
20. 'Three springtimes came and went': "Many Lives In One" pp.199–200

Chapter 18: The Greatest Lesson Learnt

1. 'Another vital lesson that life brought': "Many Lives In One" p.200
2. Acting as consulting solicitor to the Trust, Marie drafted their constitution in 1946
3. 'The object of Ahimsa is to provide a beauty spot': National Trust of NSW Draft Plan of Management, April 1982, p.2
4. 'There followed the most ridiculous newspaper': "Many Lives In One" p.202
5. As Roslyn walked up: Roslyn Muston in conversation with the author (2000)
6. Roslyn found her awe-inspiring, 'Very alert': Roslyn Muston to Gillian Coote
7. Roslyn admired her tremendously: Roslyn Muston in conversation with the author (2000)
8. 'And every time I felt like buckling': ibid.
9. Vreni learned to stand up to: Vreni Fallding in conversation with the author (1996)
10. Despite the 'agony and exhaustion': "Many Lives In One" p.203
11. Marie recognised that her physical progress: ibid. p.67
12. 'She'd say: "Right, we'll be doing dyeing today"': Margaret Ravizza in conversation with the author (1999)
13. 'China came into it a lot. She was proud of it': ibid.

14. 'I was given a good but not a brilliant brain': "Many Lives In One" p.11
15. '...The bush is necessary, not only for us who reside near': Garden Club of Australia, May 1974 edition. Marie Byles papers, SLNSW
16. 'There was a group of us': Pat Fleet in conversation with the author (1999)
17. 'I can't remember what happened': Griselda Brown

Chapter 19: Adventurous Spirit

1. The National Campaign Coordinator of one political party: Fergus McPherson, National Campaign Coordinator the Australia Party, letter to Marie Byles 23.8.1972. Marie Byles papers, SLNSW
2. The next thirteen months consisted of: Marie Byles to Ayako 25.8.75
3. 'having given up his wish': Marie Byles letter to Ayako 21.8.75
4. Writing to Griselda, Marie revealed that she had an annual medical check up: Marie Byles letter to Griselda Brown 19.2.78
5. Gaudron was encouraged, noting that 'the hurdles they had to jump had been much higher': Justice Mary Gaudron, speech to the 50th anniversary of the WLA, 1997 http://www.hcourt.gov.au/speeches/gaudronj/gaudronj_wlasp.htm
6. 'No, the quiet of the country does not banish thoughts': Marie Byles letter to Griselda Brown, 31.3.78
7. Jung called it 'the risk of inner experience': C.G. Jung (1993) *Memories, Dreams, Reflections* Ed. Aniela Jaffé FontanaPress London p.164
8. 'I should like to think that': Many Lives In One p.206
9. When Ruth Milton visited: Ruth Milton in conversation with author (1998)
10. 'The greatest lesson learned': "Many Lives In One" p.206
11. 'I know that she was so terribly pleased to see me': Griselda Brown
12. 'There was a terrific struggle at the end because Marie': Griselda Brown
13. On about the sixth day there was, Dot recalled: Dot Butler to Gillian Coote
14. 'Whatever you might say about her, she was a woman of a special calibre': Laurence Mills (Bikkhu Khantipalo) in conversation with the author (2000)
15. 'So many gods': Ella Wheeler Wilcox (1850–1899) "The World's Need"
16. 'The only pleasant thing about the [documentary]': Marie Byles, "Can Bushwalkers Save the Bush?" Marie Byles papers, SLNSW

Index

Acknowledgements

It has been my great pleasure and privilege to meet a range of people related to Marie through the fields of bushwalking, feminism, law and Buddhism. This project has been an ongoing education for me over many years.

My deep appreciation to Marie's relatives, friends and contemporaries who gave information and encouragement in researching and writing this biography:

Marie's neighbours, John and Freni Fallding, epitomised the beliefs and virtues to which the Ahimsa community aspired. Their children, Martin and Heidi Fallding.

Erika Wohlwill and her daughters, Monica Smith, Renata Kelleher, and Sabine Erika.

Alex Colley AM of the SBW, conservationist extraordinaire, gave unlimited time to discuss Marie and the early bushwalking and conservation movements of NSW.

Dot Butler, "the barefoot bushwalker", Alex's beloved partner and Marie's old friend.

Many contemporaries from the SBW including Wilf Hilder and Shirley Dean.

Marie's ex-staff members: Ruth Milton, Wyn Fensom, Pearle Giddens (née Pitcher), June Taylor, Peg Willis's son David, Maria Haber and her son Edwin.

Marie's ex-law partners: Leonard Giovanelli, Helen Larcombe, and Robert Moin.

Contemporaries in the legal profession: Margaret Crawley, Aline Fenwick, Judith King, Kay Loder, Vincent Pike, Janet Coombs, Sir Laurence Street, Nerida Cohen and her son Jonathon Goodman, Justice Mary Gaudron. Justice Elizabeth Evatt.

Marie's family: Peter de Beuzeville, Babette de Beuzeville, Louise de Beuzeville, John Byles, Ralph Byles, June Byles, Margaret Thirlwell.

Marie's Ahimsa friends: Margaret Cummins, David Ravizza, Joe Ravizza, Frank Traeker. Julie James Bailey (daughter of Florence James).

Marie's Buddhist friends: Ayako Isayama, Griselda Brown, Bart Brown, May Thet Tun, Elva and Jurgis Mniksevicus. Acquaintances: Laurence Mills (Bikkhu Khantipalo), Graeme Lyall from the Buddhist Council of New South Wales.

Marie's Bushcare friends: Shiela Woods, Eva Jones, Robin Buchanan, Roslyn Dey.

Alexander Technique: Rosemary Friend, Roslyn McLeod, Marcia Murray.

Yoga: Nancy Phelan.

Kosciusko National Park: Dr Geoff Mosley illuminated the philosophical differences between Marie and Myles Dunphy; Nev Gare provided background information on Baldur Byles and the evolution of the Park.

Editorial support:

Dr Ian Mills aided me in unravelling Marie's contradictions and clarifying her intertwining personal and philosophical issues, her 'divine discontent'.

Kay Jones helped structure the work initially. Kate McAllan's positive feedback gave me encouragement. Laurel Cohn greatly enhanced the final draft.

Neil Conning contributed specialised advice and general support, for Marcus.

Friends gave valued feedback on various drafts: Chandu Bickford, Margaret Chambers, Meredith Bubner and Jane Howat.

Teachers at TAFE and university encouraged my belief that I could tell this story and see the project through. Appreciation also to Jan Cornall of Writers Lab.

Lauren Statham of Alice Graphics helped me to realise my vision for the book.

Resources:

Books by Marie Byles

By Cargo Boat and Mountain – the unconventional experiences of a woman on tramp around the world Seeley, Service & Co., London (1931)

Footprints of Gautama Buddha Rider and Co., London (1957)

Journey Into Burmese Silence George Allen & Unwin, London (1962)

The Lotus and the Spinning Wheel George Allen & Unwin, London (1963)

Paths to Inner Calm George Allen & Unwin, London (1965)

Stand Straight Without Pain Fowler & Co., London (1978)

A New Road To Ancient Truth, by Tenko Nishida, George Allen & Unwin, London (1969) Translated by Makoto Ohashi in collaboration with Marie Byles.

"Many Lives In One" Marie Byles' unpublished autobiography, National Trust of Australia (NSW), (manuscript pages numbered by this author: 1–end).

Marie Byles' other unpublished manuscripts, held in State Library of NSW:
  "The Black Dragon and the White" (1939)
  "Hidden Light from Japan" (1966)

Marie Byles' papers held in State Library of New South Wales (ML MSS 3833).

All photographs from Marie Byles' photographic collection, State Library of NSW (PXA 1735).

Other resources

Joan O'Brien's "A History of Women in the Legal Profession in New South Wales" (1986). Joan generously gave her time to educate me about the significance of Marie's contributions in the field of law. Her Master's thesis allowed me to place them in their proper historical context.

Joan Webb's "Marie Beuzeville Byles, a life" gave insight into Marie's wider contributions (State Library of NSW, Marie Byles papers, ML MSS 9385).

Paul Croucher's *A History of Buddhism in Australia 1848–1988* was an invaluable resource, putting Marie's involvement into perspective.

Alex Colley's anthology of the Sydney Bush Walkers club journals and the NSW Federation of Bushwalking Clubs journals (*The Sydney Bushwalker/The Bushwalker*) contained articles on Marie's adventures and conservation concerns.

Dot Butler's *The Barefoot Bushwalker*, (ABC Books, Sydney, 1991) also brought those times vividly to life.

John McFarlane's *The Golden Hope: Presbyterian Ladies' College, Sydney 1988–1985*, generously provided by Pymble PLC, conveyed the school's high values.

Jeanette Blomfield's *Hawkesbury to Hunter Coastal Walking* opened up my explorations to the splendour of Bouddi National Park.

Beecroft-Cheltenham History Group's *Beecroft and Cheltenham: the Shaping of a Sydney Community to 1914* (1995).

Beryl Strom's *Bouddi Peninsula Study* Association for Environmental Education (NSW) Central Coast Region.

Gillian Coote's documentary *A Singular Woman* (1983). Gillian kindly gave permission to quote from transcripts of interviews with Marie's contemporaries.

Chris Ronalds AM SC "Marie Byles: A Reflection on her Life as a Legal Practitioner" paper given at the National Trust, Sydney, in 2005, on her personal reminiscences and Marie's legacy for future generations of women in law.

Florence James' papers, State Library of NSW, MLMSS 5877.

Correspondence between Marie Byles and Dora de Beer, The Hocken Collections, University of Otago, New Zealand

Gratitude to:

The State Library of NSW for access to and assistance with Marie Byles' papers and photographic material.

The National Trust of Australia (NSW) for:
- permission to reproduce photographs from Marie Byles' photographic collection held in the State Library of NSW
- access to Marie Byles' papers including articles written by Ian Stephenson and Joan Ecob; and transcripts of interviews recorded for *A Singular Woman* – archive/library manager, Julie Blyth
- The Trust's exhibition, "Marie Byles: A Spirited Life" – curator, Julie Peterson
- Thanks to Dr Roslyn Muston, Environment Director, responsible for management of Ahimsa, for her reminiscences of Marie and Ahimsa

The Bouddi Society for supporting this publication; and Dr David Dufty for guiding me through Bouddi National Park.

Printed in Australia
AUHW011259270820
333174AU00016B/537

9 780646 941417